ROOM TWO MORE GUNS

the intriguing history of the Personal Column of

Also published by Allen & Unwin

THE FIRST CUCKOO
Letters to *The Times* 1900–1980

THE SECOND CUCKOO
A further selection of witty, amusing and
memorable letters to *The Times*

THE THIRD CUCKOO
More classic letters to *The Times*
chosen and introduced by
Kenneth Gregory

AMAZING TIMES

MORE AMAZING TIMES
A selection of the most amusing and
amazing articles from *The Times*
chosen by Stephen Winkworth

ACCIDENTAL TIMES
A selection of bizarre and amusing Victorian
accidents from *The Times*
compiled by Jane Lambert

ROOM TWO MORE GUNS

the intriguing history of the
Personal Column of

STEPHEN WINKWORTH

Jacket illustration by
Michael ffolkes

London
GEORGE ALLEN & UNWIN
Boston   Sydney

First published in 1986
This book is copyright under the Berne Convention.
No reproduction without permission. All rights reserved.

George Allen & Unwin (Publishers) Ltd.,
40 Museum Street, London WC1A 1LU, UK

George Allen & Unwin (Publishers) Ltd.,
Park Lane, Hemel Hempstead, Herts HP2 4TE, UK

Allen & Unwin Inc.,
8 Winchester Place, Winchester, Mass. 01890, USA

George Allen & Unwin Australia Pty Ltd.,
8 Napier Street, North Sydney, NSW 2060, Australia

George Allen & Unwin with the
Port Nicholson Press
PO Box 11-838 Wellington, New Zealand

© Stephen Winkworth, 1986

British Library Cataloguing in Publication Data

Winkworth, Stephen
  Room two more guns: the intriguing
history of the Personal column of the
Times.
1. Times   2. Personals – Great Britain –
History
I. Title
070.4'42   PN5129.L7T5

ISBN 0–04–808055–1

Set in 10 on 11 point Times by Nene Phototypesetters Ltd, Northampton
and printed in Great Britain by
Richard Clay (The Chaucer Press) Ltd, Bungay, Suffolk

Contents

Acknowledgements

The author would like to express his thanks to all those advertisers from Charles II to Conan Doyle, without whose creative efforts this book could not have been written. Valuable contributions to the study of personal column advertising have recently been made by Miles Kington, Katherine Whitehorn and Irving Wallace (in a chapter of his book *The Sunday Gentleman*, Cassell 1966). What limited understanding of cryptanalysis I now possess I owe largely to David Kahn's book *The Codebreakers* (Weidenfeld & Nicolson 1966), which threw light on many dark corners of the personal column. My special thanks are also due to Rupert Allason; Mrs P. M. Clegg, Curator of Harrogate Museums; John Ebdon, Director of the London Planetarium; Miss Jane Evans, Curator of Woodspring Museum; Mrs John Hannam; Miss Caroline Hobhouse; Mrs V. M. Lakin; Donald McCormick; Derek Reid, Head of Mycology Section, The Royal Botanic Gardens, Kew; Michael Richey, Editor of *The Journal of Navigation*, Royal Institute of Navigation; The Rev. Charles Sinnickson; Graham Smith, Archivist of H.M. Customs; The Rev. David Vincent. Finally, I am greatly indebted to Peter Leek, who edited the typescript with a patient and perceptive eye, and made invaluable contributions to all aspects of this book.

1 *A Sporting Challenge*

Every literate English man and woman has some notion as to the contents of the classified advertising columns of *The Times*: births, deaths, marriages, 'In Memoriam', charities, entertainments, 'prize courts', business opportunities, Club announcements – and, of course, that rag-bag of oddities, 'Personal'. Young men with public school backgrounds, no experience and powerful motorcycles, want jobs abroad, preferably involving danger; people known only by initials cancel arrangements to meet under the clocks of railway stations; vital documents, locked in attaché cases, have been left in taxi cabs; jewellery of astonishing value has been dropped somewhere between Lowndes Square and Holland Park; distinguished authors and actors have small flats to let, and animals with idiotic names roam at large all over the home counties. Such is the stereotype. It is a convenient one, and the personal column is often drawn upon by novelists when the plot is sticking or a change of gear is needed. A stock property of the literary imagination, it serves much the same purpose as the telephone in films: the voice from 'somewhere else', interrupting and redirecting events.

In point of fact it was entirely by chance that he had gone into the scent business. His eye had been caught by an advertisement in *The Times*, a small factory for sale very cheap . . . just luck.

A thousand novels have used the device (the above example is from Aldous Huxley's *Eyeless in Gaza*).

There is, in short, an archetypal image that can be relied on to convey the right impression when a casual reference needs dropping in writing or conversation.

1

Archetypes – those familiar ideas shared by large numbers of people – have the peculiarly fascinating property of never conforming to expectations when they are closely examined, and it is almost always entertaining to find out what they are really like. I had no idea, for example, how funny personal column advertisers can be, usually unintentionally, or how grotesquely snobbish. Or that people should write, as they did in the 1920s, 'My spring suit just loud enough asphyxiate snakes who dare hiss "unfashionable" ' or 'Would the person in the green Tyrolean hat note that although it may be a custom on his own course to pocket golf balls on the fairway, it is not done elsewhere.' It also came as a considerable surprise that, far from being some sort of late Victorian addition which was allowed gradually to push news off the front page, the personal column lay at the very core of its founder's conception of the newspaper in 1784. In fact it positively dominated his thinking. Indeed, it would not be too fanciful to suggest that if *Exchange and Mart* were to add a page or two of news to their classified advertising they would be following in the honoured two-hundred-year-old tradition of *The Times*, and might in due course grow up to become a 'real' newspaper and a pillar of the Establishment.

This is a bold claim. To substantiate it one has to look at the origins of classified advertising in the eighteenth century. Take, for example, the Duke of Portland's wager. In 1749 the Duke of Portland and the Earl of Chesterfield were discussing the question of human gullibility and the persuasive power of advertising. The Duke advanced the claim that people were foolish enough and curious enough to pay good money to see 'the most impossible thing in the world' performed, if it were well advertised. The Earl of Chesterfield challenged this assertion. 'Surely, if a man should say, for example, he would jump into a quart bottle, no one would believe him.' The Duke replied that on the contrary he was prepared to bet they would believe as much, and more; and he would wager a hundred pounds on it. The two men composed an advertisement, which was placed in a newspaper called *The General Advertiser*:

At the new theatre in the Haymarket, on Monday next, the 16th instant, is to be seen a person who performs the most surprising thing – viz., he presents you with a common wine bottle, which any of the spectators may first examine; this bottle is placed on a table in the middle of the stage, and he (without any equivocation) goes into it, in the sight of all the spectators, and sings in it; during his stay in the bottle any person may handle it, and see plainly that it does not exceed a common tavern bottle. Tickets to be had at the theatre. To begin a half hour after six o'clock.

The effects of this advertisement were beyond all expectations. The theatre was sold out, with seats priced at up to seven shillings each, and the building was packed from pit to gallery. When the appointed hour came and went without anyone appearing, the crowd grew restless. In vain the manager came out and apologised for the delay. The minutes passed, boos and hisses began to fill the air; then suddenly a top-hatted buck in a box threw a lighted candle at the stage. Pandemonium broke out, and the audience started ripping down the curtains and tearing up the furniture. The theatre was gutted. But the Duke of Portland's wager was won.

Nor was this the beginning of personal column advertisements. A century before, in Cromwell's day, the pamphlets and 'mercuries' of the cavaliers and roundheads often carried announcements: for instance, Milton's pamphlets were advertised in *Mercurius Politicus* and the *errata* for his *Areopagitica* were printed in the same columns.

But perhaps the honours for the first personal column announcement to display both wit and style should go to one which appeared in the *Mercurius Publicus* on 29 June 1660. It is also a very special advertisement in another sense, for it is, so far as I am aware, the only personal column advertisement composed and inserted by a royal hand. Many other famous people, from Winston Churchill to Mrs John F. Kennedy, have advertised in the personal column of *The Times*, but this is, so far as research has revealed to date, the only royal advertisement (unless one is prepared to count 'Anastasia'). It is printed in italics, with a little hand pointing to it in the margin:

> *We must call upon you again for a black dog, between a greyhound and a spaniel, no white about him, only a streak on his breast, and tayl a little bobbed. It is His Majesty's own dog, and doubtless was stolen for the dog was not born nor bred in England, and would never forsake his Master. Whosoever finds him may acquaint any at Whitehall, for the dog was better known at court than those who stole him. Will they never leave off robbing His Majesty? Must He not keep a dog? This dog's place (though better than some imagine) is the only place which nobody offers to beg.*

A personal column advertisement by the poet John Dryden seems commonplace after that, though dark deeds are spoken of and royalty invoked:

Whereas John Dryden Esq was on Monday the 18th instant, at night, barbarously assaulted and wounded, in Rose Street in Covent Garden, by divers men unknown; if any person shall make discovery of the said offenders to the said Mr Dryden, or to any justice of the Peace, he shall not only receive fifty pounds, which is deposited in the hands of Mr Blanchard, goldsmith, next door to Temple Bar, for the said purpose, but if he be a principal or an accessory in the said fact, His Majesty is graciously pleased to promise him his pardon for the same.

The London Gazette, 22 December 1679

Dryden, a loyal supporter of Charles II, had been made Poet Laureate the year before, so talk of a royal pardon was no empty formality.

Indeed, the history of personal column advertisements has its darker side. Negro slaves were regularly bought and sold through the press:

A black boy, twelve years of age, fit to wait on a gentleman, to be disposed of at Denis's Coffee-house in Finch Lane, near the Royal Exchange.

The Tatler, 1709

And there were romantic advertisements too, in those early days:

A gentleman who, on the twentieth instant, had the honour to conduct a lady out of a boat at Whitehall Stairs, desires to know where he may wait on her to disclose a matter of concern. A letter directed to Mr Samuel Reeves, to be left with Mr May, at the Golden Head, the upper end of New Southampton Street, Covent Garden.

The Tatler, 21 March 1709

The first book on the subject of personal column advertisements appeared in 1750, and was made up of such gallant offers and proposals. Entitled *Love At First Sight, Or The Gay In A Flutter*, it contained a selection of the most salacious and diverting announcements, and casts a fascinating light on activities in the neighbourhood of Covent Garden, where the flightier elements were to be found.

The claim is made by Stephen Leacock in *Moonbeams from a Larger Lunacy* that the first newspaper was founded on the principle 'whether this be true or not we cannot tell; but it is paid for'. This may be something of an exaggeration, but certainly by the latter half of the eighteenth century a tradition had become well established whereby news sheets, like the taverns and coffee-houses in which they were read, served as a forum for the exchange of information and for the conduct of business of every description. It was John Walter's intention in 1784, when he conceived the notion of using his remarkable new 'logographical' printing press to print a new broadsheet, *The Universal Daily Register*, to 'facilitate the commercial intercourse between the different parts of the community through the channel of advertisements'.

'The credit of the paper,' he announces, 'shall stand pledged not to the truthful reporting of news, or anything of that sort, but for the convenience of advertising correspondents, their favours shall *to a certainty* be inserted on the very day that they shall direct.' A letter on the back page signed 'Gregory Gazette', but presumably written by the same pen, describes the sort of advertisements the newspaper is likely to contain:

> The Universal Register, it is expected, will be carried on to the satisfaction of an impartial public. Its plan being liberal and comprehensive: masters who want servants, or servants masters; traders, who wish to buy or sell goods; the fair, whether maids or widows, who sigh for husbands and help-mates; in a word, all sorts and sizes, denominations and descriptions of men, have nothing to do but advertise in the Universal Register – and they will immediately hear something to their advantage.

In short, advertisements rather than news were to be given pride of place: advertisements from which one could, in that phrase so familiar to readers of *The Times* personal column, expect to 'hear something to one's advantage'. News, 'although highly acceptable in itself', came second, with a pun on the four points of the compass from which the word N-E-W-S is composed. The very name Walter chose for his newspaper – *The Universal Daily Register* (the newspaper was not to adopt the title *The Times* for three years) – is significant: it was, primarily, to be a vehicle for personal announcements and public advertisements. Indeed Walter's declared attitude towards his advertisers shows how strongly he felt on the subject:

> A newspaper in this particular ought to resemble an Inn, where the proprietor is obliged to give the use of his house to all travellers who are ready to pay for it and against whose persons there is no legal or moral objection.

These were liberal and far-sighted principles, and very democratic ones; he was not going to preach or propagandise, but simply record salient facts such as City news, law reports and shipping movements – and throw open the rest of the space to 'travellers ready to pay for it'. The seeds of the advertising industry as we know it today had been planted in the gazettes and mercuries of the previous century, and the first shoots were now pushing up strongly through the cobbles of Printing House Square. The personal column is no chance offshoot: it is the last freak survivor of an ancient species which has itself branched out into monstrous and unrecognisable forms.

If it were to be assessed by the taxonomists of the Natural History Museum (let us wander down the corridors from the Botany to the Palaeontology Department), the column would have to be classified as an absurdly lightweight, delicate-boned species, a sub-branch of the genus that produced first the pseudosuchians of Madison Avenue and finally *Tyrannosaurus Saatchi*; a species that was, nonetheless, gifted with the power of flight. Unfortunately it uses this power at rare intervals, and only the most dedicated and patient observers have actually seen it in the air. No casual browser glancing through the files of *The Times* is likely to surprise it doing anything very spectacular: those odd and memorable messages of which this book is composed are strung out at intervals of months or years.

Why then, in the days when it graced the front page, did people read the personal column so assiduously? What was there in those mundane small notices that held the attention day after day? For hold the attention they undoubtedly did. Surveys have shown many times over that it came high on the list of those parts of the newspaper most frequently read – too high to be flattering to many of those who spend their time writing the rest and only just below the letters, which are not written by professionals either.

That unpremeditated and unpredictable amateur quality is an essential part of its charm. For who by consciously trying could have produced anything as unexpected as those outbursts against footballers during the First World War ('Wanted. Petticoats for footballers . . .') or that business of the lady with the lisp who aroused the anger of the person sitting behind her at the Lyric Theatre, Hammersmith, in 1923 (there turned out to have been six ladies with lisps present in the audience), or all those extraordinary inventors' appeals? Indeed when the column acts as a soap box or as a safety valve for the expression of ideas and prejudices it often achieves its greatest heights of eloquence and its wildest flights of absurdity. In fact it performs a valuable function as a forum for airing strongly held opinions, just as Speakers' Corner does, though the cost is beyond the pocket of the average pavement orator.

Perhaps the column should be reinstated on the front page, with a Government grant, as a hitherto overlooked facet of the mechanism of democracy?

The personal column has had some eminent fans and staunch supporters, including writers as diverse as Surtees, Dickens, Hazlitt, Hardy and, of course, Conan Doyle. Church leaders both Anglican and Catholic have enthused about it – Cardinal Newman and more than one Archbishop of Canterbury among them. Politicians from Disraeli to Churchill have found it intriguing and instructive. Even royalty has not scorned to declare an interest. Queen Victoria mentions it as a royal hobby and our reigning Queen is said to have shared her great-grandmother's enjoyment of it – though neither, so far as I am aware, has followed Charles II's example and inserted their own advertisement.

This is not the first book to be devoted to the subject since *The Gay In A Flutter*. In 1881 Chatto & Windus published *The Agony Column* by a writer named Alice Clay as part of their Mayfair series, intended as 'light drawing room reading' and including *Puniana* by the Hon. Hugh Rowley, *Gastronomy as a Fine Art* by Brillat-Savarin, the speeches of Charles Dickens, some plays by W. S. Gilbert and *The Book of Clerical Anecdotes* by a certain Jacob Larwood. Alice Clay does not comment on her selection, which covers the years 1800–70, but there is an introduction in which she makes much of how 'mysterious' the messages of the personal column are and somewhat coyly invites the reader to pry into romantic secrets, showing how the simple 'substitution' codes employed by lovers in those days could be unpicked, like so much needlework, to reveal the tender messages within. It is all light, gossipy stuff. Her interest is principally in the romantic advertisements, and she shows no sign of possessing a sense of humour. She also fails to see – at least I hope and believe that she fails to see – that some of the advertisements go distinctly beyond the limits of Victorian propriety. But since *The Times* had also failed to notice this, she can hardly be blamed. There was a special thrill for Victorian lovers in seeing their secret *tendresses* printed publicly, but in a form which only they (as they thought) could recognise. Alice Clay notes, for example, the claim of 'S.B.' to be 'a strict disciplinarian and not afraid of a rather unruly pupil', but imagines it to be some kind of schoolroom jape; she is quite unaware of the metaphor of sexual innuendo.

Perhaps the main reason for the personal column's special appeal is that it is the perfect text for a daydream. It does not have to offer bizarre insights or elegant wording to be worth reading. It takes the lid off the world and shows the reader a random assortment of things that are happening – and however prosaic those things are in themselves, they reveal just enough to allow the imagination to roam or relish delicious ambiguities. Take an average page from the files during the period just after the First World War:

> Vauxhall. – Nothing to fear. – Write B.L.

Curiously appropriate today, in view of the advertiser's initials and the state of the car industry. But no, that cannot be it, not in the 1920s. More likely, in a squalid back street behind Vauxhall Tavern the net curtain of a small terraced house slowly parts and a terrified woman's face peers out. B.L., confidently bowler-hatted, is standing on the street outside, briefcase bulging with documents which will ensure that a husband is brought to heel and the mortgage is not foreclosed. Or, again:

> Spaniel or retriever taken to train; reasonable terms.

The limousine draws up at Waterloo. The elegantly groomed animal, diamanté collar gleaming, is escorted by an expert dog-handler in black leather uniform to its own specially reserved first class compartment . . .

And it is possible to dream of advertisements one would like to insert oneself. E. F. Benson's Major Flint 'in gaseous mood' dreams up a challenge which he plans to issue through the personal column:

> 'A sporting challenge in *The Times*. "Retired Major of H.M. Forces" – The King, God bless him – " (and he took a substantial sip); "retired Major aged 54, challenges any gentleman of 50 years or over . . . to a shooting match in the morning, followed by half a dozen rounds with 4 oz gloves, a game of golf, 18 holes, in the afternoon, and a billiard match of 200 up after tea." Ha! ha! I shouldn't feel much anxiety as to the result.'

Like so many of Major Flint's daydreams, it never turns into reality.

A small monograph could be written on such fictional advertisements, for many have passed into that limbo where they are half-remembered as true. 'Volcano for sale' is one of them, but, like the famous headlines 'Fog in Channel, Continent isolated' and 'Small Earthquake in Chile'[1], the myth evaporates in the bright light of research. A volcano was indeed once offered for sale and the fact is reported in *The Times*, but there is no advertisement for the volcano in the personal column. There are other delusions –

---

[1] See *More Amazing Times*, chosen by Stephen Winkworth, Allen & Unwin, 1985, pp 2–4.

'Robinson Crusoe' and 'Girl Friday', for instance, do not offer an escape to the South Seas but boring jobs in the City; and 'Daring young man, public school educated, offers to do anything legal, though crime, provided it is amusing enough, also acceptable.' never appeared. However, something like it is used by 'Sapper' in one of the Bulldog Drummond books:

> Demobilized officer finding peace incredibly tedious, would welcome diversions. Legitimate preferred, but crime, if of a comparatively humorous description, no objection. Reply at once Box X10.

This was, incidentally, the advertisement through which Phyllis got Bulldog Drummond. The Bulldog himself occasionally featured in the real-life *Times*, though as these were 'book-plugging' advertisements the management put him firmly 'below the line' – that fine line which in later years attempts to separate 'trade' from 'personal':

> Algy and Peter! I say, you mugs, old man Peterson's on the war-path again. Meet me usual place. – Bull-dog Drummond.
> *2 January 1924*

There are also, while we are still in the realm of daydream, those advertisements which nearly appeared, such as the one that Vivien Eliot, wife of Thomas Stearns, at a critical point in their stormy relationship, intended to insert on 17 September 1934, two years after Eliot had walked out:

> Will T. S. Eliot please return to his home 68 Clarence Gate Gardens which he abandoned September 17 1932. Keys with W. L. J.

If in fact Eliot had chosen to consult the front page of his *Times* on 17 September 1934, he might have found inspiration in the following cryptic appeal (perhaps from Vivien, writing in code):

> Harassed parent is asked – What Saint floated upstream? What Saint taught the devil not to poke his nose into the metal shop? Box 730 . . .

Possibly the most famous advertisement which actually appeared and was answered is this:

> Exploring and sporting expedition, under experienced guidance, leaving England June, to explore rivers Central Brazil, if possible ascertain fate Colonel Fawcett; abundance game, big and small; exceptional fishing; ROOM TWO MORE GUNS;

9

highest references expected and given. – Write Box S.1150.
14 and 15 April 1932

This caught the eye of Peter Fleming, Ian Fleming's elder brother. Here was a persistent devotee of the personal column and self-confessed daydreamer who was, for once, tempted to put those dreams into reality. His work at the time, as literary editor of the *Spectator*, was not of so pressing a nature that he could not afford a sabbatical. He had, he explains in the first chapter of his book *Brazilian Adventure*, 'a curiously distinct vision of two men with red faces deciding, in the bar of the Royal Automobile Club, that what they wanted was a couple of suckers to put up a thou'. Nevertheless, despite his doubts, he wrote off to Box S.1150 and found himself embarking on an adventure 'for which Rider Haggard might have written the plot and Conrad designed the scenery' on the limitless rivers and high plateaux of the Matto Grosso in central Brazil.

No personal column enthusiast should neglect to read *Brazilian Adventure*. Fleming and his companions failed to get within fifty miles of the area where they believed Fawcett might have disappeared; but much of the charm of the book lies in its honesty and ever present sense of humour, and it did for the *Wide World Magazine* school of writing, which Fleming constantly guys, rather what Stella Gibbons's *Cold Comfort Farm* did for imitators of Hardy. Its opening chapter is nothing less than a paean of praise for the personal column of *The Times*. Fleming confesses that he always reads it first 'and the news, if there is time, afterwards'. In hindsight, this was a rash remark for a man who was to become a *Times* staff writer; nevertheless he frankly admits that he prefers the agony column's 'world of romance' to 'that great stage of fools to which the editorial pages of *The Times* so faithfully hold up a mirror'.

What a lot would never have happened if the author of *Brazilian Adventure* had not been such a devoted reader of the personal column. Peter Fleming, the toiler in Grubb Street, unenhanced by the glamour of the Matto Grosso, might not have married Celia Johnson, star of such films as *Brief Encounter* (very 'personal column' – all those snatched meetings in railway stations) and his brother Ian might not have been impelled by jealousy to invent James Bond. In other words, the world would have been deprived of at least three archetypes.

We might also have been deprived of a fourth. *The Times* had already carried a number of articles on the various attempts to ascertain the fate of the lost Colonel Fawcett, who had disappeared, with his son and another young man, into the central Bazilian plateau in 1925, never to be seen again. The 'fourth archetype', not exactly a result of Fleming's reply to that advertisement, but inseparable, at least in daydream logic, from the rest, surfaces in one of these earlier articles. On the evidence of a manuscript dating back to 1743 Fawcett, a thin wiry man of incredible toughness, who was something of a mystic as well as a man of action and skilled geographer, convinced himself that there was a lost world somewhere between the upper reaches of the Rio Xingu and the Rio das Mortes, both northward-flowing tributaries of the Amazon. Surrounded by the high, impregnable walls of the Serra do Roncador there lay hidden amid the jungle the ruins of a massive city of incredible antiquity, deserted following an earthquake aeons ago. It was not actually El Dorado, though it certainly had more than a gleam of gold about it, as well as a mass of indecipherable hieroglyphics and thrilling evidences of a lost civilisation far more advanced than anything hitherto discovered by archaeologists.

This was a rich time for lost worlds. Howard Carter's excavations of the Valley of Kings had revealed dazzling treasures astonishingly well preserved. Conan Doyle had published in 1912 his story of another lost world, surrounded also by high walls of basalt and populated by prehistoric animals (the first creature the two explorers, Challenger and Summerlee, come across is of course a giant pterosaur).

Unfortunately for romantics and dreamers everywhere, Fawcett's lost world of the Serra do Roncador (an appropriate name, incidentally, so far as daydreaming is concerned, for it means the 'snoring mountains') turned out to be purely imaginary. This much at least was established by Fleming's expedition. Conan Doyle's basalt cliffs, on the other hand, are very much all there today, for the area he was thinking of, in the Roraima mountains of southern Venezuela, does indeed boast a high plateau, since visited by various expeditions, none of which have discovered evidence of the survival of prehistoric life, though they have found some weird and unusual mosses. By one of those pleasing criss-cross ironies which show that real life is doing its best to keep up with fiction, the explorer Jimmie Angel, who landed a plane on top of Conan Doyle's 'Lost World' and discovered the Angel Falls, the world's highest waterfall, crashing down over a mile of basalt rocks into the valley below him, was later to take up Fleming's suggestion and mount his own (equally unsuccessful) Fawcett hunt by air.

But we are losing sight of our fourth archetype. It centres on the report of a Swiss trapper named Stephen Rattin who turned up at the British Consulate in São Paulo in March 1932 with an extraordinary story. The story is given in a *Times* article which Fleming read ten days after he had seen the advertisement in the personal column and it was as a result of reading this article, which describes the proposed expedition, that he decided to write to Box S.1150. Rattin relates how he had met and talked with Colonel Fawcett the previous October, in the course of a trapping expedition across the Matto Grosso. With two companions, a Swiss and an Argentine, he was washing clothes at sunset in a small stream, when they were surprised by Indians. Although he spoke many Indian dialects, he was unfamiliar with the one spoken by this tribe; however, he was able to convey to the Indians his wish to be on friendly terms and signified his sociable intentions by suggesting they should all get drunk on something called 'xixa'. This is apparently an irresistible social gambit when encountering unfriendly Indians in the wild. Rattin and his companions were then escorted to the camp, where they found a large number of Indians, including women and children. The whole party settled into groups, squatting on the ground, and 'xixa' was duly produced and drunk in large quantities.

During the drinking bout Rattin became aware of the presence of a white man – a man whom he described as being tall, old and white-bearded, with long yellowish hair reaching down to his shoulders. As soon as he realised Rattin's interest in this venerable figure, the Indian chief became suspicious and told a warrior to go and sit beside the old man. Rattin's interest in the old man was more than matched by the old man's lively interest in Rattin, but the Indians did their best to keep the two white men apart. As the night wore on and most of the Indians became drunk, Rattin managed to approach the old fellow, who asked him if he was English. Rattin said 'no', and a difficult conversation ensued. (It must be explained that Rattin barely spoke English – and both parties had done full justice to the ample supplies of 'xixa'.) From this conversation not much coherent information emerged except that the white-bearded old man had once been a colonel in the British Army. Rattin was then shown some blocks of wood on which inscriptions had been carved with a sharp stone. He attempted, with complete lack of success, to copy them onto a piece of paper he happened to have in his pocket. (Rattin's account does not explain what these inscriptions were about, nor why he failed to copy them – though we can guess at the reason for that. Could they have been the hieroglyphics of the lost civilisation Fawcett was searching for, which he had memorised from his reading of the account of the expedition of 1743? Fleming, whose interest in the Rattin episode was purely practical, brushes them aside as 'meaningless carvings on a tree'.)

The Colonel then told Rattin that 'his son was sleeping', whereupon he began to cry. According to Fleming (this detail is absent from *The Times* report), a signet ring was also produced, but not taken by Rattin; Mrs Fawcett later confirmed that the ring described sounded like the one her husband always wore. Before the two men parted, the Colonel, who oddly enough failed to mention his name, asked Rattin on his return to civilisation to go to the nearest British Consul and tell a certain Major Paget that he, Colonel 'X', was held captive. This Major Paget was, it seems (and this is a detail the Swiss trapper could not have known), a close friend of Colonel Fawcett.

A final touch is added by *The Times*, to the effect that a Mr C. Lanarche, an American naturalist, who had recently passed through São Paulo, believed Fawcett still to be alive, since the Indians often regarded white men as 'mascots' and some Peruvian or Paraguayan trappers with whom he had camped on the banks of another north-flowing tributary of the Amazon, the Tapajoz, had told him they often came across white men living among the Indians. Their chiefs, he explained, had a weakness for white servants – who were treated well, though any attempt at escape was punished by death.

Readers who are familiar with Evelyn Waugh's *A Handful of Dust* (published in 1934, two years after the above report had appeared in *The Times*) will recognise the 'fourth archetype'. In the penultimate chapter of that book the hero, Anthony Last, becomes ensnared by a Mr Todd, an autocratic and illiterate recluse living in a remote part of the Matto Grosso. It is evident that Waugh must have drawn inspiration from reports, such as the one in *The Times*, giving Lanarche's highly suggestive remarks about 'mascots' whose escape is punished by death. In the earlier, fuller version of the story published in the American edition and also separately as a short story entitled *The Man Who Liked Dickens*, the carved wooden blocks become carved wooden crosses on simple graves. In both versions the ring becomes a watch and 'xixa' enters repeatedly into the story, first as 'cassiri' then as 'pivari'.

Few personal column advertisements trail quite so many clouds of glory, but reflections of what Fleming calls 'that great stage of fools' are scattered about unpredictably at intervals throughout the two hundred years of the column's existence. Peace proclamations appear in it (for instance in 1802); Hardy's action at Trafalgar is recorded, as is the sinking of the *Lusitania*, the Wall Street crash and sundry strikes, the effects of which advertisers ingeniously seek to mitigate or exploit ('Fully trained chauffeur at your disposal', for example, during the general strike of 1926); and in 1939 the outbreak of the Second World War is announced above the personal column in letters nearly half an inch high.

13

What the column is perhaps best at is reflecting the mood of the nation and changing codes of behaviour:

Cadet, old military family . . . having achieved modicum commercial success, desires resume social intercourse with such of the breed as do not consider trade ignoble. Requisites, brains and birth. Profiteers and plutocrats taboo. Dancing anathema.

What a lot that says about England in 1920!

2 An Inn for All Travellers

As John Walter's *Universal Daily Register* gained in popularity, the
personal column gradually emerged from the mixture of shipping announcements, advertisements for patent medicines and
theatrical performances, sales by candle and sales by auction, puffs
for turtle soup and books of verse which jostled together on the
front page. Within a month or two the custom of placing the more
strictly personal material at the top of the second column of the page
was established, but it was not until nearly a hundred years later that
this tacit separation was made explicit by the addition of the heading
'Personal &c.'

In those early days advertising space was filled both by lifting
advertisements from other newspapers (Mr Walter, with admirable
cheek, would follow this up by sending a bill to the advertiser) and
sometimes by the practice, which has been repeated in more recent
times, of inventing material. In a satirical vein, Walter lists the
'wants' of London 'Society' in 1785:

WANTED

By several superannuated ladies – female fripperies to make
them look young and handsome.

By many people – as much charity for others as they have for
themselves.

By half a million in our metropolis – honest hearts and sound
bottoms.[1]

---

[1] 'Bottom' in the eighteenth century meant an underlying seriousness of purpose,
as well as coolness and courage – rather the equivalent of 'guts' today. The metaphor
is that of a ship's bottom.

15

By hundreds of both sexes – to be placed on the pension list, and like beggars to be clothed and fed by the public.
By gamblers – to pick their neighbours' pockets.
By certain lawyers and physicians – tender hearts and consciences.
By several ladies – attentive Cicisbeos, instead of snoring stupid husbands.[1]
By many thousands of husbands and wives – to be divorced.
By several persons who figure in high life – ease, grace and dignity of deportment.
By ditto – cork-rumps on a new construction, artificial teeth and hair, with a few single eyes.
By certain schoolmasters – learning and temper.
By several public speakers – a quick conception, and an easy delivery.
By Ireland – a parliamentary reform, protecting duties, commercial equalizations and a trade to Portugal.

Walter was seeking both to entertain his readers and to encourage them to use the advertising columns of the newspaper. By demonstrating that such advertisements could be witty he was setting an example and establishing a tradition for which the personal column of *The Times* was later to become famous. Unquestionably he expected many advertisements of a romantic or matrimonial nature; however, advertisers of this kind are slow to seize on new media and it was not until the end of the following year that the first 'matrimonial' appeared. The earliest advertisements which could strictly speaking be termed 'non-trade' – lost and found, wanted, and so forth – are intermixed with a humus of tradesmen's announcements, sometimes of remarkable quality, and at this date these are often the most interesting material in the column. The more delicate 'personal' outgrowths which later spring to life must be seen against this rich background.

A delicious example is Mr Jenkins' announcement concerning 'teas'. If ever words could be said to prostrate themselves, these do, for Mr Jenkins, acutely aware of the competition posed by his rival the Percy Coffee House, next door, does not merely thank his clients for their attention, but:

impressed with the deepest sense of gratitude, humbly begs leave to return his unfeigned thanks to the nobility and gentry who, notwithstanding the many allurements held out by pretenders to public favour, have continued to patronize and

[1] A 'Cicisbeo' was a *cavalier servente*.

favour him with their commands. He assures his friends in particular that the remembrance of the obligation he is under will only cease with his life. And as the only means within his power to convince them of what he here asserts is to serve them with every article of the best at the lowest price, he pledges himself that no assiduity shall be wanting to give the same satisfaction which he flatters himself he has given heretofore.

Meanwhile in the coffee house next door not only coffee and fine words would have been exchanged, but goods of all kinds, and financial transactions of considerable importance broached and debated: 'Barks and brigantines for sale at New Lloyds Coffee House over to the northwest corner of the Royal Exchange'. The New Lloyds Coffee House was, of course, the original site of that venerable City institution, Lloyds of London.

Jostling for place on the newspaper's front page are such commodities as 'Sharp's Concave Razors', 'Middleton's Lead Pencils' and 'Velno's Vegetable Syrup'. The latter, it appears, is available from two rival manufacturers. With calculated tactlessness, the announcements of the two rivals were on one occasion placed one above the other. There follow a series of 'Cautions' from each, explaining that the other is an impostor. This use of the word 'Caution' became widespread in later years, and is a constant theme in nineteenth-century advertising.

The 'vegetable syrups', it seems, are good at curing almost everything but really come into their own when dealing with 'scorbutic and venereal disorders'. Also in this field, though aiming at a slightly different market, is something called 'The Compound Water'. This is advertised under the heading 'Health', as though it were the announcement of some public institution:

The passions prevailing, the consideration is, the balance of utility from the unerring maxim, that it is better to preserve or defend Constitutional Health, than to be content with it impaired with poisonous medicine, is the consideration under which is offered to the Public a safe, inoffensive, delicate, specific Venereal Antidote.

Many years use of this external application in America, the West Indies, and Europe, and from trials with infected persons after several hours intercourse (and never known to fail) pronounces it to be a select gift in the Mystery of Chymistry.

To be had in pint and half-pint bottles, No 55, facing Anderson's Coffee House, Fleet Street, and No 91 Blackman Street, Southwark. Ask for the Compound Water.

17

Captains of ships and gentlemen travelling, will do well to attend to the above, as it will retain its virtue in all climates.

Good allowance to those that take a quantity.

Despite a somewhat breathless start, there is a compelling urgency about this – centred on the key phrase 'and never known to fail' – which might impel readers to rush out at once and head for 55 Fleet Street. To save modern readers the trouble, it should be mentioned that this is now the address of a branch of the Anglia Building Society.

Dangers such as those alluded to in the above advertisement were not experienced solely by captains of ships and those travelling to the Americas, as is made plain in a 'house' announcement inserted by Walter in March headed 'Hints for Magistrates'. Readers who are not much taken by the modern fashion for wine-bars will find their prejudices reinforced by this condemnation of their eighteenth-century equivalent:

Attention to be paid to gin-shops, alias Wine Vaults; each of these is a Pandora's box, pregnant with evils and diseases. It is in these places the murderer and robber irradicate the feelings of human nature, by the use of spirituous liquors; it is here they stimulate their minds to acts of horror; it is here the trades-man's wife squanders the earnings of her husband; it is from these shops the abandoned prostitute issues into the streets, to seduce the innocence of youth from the path of virtue.

A visitation should be repeatedly made to a coffee house not a hundred miles from Soho, where demireps hold nocturnal revels, and where every species of debauchery is practised.

Further evidence of the cyclical nature of fashion is provided by the advertisements for 'ginseng tea'. Again, breathless enthusiasm is the keynote:

It has been introduced into England, which, with other curious herbs of our own growth, by extracting the salts, is rendered superior to all the tea exported from China, the common people cannot purchase the root in China on account of the price. This extraordinary discovery to England will be the saving of more lives than the sword has destroyed, which time will produce.

The writer, clearly anxious to get his message across with the utmost urgency, regardless of order or syntax, explains the benefits of ginseng and the difference between this valuable root and the other teas which:

by being adulterated, as too frequently is the case, both by the Chinese before they come to England, and when they come are adulterated here, and the leaves dried again after being made use of, is the most prejudicial thing for the nerves, and by the nerves being hurt disorders the whole frame. Such are the virtues ascribed to this celebrated root.

Spoken from the heart, clearly, by a man well acquainted with the damaging effect on the nervous system of adulterated tea.

Another curious import, also enjoying a revival of interest today, is:

Diona Musipula or Venus's Fly Trap. – In fine order for planting, just arrived from Mr Young, Botanist to His Majesty. Also the plants called Fothergalia, Andromeda, Gloriosa foliis, Sempervirens, Gordonia, Utopia, etc, collected with many new and rare seeds in that long journey by land, from Philadelphia to Cape Fear, some of which are evergreens, and such as were never before imported. To be sold at Brooke's Menagerie, New Road, Tottenham Court.

30 April 1785

Such advertisements, whether for rare plants, birds, minerals or other products of the expeditions of natural historians, abound at this time; they are generally addressed 'To the Curious' – 'in plants', 'in birds', 'in minerals' etc. But patent medicines, along with such fairground marvels as dancing dogs, tightrope acts and displays of juggling, are the mainstay of the second column of the front page.

An unusual medical endorsement appears in May 1785, from one William Reeves, colourman. William Reeves is a regular advertiser, 'having devoted eighteen years in the preparing of superfine water colours in cakes', for 'patrons of the beautiful art of landscape and miniature painting, drawing etc'. His is one of the few firms still in existence today whose advertisements appeared on the front page of the newspaper during its first year: one of the others is the publisher John Murray. In a bizarre example of 'dual purpose' advertising Reeves appends his name to a lengthy statement concerning his wife's cure from a 'complicated bilious and nervous complaint' involving 'pain and wind in the stomach . . . with sighing and crying hysterics, rising in the throat, tremors, hurry and confusion, dread and fear'. As though this were not in itself sufficiently serious 'there followed a most severe vomiting of bile night and day for about five months, without one day's intermission, and however incredible it may appear, frequently brought up two or three quarts of bile in a day, and seldom anything passed the bowels or stayed on the stomach, and through violently straining the blood frequently gushed out of the nose.' All advice, needless to say, proved ineffectual, until Mr Reeves applied to a Dr Brown of Leicester Fields, whereupon a nearly miraculous cure was performed upon what sounds like a most spectacular form of illness.

William Reeves' efforts, however, pale into insignificance when compared with the work of that Alexander Pope among copy writers known only to posterity as N. Godbold, purveyor of Godbold's Vegetable Balsam. There must have been long faces and bitten fingernails at Velno's, rival purveyors of a similar substance, when Godbold's poem 'Ah! what avails the wealth that Indus brings', over eighty lines long and written in elegant heroic couplets, graced the front page of the *Universal Daily Register* in May 1785. It is an extraordinary display, quite unlike anything else that has ever appeared on the newspaper's front page.

Other poems appear in the personal column at various stages throughout its history, despite the efforts of management to suppress them, and there is even a chance that some may be attributed to famous hands, as I shall explain later. Whether this work (too long, alas, for inclusion as a whole) is by Godbold himself or by some better known versifier writing under a pseudonym as a paid hack is uncertain, but Godbold declares:

> Who reads this verse peruses not the lay
> Of hirelings base, who draw their pen for pay.

I need only point out here the masterly build up to a climax in the middle of the poem when the sickly youth, despaired of by his weeping mother and by friends and physicians alike, 'scarcely breathes, the shadow of a shade' – followed by the thumping bathos of:

> GODBOLD arrives, and in propitious hour
> Rescues the victim from death's sovereign power,
> His balsam drawn from herbs with wondrous skill
> (So Heaven ordains) his great designs fulfil . . .

Perhaps the most extraordinary thing about Godbold's epic, however, is that henceforth his name vanishes from the pages of the newspaper. Was he, with the true instinct of the supreme artist, content to slip away from the scene, knowing that his masterpiece could never be surpassed? Did the poem whip up such a tornado of customer demand that, bearing in mind the inevitably limited supplies of the precious herbs from which the balsam was composed, he was forced to take cover from the mobs who besieged his house in Bloomsbury Square? Or was he overcome by a trade rival? Perhaps Mr Velno throttled him.

Godbold's masterpiece should no doubt be classified under the heading of 'Trade'. There are, however, even at this early date, some advertisements which may be considered to be free of that taint, though Godbold's poem surely stands as a fine example of the heights which patent medicine advertisements are capable of reaching and a warning to those who might imagine that the column's 'soul' lies only in the messages of lovers, runaways, spies, cads, lunatics and the like. Some of the column's other multifarious functions also show signs of that 'soul' which somehow lives on through all the dross of daily petty transactions. Lost and found announcements, for example, and particularly those concerning animals. Here are some touching examples from the newspaper's earliest years:

> Lost, on Friday evening last from Clarges Street, Piccadilly, a brown bitch, of the Fox kind, answers to the name of Loo. Whoever will bring her to No 34 above, will receive five shillings for their trouble. She will not be advertised any more.

> Strayed into St James Park, a little rough dark brown bay filly marked 'D' the off shoulder, long tail but no shoes on. Whoever she may belong to by applying to Mr Boys, Park Keeper, St James' Street Gate, St James' Park, and paying the expenses, may have her again.

Another, from the less elegant end of the town:

> Lost, about three weeks ago, a dark Grizel Nanny Goat, without horns, from No 11 Labour-in-Vain Yard, Upper Thames Street. Whoever will bring her to the above direction, will be rewarded for their trouble.

Double the number, and add water:

> Two pigs found swimming in the Thames, near Westminster Bridge. Now safely lodged, awaiting a suitable reward, at The Swan, by Lambeth Church.

Multiply by ten and add a note of suspicion:

> Sheep stopped. Stopped, on suspicion, twenty down sheep, at Mr Brokers, Butcher, Kingsland Road. Whoever owns them, may have them again, by paying the expenses.

> Sheep, like goats, are notorious for going 'astray-ay-ay-ay-ay'

(*pace* Handel), but what about ships' anchors? For some reason –
perhaps a series of bad storms, perhaps some piratical plot – several
anchors were reported lost in 1788:

> Lost, off Gunfleet, on the 3rd inst., a Ship's Anchor, of about
> 17 to 18 cwt, with a new buoy and buoy rope, and about three
> fathom cable, belonging to the ship Two Brothers, Christopher
> Blom, Master, from Norway. Gunfleet Beacon, bearing then E
> by N by the compass about a league; and Harwich Ness steeple
> NE by N in nine and a half fathoms of water. Whoever has
> found the same, and will give notice to Messrs G. & E. Wolff &
> Co., in London, shall receive their full salvage and other
> expenses.

Later the Maplin Beacon itself was advertised as lost in these
columns, making a strange bedfellow with the endless series of
bags, books, bangles, walking sticks and precious stones. There is
no way of estimating how many of these impedimenta were ever
restored to their owners; however, on one remarkable instance, in
1798, a 'found' and a 'lost' are printed one above the other and have
every appearance of belonging to the same article:

> Found, a Bank Note. Any person producing the sum, number
> and date, upon paying the expenses of this advertisement will
> receive the same upon applying to Mr Spry, at Mr Lane's, No
> 240 Aldersgate Street.

> Lost, a £15 Bank Note, between the Bedford Head, Maiden
> Lane, Covent Garden, and Mr Regulus's Toy and Doll Shop,
> Little Newport Street, Leicester Square. The number of the
> note not known. Whoever will bring it to the Bedford Head,
> Maiden Lane, Covent Garden, shall receive Two Guineas
> reward.

One cannot help hoping that Mr Spry was not too insistent about
wanting to know the number of the note, and one wonders whether
the gentleman from the Bedford Head eventually returned, with his
refound £15, to Mr Regulus's delightful-sounding shop, to make a
purchase which brought pleasure to some eighteenth-century child.

If the personal column has a soul, it is a soul not without defects.
One such defect – an enduring, though regrettable one – makes its
first appearance in June of the newspaper's first year:

> Whereas my wife, Mary Sermon, being lewdly inclined, and
> not content with the endearments nature hath afforded me,
> hath taken into her employ another man; this is to caution
> all persons not to trust her, as I will not pay any debts she

may contract. – The Mark of W. Sermon. Witness Benjamin Kiddell.

30 June 1785

Human nature being what it is, husbands and wives continued to be lewdly inclined, or otherwise to disagree, and such announcements are so frequent as not to be worth commenting on again, since they all fall roughly into the same pattern of legal phraseology, omitting however those details which distinguish W. Sermon's disclaimer. (In one rare instance, during the Second World War, there is a return of fire from the opposite side.) But as for lewd inclinations, a good deal more latitude was allowed to the newspaper during its earliest years, so it is not altogether surprising to find, alongside worthier publications such as *Swedenborg Vindicated* and *Sympathy Defended* (both published by John Murray):

> Harris's List of Covent Garden Ladies, or A Man of Pleasure's Calendar for the Year 1786. Containing the histories, and some other curious anecdotes of the most celebrated ladies now on the Town, or in keeping, and also of many of their keepers. Printed for the author, and sold at No 9 Little Bridges Street, next door to the one shilling gallery of the Drury Lane Playhouse.

Matrimonial inclinations, on the other hand, are scarcely catered for at all, despite Walter's expectations of being able to satisfy 'the fair, whether maids or widows, who sigh for husbands and help-mates'. Advertisements for wives, or husbands, in fact never became a common feature of the personal column. The first, from 'a gentleman', appears in December 1786:

MATRIMONY

> A gentleman of very considerable fortune, about the age of forty, offers himself as an husband to any well-educated, amiable and agreeable lady, of good character and not more than thirty years of age, and as much younger as may be, who will undertake to exercise those attentions which his particular situation requires. Though he possesses an excellent and unimpaired constitution, he is afflicted with an incurable weakness in his knees, occasioned by the kick of an ostrich, in the East Indies, which disables him from walking, rising from his chair, or getting from his bed, without assistance. That assistance he wishes to receive from the tender care of an

affectionate young lady. Fortune is not an object of his consideration. Letters addressed to M.P. at Mr Wallis's, printseller, Ludgate Street, will receive every proper attention. No other enquiry need be made, as no information can be given.

The final sentence was presumably M.P.'s defence against the wags, who might have been disposed to find something comic in what was to M.P., no doubt, a delicate and unhappy predicament.

'Kick of an ostrich' indeed! This is one of half a dozen well-known gems from the personal column which are repeated by everyone who has ever had anything to say on the subject. In most of these articles – one suspects they read each other rather than the original – the piece is wrongly dated and is quoted in such a way as to give the impression that the column was full of such advertisements in those days. Some writers have even invented a few of their own in a similar vein, to add spice. Anyone who has studied the early years of the column carefully might imagine, as I did, that this piece too was an invention; but, *rara avis* though it is, it did indeed appear, though there is nothing else remotely like it. It first came to prominence when *The Times* reprinted it in a series of advertisements published shortly after the Second World War, designed to encourage advertising in the classified columns.

The first matrimonial advertisement by a lady appears about a year later. It was inserted by 'a lady, about twenty-five years of age, who has been flattered with the idea of possessing an agreeable person, and who, without any flattery at all, is in the actual possession of an independent fortune'. Why, then, one wonders, would she need to advertise, for, to turn the tables on Jane Austen, 'it is a truth universally acknowledged that a single woman' (especially one with an agreeable person) 'in possession of a good fortune, need not wait long for a husband'? In this case, as it turns out, all was not well, for 'the ill usage of her relations has obliged her to separate herself from them; and they, in revenge, not only employ their utmost malice to disturb her repose, but threaten prosecutions to deprive her of her fortune'. Indeed there is the making of a Jane Austen novel here, for the final words of the advertisement are 'Any such gentleman, therefore, who will stand forth as her protector, to save her from the tyranny of her family on the one hand, and the impositions of lawyers on the other, shall be rewarded with the object he has protected, and the fortune he has preserved.'

Nor would it be too fanciful to hear the voice of Jane Austen in the following, which appeared not long afterwards:

> Wanted – A young woman of genteel appearance and agreeable temper, to attend upon a lady going to Bath; a person that can be well recommended, and of creditable friends, who has not been in a similar capacity will not be objected to.

Jane Austen would have been fifteen when the above appeared. Four years before the publication of *Northanger Abbey* in 1818, a young lady of quite exquisite gentility – the perfect companion for a season at Bath – advertises for a post as companion, and indeed apologises for having to do so:

> A young lady wishes to be received as inmate by a lady of a gay and lively disposition, who requires an intelligent and confidential companion. She would have no objection to contribute something towards her expenses, but her circumstances being limited, it could be nothing very liberal, though it might be some object of consideration with a lady, who would find it inconvenient to enter into the expenses incurred by an additional inmate. Though reduced to the necessity of making her wishes and application known through the medium of a newspaper, the advertiser would nevertheless be found, on further enquiry, an acquaintance fully to answer the requisites described, and might prove an agreeable and useful acquisition to a lady of the above description. A letter addressed to the care of Mrs Smith, 20 Great Castle Street, Cavendish Square, will receive punctual attention.

Also in reduced circumstances, though more robust in her attitude, is the 'middle aged woman who has seen better days' who advertises in 1798. She is looking for a widower with children 'to whom she would pay every tender attention', while she herself would become 'a useful and cheerful intimate of the household'.

Another valetudinarian advertises in April 1802 'To settled and single ladies, who are so situated as to command that happiness in life which the sexes, when dispositions are mutually attempered, constitute in each other.' As though that were not enough to destroy his chances, he goes on – like the young lady of exquisite gentility – to apologise for advertising and for being 'destitute of further introduction than the recommendation of expressing himself'. He is, he declares, 'desirous of becoming allied with some provided-for female of sentiment, who has no objection to alter her state for the society of an infirm, but (to be candid) affectionate and considerate man, of little more than 30, whose particular wish it is to be fixed and settled; but whose dependence having been rendered very limited, his intentions of quitting the Mother country to improve his circumstances will be changed only by some connection as above stated'. There is a peevishness about this which makes one hope for their sake that the ladies who read it chose to remain as settled and single as they were when they picked up their newspapers. But selfishness, emotional tepidity, materialism, cowardice and ground-less self-esteem so pervade the advertisement that any woman stupid enough to fall for it would have had only herself to blame for the choice of the miserable life of unrewarded self-sacrifice it clearly offers. Here are this latter-day Caspar Milquetoast's closing words:

> As society and the means of genteel support are objects which duty directs to precede a too great warmth of affection, any amiable and judicious woman, situated as before represented, whose sentiments may have a coincidence with those now tendered, may command an interview, by a correspondence addressed to A.B. at Mrs Stevens's, No 3 Downing Street, Westminster.

Was the composer of so off-putting an advertisement really looking for a wife at all? B.M., who advertises in 1787, was not. 'Wanted – A sincere friend', he announces. All B.M.'s friends, it seems, had for various reasons deserted him. Either they had fallen sick and died just when he needed them most or they had gone away, or got married, or otherwise behaved unsatisfactorily. But lest modern readers be tempted to read the wrong meaning into all this, B.M. goes on to explain 'The advertiser is a creditable householder, in a genteel line of life, from which he derives a decent income, yet is at present so circumstanced as to have occasion for the use of £80 or £100 for a year and a half, or two years' and he further specifies that he is prepared to pay five per cent interest to this friend, and will repay by instalments and deal with principals only.'

The severely practical purpose which lay so close to the surface of this advertisement is present in most of the matrimonial advertise-ments as well. Even old 'Ostrich Kick' is careful to point out that whereas he is in possession of a very considerable fortune, the same 'is not an object of consideration' in the future Mrs Ostrich Kick. That unfortunate weakness of the knees was not accompanied by a corresponding weakness of the head.

Matrimonial and 'lonely hearts' advertisements never took root in the personal column, and were banned altogether following the shocking Red Barn murders of 1828. The murderer, William Corder, stealthily killed a girl named Maria Marten, then adver-tised in the *Morning Herald* of 13 November 1827 (and in the *Sunday Times* ten days later, but never in *The Times* itself) stating that he had 'lately lost the chief of his family by the hand of providence, which has occasioned discord among the remainder' and was looking for a new wife. One of the forty-five letters Corder received as a result of this announcement was from Mary Moore, whom he eventually married, before killing her in turn. This produced a powerful revulsion against the idea of matrimonial advertisements. As one contemporary remarked, they 'generally emanate from speculative, sensual and sordid men, whose aim is to obtain a mistress, or a fortune, rather than a wife'. The examples I have quoted seem to bear this out. Readers of *The Times* should be thankful that the paper did not allow them after this, for they would have unbalanced the personal column, pushing out better material, and *en masse* they make dull reading.

The same is certainly not true of messages between lovers. A daily smattering of them is very much the hallmark of *The Times*. Such *cris de coeur* grew in number towards the middle of the nineteenth century, by which time the second column of the front page had already been popularly dubbed 'the Agony Column' (before the phrase came to be used for replies to readers' letters in the 'Miss Lonelyhearts' sense). Once romantic messages had become fashionable, they remained current for a further span of twenty or thirty years – for the personal column is much given to imitation and in many instances pioneering messages of one kind or another are followed by a host of variations on the same theme. The most remarkable instance of this are the Collinson cryptograms in the middle of the nineteenth century, which attracted a continual barrage of other coded material lasting for another decade and a half after Collinson's six years of cryptic activity.

The earliest 'gallant' advertisement appears in December 1800. It has a politely male-chauvinist flavour, distinctly a product of the eighteenth century:

A Card. – If the lady who a gentleman handed into her carriage from Covent Garden Theatre, on Wednesday the third of this month will oblige the Advertiser with a line to Z.Z., Spring Garden Coffee House, saying if married or single, she will quiet the mind of a young nobleman who has tried, but in vain, to find the lady. The carriage was ordered to Bond Street. The lady may depend on honour and secrecy. Nothing but the most honourable interview is intended. The lady was in mourning, and sufficiently clothed to distinguish her for possessing every virtue and charm that man could desire in a female he would make choice of for a wife. Deception will be detected, as the lady's person can never be forgot.

A very different tone is displayed by the following, which appeared four years later. Had its author been reading too many Gothic novels?

> To M---a M---e. 'Forget' you? By Heaven I cannot! Engraven on my soul is your memory, in deepest characters, which Time will vainly endeavour to efface, contracted as now must be its span; since without one remonstrance, one expostulation, you can resolve forever to forget me. Wherefore, then, often warned, persist in exciting a reluctant, indeed, but never more unfeigned sensibility, only to wound it? Do I deserve this? Is it generous? Is it equitable? But severe no longer; welcome now is the mandate of authority, enjoining oblivion of – 'Orl---o'

The name Orlando had taken on a new popularity since the publication of John Hoole's translation of *Orlando Furioso*, Ariosto's poem, a few years earlier in 1783 and remained a favourite pseudonym for 'romantic' advertisers in the personal column well into the twentieth century. Another popular name was Leander. This carried rather more desperate connotations, since, as it will be remembered, Leander drowned while swimming across the Hellespont one night on his way to see his beloved Hero, a priestess of Aphrodite, who in turn was so upset that she threw herself into the sea:

> Incognita's elegant and well composed epistle, of the 19th instant, has had all the impression that possibly could be expected: another, with real name and place of abode, may safely be ventured. An immediate intercourse is earnestly requested by – 'Leander'.
>
> *23 December 1802*

Agony of a less romantic kind also appears:

> If the youth that left Islington on Sunday evening can remember that he ever had a mother, he is informed that he will soon be deprived of that blessing, except he immediately writes with particulars, or personally appears before her. His friend will redress any circumstance, and settle every point to his satisfaction.—West Smithfield
>
> *21 September 1804*

This is perhaps one of the most strongly worded, but 'Come home' messages are considerably more frequent than those of lovers at this date. Most simply state 'Will so-and-so, who left such-and-such a district not long ago, kindly communicate with his father (mother, family etc) who would be glad of any news of him.' Sometimes there is a veiled threat that if 'so-and-so' does not return various unpleasant things may happen, and from time to time they are so worded as to make it transparently obvious why 'so-and-so' felt impelled to leave in the first place.

Another desperate mother – or perhaps it is the same one, if desperation can be sustained at this pitch for twelve years – appeals in 1816: 'Philip. – Would Philip like to hear of his mother's death?'

There are other appeals of a more venal kind. Ever since *The Times* started the practice by endorsing a charitable case on its front page in June 1787, an increasing number of advertisements had begun to appear appealing for money. On 13 July 1808 a sort of prototypal Jeffrey Archer makes an announcement detailing the way in which he has been unjustly deprived of a fortune through an unfortunate speculation and is now reduced to penury. Rather than writing a best-selling novel about the incident, however, he restricts himself to a public notice setting out the case. This notice, he explains, is on display in the bar of the Globe Tavern, Fleet Street. 'The particulars of his sufferings, and the circumstances which led up to them, may be seen by application at the bar of the Globe, signed by persons of distinction and respectability, and what trifle humanity may be induced to contribute, will be received at the site, and strictly appropriated to the relief of the object of this appeal.'

There are few other truly 'personal' advertisements during these early years. There are occasional mystifying messages such as 'The answer of a letter to an officer at Hereford is "That he was"' (13 February 1800), or, more intriguingly, towards the end of the year 1810, 'If the gentleman, whose conversation was interrupted a fortnight ago by the exclamation "Sir, you will lose your handkerchief" and also by a carriage driving suddenly into Portland Place, wishes to renew it, he will find that the curiosity that then lay dormant has since been excited.' The earliest example of a really cryptic message is the appearance in January 1800 of the two letters 'J.B.' on their own, with no signature. No doubt this meant something to someone, but it is probably a signal rather than a cipher, for the vogue for codes in the column did not start until much later. There is, however, one remarkable early use of code, in 1821–1824. This is interesting not only because it appears over twenty years before coded messages began to become popular, but because it has never been decoded. Had it appeared a few years later and had Babbage seen it, the story might have been different. The 1821–1824 series is given in the Appendix.

Mysteries and curiosities such as these are extremely rare until many years later. Most of the day to day material is made up of advertisements such as the following:

> Wanted. – A light elegant second-hand chariot, not the worse for being a little used, the body hung on whip springs, and a barouche seat on springs large enough for two persons. Price from 120 to 150 guineas. Address, post paid, to Messrs Haily and Paines, Royal Exchange.

The above dates from 1807, but could be considered a prototype of the kind of used car advertisement which has always been a staple of the column and continues to this day.

A major concern of advertisers during the earlier years is to assure the readers of the genuineness of their product. 'Beware imitators' warn rival manufacturers, 'none other genuine' – and, of course, 'Caution'.

> Real Bear's Grease. Mr Vickey informs Ladies and Gentlemen that he has killed another fat bear and that they may have the grease in its real state, cut off from the animal in the presence of their servants; or that rendered down in pots, from one shilling to one guinea each; at his house, No 139 Billingsgate Street, near the London Tavern. The above is the only thing possible to make the hair grow thick and long, recover it after sickness, and preserve it on the head during life. The fat rendered down, and made fit for sale, is sold upon oath.
>
> *18 March 1786*

It is as though a butter manufacturer were to announce today 'Mr United Dairies informs the public that he has rounded up a herd of cows, and will milk them in the presence of your staff and churn it into butter in front of their very eyes and wrap it in 450gm foil packs while they watch.' Advertisers adopted a similarly dramatic stance when they announced that they had 'landed a fine lively turtle' from which soup was to be made and sold in pots.

Even more exotic fare was popular: reindeer tongues enjoyed a vogue at the turn of the eighteenth century, at 10s 6d a dozen; there were also East and West Indian preserved ginger, guava jelly, mangoes 'and all sorts of rich sauces and pickles, as Japan Soy, Cheroque, zoobditty, Quin sauce[1]; Japan and Patna rice at 2d and 3d halfpenny a pound; the real Bengal currie powder, the only cold drawn castor oil, and genuine tapioca.' All these goods, together with 'China ware very cheap, Indian floor mats and Chinese ink' were for sale in January 1788. And, to wash down the reindeer tongues and Bengal curry, what better than 'that excellent anti-scorbutic almost now universally drunk at table, Spruce Beer'. This

---

[1] 'Cheroque' is a walnut ketchup. 'Zoobditty' is a mystery.

concoction was made, improbably enough, by the Swedish Army, from the leaves and tops of the fir. They had devised a good military bottle to contain this potent brew – 'The corks are wired down that they may not be driven out by its expansive force.'

Common ale and beer were not advertised at this time, perhaps because their manufacture was small-scale, conducted piecemeal and for the most part on site by individual inns and ale-houses. Large breweries with brand-names to promote were as yet unknown. However, a mere twenty years later, in 1822, beer is being advertised in a way that suggests that small-scale brewing – 'home brewing' – has become a rarity, leaving the true enthusiast, like his modern counterpart, with an endless search for the few remaining traditional ale-houses where the magic substance was still to be found. The words of this announcement conjure up a mouth-watering picture of an age of innocence among publicans and an Arcadian springtime for beer-drinkers. Reading it one is assailed by a curious confusion of the sense of time: a sort of blending of the centuries, such as can occur in rare instances in certain very musty old public houses. Is this the perfect pub, and was Mr Bush the archetypal landlord? Should the Bell be the Mecca for pilgrims in the Campaign for Real Ale? Alas, the Bell has vanished and has been replaced by a modern office block, but here is its advertisement from October 1822:

> To the admirers of the Genuine Home-Brewed, in the highest state of perfection: the general approbation so warmly bestowed upon the Home Brewed Ale, Stout and Porter, of the Bell Inn Brewery, Warwick Lane, having excited in many a desire to become acquainted with this brew and superior process of brewing from malt and hops only, W. Bush begs to inform Country Brewers and Private Families, that he is willing to give instructions, on moderate terms, to such as will attend his brewings, where every information necessary to ensure a complete and practical knowledge of the process may be obtained.
>
> The following reduction in prices has just taken place: Porter 4d, Stout 5d, Ale 6d per pot, and the same article sent in casks or bottles, according to order. Choice Wines and Spirits. Families supplied with Hops and Malt, ground or unground, in any quantity.
>
> N.B. As the above are offered at a very small profit, no credit can be allowed.

Genuineness was even more important and more difficult to ensure when it came to wine:

Poison Detected. – An artifice is practised by the dealers in wines, cyder, etc, when they become sour, to recover their former sweetness and flavour by one of the most pernicious drugs that can enter the human frame, and which the taste cannot perceive. Those who wish to guard against the bad effects of such diabolical practises may be supplied with a Chemical Preparation for the purpose, which will instantly expose such hidden mischief. Sold for the proprietor, by Mr Goldberg, Perfumer to Her Majesty, Cornhill, in bottles at 2/6d each and nowhere else in London.

24 May 1787

One could imagine this product being much in demand in 1787. The passage of time is more clearly evident from the announcements of the quack and patent medicine manufacturers, who dominated the advertising space at this time. Many bore long and florid testimonials, and although none went quite to the lengths of N. Godbold, many were elaborately written. Such advertisements must have constituted one of the newspaper's most reliable sources of income at this date. A high proportion of them openly declare their efficacy in curing the 'venereal affliction', and they frequently devote much space to attacking each other, or debunking rival forms of treatment. 'Salivation exploded', announces one, in a vituperative attack against the popular use of mercury as a treatment for syphilis (one of the side effects of the treatment was the production of excess saliva in the patient's mouth). Words are not minced in such advertisements, and many are quite gruesome. Their frankness is however preferable in some respects to what was to follow, for soon a species of insinuating, whispering cant had developed, aimed at arousing anxiety and, above all, guilt in the reader. Leaders in this field are Messrs Currie & Co, 'Regular Surgeons', who in 1806 announce:

A radical cure in all cases of infection and disease, which have hitherto baffled the virtue of every medicine, but that of mercury. Their mode of treatment has proved itself equally beneficial in the cure of those maladies, relaxations and debilities, both of body and mind, resulting from a long residence in hot climates, from licentiousness of living, from the intemperate pursuit of excessive pleasure, and the fatal indulgence particularly to the younger classes of both sexes in an insidious and destructive habit.

The cure consisted of 'advice and medicines' and could be obtained either by direct consultation or by letter 'post paid, enclosing a

Bank Note' (surprisingly, the denomination of the bank note is not specified). The wording is deliberately vague and carefully calculated to worry the nervous while simultaneously offering to cure them – a technique perfected by the travelling 'medical museums', which enticed inside curious and credulous people, frightened them with waxwork models of disease and medical curiosities in preserving jars, then offered salvation through quack medicines and leaflets exhorting plain living.

The following advertisement from 1798 manages to combine a degree of euphemism with an unmistakably eighteenth-century frankness of intention:

> Pregnancy. – Ladies who, from the consequences of indiscretion, may be desirous of medical aid, or perhaps find temporary seclusion from the world necessary, may be accommodated . . . by a medical gentleman whose honour and secrecy may be safely confided in, whose advice and friendship, if early sought for, may be productive of unexpected benefit, and the means of preserving reputation unsullied. As the plan is established with the most scrupulous attention to privacy, to repress idle curiosity, and improper application, a Guinea will be expected . . .

A certain delicacy was also employed by the manufacturers of Leake's Genuine Pills, sold by 'His Majesty's Royal Letters Patent' (in view of what they claimed to treat they could hardly have been sold by Royal Appointment). To preserve the privacy of purchasers of 'Leake's Venereal Antidote' there were, it was explained, 'two back doors and Lights in the Passages at Night'. Another herbal extract, named 'the Infalliable Tincture', was sold from 74 St James's Street at 7s 6d the pint bottle by a lady 'acting more from a principle of humanity than emolument'. Furthermore, it was actually given away gratis on Fridays (but only between ten and twelve o'clock) 'because there are many who labour under the complaints, and have it not in their power to purchase this sovereign medicine'. One might see in this, according to one's point of view, an early foreshadowing of the National Health Service or perhaps the original 'loss leader' by the original 'ethical pharmaceutical company'. Cynicism urges the latter view, despite the lady's protestation that she thought it 'a duty incumbent upon her to offer this tincture from the experience she has had of its unerring qualities', for the wording of the advertisement makes it clear that there was more humbug than humanitarianism in the offer. Perhaps it led too little and lost too much, for by 1789 the 'Infalliable Tincture' had disappeared from the pages of *The Times*.

Not long after this there appears a series of advertisements for something called 'Spilsbury's Patent Antiscorbutic Drops', in which for a brief moment great heights of the copywriter's art are reached. If Godbold is the Pope of advertising, Spilsbury is its Poe and Elizabeth Leek his Eulalie.

'Elizabeth Leek had at first a small spot, of a brownish cast, on her wrist', begins Spilsbury's first announcement, in February 1805. What is it about this opening which is at the same time so compulsively memorable and yet so quietly sinister? (The name 'Leek', by the way, may have been a sideswipe at the rival manufacturer, 'Leake's Genuine Pills'.) Few readers of *The Times* can have failed to shudder at these words, coiled evilly at the foot of the personal column beneath a clutter of Patent Bedsteads and Incomparable Razor Strops ('under Ducal Patronage'). Here, in its entirety, is the saga of Elizabeth Leek:

Elizabeth Leek had at first a small spot, of a brownish cast, on her wrist; she paid no attention to it, conceiving it required none: it began to spread, producing a watery humour, accompanied with a dry scurfy surface, inflamed, with violent itching. When she applied for the medicine, Spilsbury's Patent Antiscorbutic Drops, the disease had spread over both arms, and they exhibited the appearance of a continued raw surface, so that she was unable to draw on her gloves. Having taken the first bottle, they amended surprisingly, and after taking six bottles scarcely anything remained save a roughness of skin. Elizabeth Leek.

Joseph Tucker, No 11 Tottenham Street, Tottenham Court Road, vouches for the veracity of this statement.

Remarks on the genuine medicine: 'By the King's Patent' must be expressed in words at length on the bottle, in the bill of directions and the wrapper covering each bottle of medicine. The stamp (that is the King's Duty) is printed in black ink instead of red ink: the cork in the mouth of the bottle is always sealed with red sealing wax.

Mr Spilsbury attends as usual at the Dispensary.

6 February 1806

The detail about the gloves touches some deep dream-symbol, and the mumbo-jumbo about red and black ink adds a masterly touch of authority. Satisfied, as well he might be, by the results of this pioneering effort, Spilsbury went on in July of the same year to write a second tale of mystery beginning with the words 'Jane Taylor, aged 34, broke out four years ago, in a large blotch on her left leg. It continued, spreading, until it arrived about the knee.' After which, the course of events followed much the same path as they did for Elizabeth Leek – ending, naturally, with salvation through Spilsbury. In October we have 'Sarah Lekford, aged 35 years: when first this case of scrophula made its appearance, it was in the absorbent glands in the neck'. There is here a marked falling-off in both style and substance. Spilsbury's decline, hastened no doubt by over-indulgence in his own antiscorbutic preparations (which were probably highly alcoholic), is henceforth precipitous, until by the end of the year he has abandoned all attempts at fictional creativity and is grovelling before the feet of the medical profession with windy announcements beginning 'The case of scrophula which we have submitted to the public is extremely interesting' and going on with much babble about the King's Evil. It is sad, though not surprising, to discover that Spilsbury makes no further appearances in print after 1806.

To this short excursus on the connections between patent medicines and the poets there must be added one more name: Byron. Extending the range of our interest somewhat to other items in the chemist's shop, it is known that Lord Byron never troubled to deny the charge that he once received £600 from Mrs Warren for composing verses in praise of her blacking:

> Friend, said Aminadab to Obadiah,
> Why such amazement do thy features show?
> To see, Aminadab, thy boots on fire,
> And thou stand harmless in the burning glow!
> Ah, Friend, dost thou so of discernment lack –
> Art thou so far to common knowledge barren,
> Not to perceive 'tis but the radiant black
> That's manufactured by friend Robert Warren?

When asked who it was that had composed these fine verses so widely featured in her advertising (George Cruikshank, by the way, illustrated her posters with a cat spitting at its own reflection in the toe of a boot), Mrs Warren is said to have replied 'La, Sir, we keeps a poet!' Incidentally, the same remark is attributed in 1855 to Mr Packwood, a manufacturer of razor strops. What cannot be denied, however, is that in 1812 there appears an advertisement bearing the poet's name. His biographers have commented on his continual and excessive use of aperients. Are 'Byron's Pills for Removing Costiveness' a mere coincidence? The phrasing of the advertisement is graphic enough: 'When the stomach or intestines are surcharged with bile, these pills unite with, gently dissolve and carry down their contents; nor do they leave the bowels in a state of imbecillity, but induce that temperament necessary to health, so much to be desired by bilious persons.' They are recommended especially for 'seafaring men, elderly and sedentary persons, and those who drink to excess'. Byron certainly drank to excess, but poets are not mentioned.

Literary style in the small advertisements was not confined, in these early years, to commercial advertisers. The following vituperatively sarcastic outburst against a public lottery inspector was published in 1789, before the laws of libel put such language beyond reach:

Three hundred guineas reward. – For T. Wood, Inspector of Lottery Offices. If Mr T. Wood will support upon oath, what he has ventured with uncommon audacity to affirm, we undertake to give him three hundred guineas for doing himself that justice which every honest, innocent man would anxiously seek, even without any pecuniary incentive. His deposition to state unequivocally:

That he is not the said T. Wood who, after hiding himself in a private room, and the door being broke open, was apprehended for being concerned in the fraud and conspiracy of subborning a bluecoat boy to steal a ticket from the lottery wheel, to have it apparently redrawn at a stated time, for sinister purposes.

That he knows nothing of the said T. Wood, and was never apprehended upon such a charge.

That he never assumed another name at Boulogne, in France; or negotiated any bills, in any name but his own.

That he has not been a general common informer under various penal statutes.

That he never kept any Insurance Offices himself, nor shut them up, leaving the adventurers unpaid.

The connection between insurance and gambling is one which would hardly be looked upon with favour in the City today; however, not all insurance was carried on in this fashion. Lloyd's, though still referred to as a coffee house, was rapidly establishing itself as the centre for this business. An advertisement from 1805, for instance, speaks of 'a steady, respectable man, well acquainted with the business of the rooms' who wishes to be employed 'by any house of consideration' to effect their insurance, or to 'devote his whole time to the concerns of such a house, being well qualified for any department, where experience, attention and integrity are desirable'. He gives his address as 'R. R. at Lloyd's Coffee House'.

This was a time of rapid growth and consolidation for financial institutions of every kind. 'Money!', announces an advertiser in 1789, 'Certain noblemen, gentlemen and ladies may have occasion for a temporary or permanent speedy supply of Money!' Which of us does not? At all events, it seemed that this universally felt need could easily be met by a Mr R., of 17 Essex Street, off the Strand, where ladies and gentlemen might 'depend on the greatest candour and delicacy in every respect'. But Mr R., as the advertisement later makes clear, was not a philanthropist but a moneylender.

Another advertiser at about this time declares:

Money lent and fortunes increased. – Money in two hours to merchants, noblemen, and others, for Bills or Notes of Hand, or on Annuities, or any kind of security, real or personal, for any length of time. The advertisers never procrastinate; they either decline the business when it is impracticable, or do it out of hand, and always with profound secrecy. Those who have money may lay it out with great advantage by applying, or addressing (post paid) to the Discount Office, No 93 Norton Street, Portland Street, or to the Agent, at the private door, No 17 Ludgate Hill.

In September 1790 the column carried an advertisement with a zany mixture of the amateurish and the improbable. It was inserted by a gentleman – or perhaps a rogue – with an unlikely choice of hobbies, collecting debts 'for amusement':

Wanted, by a middle aged person who has a small income of his own, some employ for exercise and amusement in the way of collecting debts, rents or otherwise; salary will be no object.

The man was, at the very least, a sadist and clearly there would have been scope for greatly augmenting that 'small income' in all sorts of unscrupulous ways.

Educational establishments of one kind or another occupied a fair proportion of the advertising columns. An important-looking announcement heads the personal column in July 1795 with the words 'At a very numerous and respectable meeting of masters of boarding schools, in the vicinity of London, held at the Crown and Anchor Tavern, in the Strand, the Rev. Dr Rutherford in the Chair.' At the meeting, it seems, there was a unanimous demand for an increase in boarding school fees.

The tavern played an important role in the life of the schoolmaster at the turn of the eighteenth century and the beginning of the nineteenth:

Castle Hedingham Academy, one of the most pleasant and healthy villages in the county of Essex. – J. Jonas (late assistant in the academy of Mr S. Lyon Hebrew teacher to the University of Cambridge) begs to inform his friends and the public in general that he has opened a seminary for the tuition of young gentlemen, and hopes, by the strictest assiduity and attention to the instruction and morals of his pupils, to merit the favours and patronage of those who may place their children under his care. Terms, 18 guineas per annum, washing and every other expense included, except books, clothing and medicine. School opens on Wednesday 7th instant, until which time letters post paid addressed to J. Jonas to be left at the Bar of the Green Dragon Inn, Bishopsgate Street (where J.J. may be seen every day from 11 o'clock in the forenoon till 3).

3 January 1806

Such advertisements enable one to build up a fair picture of daily life at this time. There is another kind of advertisement, however, which provides not only detailed descriptions of people, but often dramatic stories, told in a few simple words. These advertisements, which appear with increasing frequency in the early years of the nineteenth century, always start by offering a 'reward':

One hundred guineas reward. – Whereas Lavinia Robinson, one of the daughters of the late William Robinson, of Manchester, wireworker, was, on the evening of Thursday the 16th day of December last, in the company of a gentleman (to whom she was on the point of marriage) in the parlour of her sister's house in Bridge Street, Manchester, after her sister, who was unwed, had retired to rest. In the morning it was discovered that she had not been in bed, and a note, purporting to be in her handwriting, was found in the parlour, from which there is reason to fear that she is no longer living. Her family and friends have been plunged by this unhappy event into the greatest distress. They feel the most painful anxiety to obtain some intelligence respecting this unfortunate young lady, and as an inducement to strangers to exert themselves upon the occasion, a Reward of Thirty Guineas (free of all expenses) is hereby offered to be paid by Mr John Redhead, solicitor, St Ann's Church-yard, Manchester, to any person who shall be the means of discovering, alive or dead, the lady who is the subject of this advertisement. She was 20 years of age, of a middle size and good figure, of a fair complexion, with long light brown hair. She had on a fawn coloured twilled stuff dress, a pink and yellow shot figured silk handkerchief on her neck, a brown cloth mantle, a black cottage bonnet, and her linen is marked L.R. We, the Borough-reeve and Constables of Manchester, as a further stimulus to the exertions of strangers, do hereby offer a Reward of Seventy Guineas, in addition to the above reward of Thirty Guineas. Thomas Hardman, Boroughreeve. Thomas S. Potter, James Touchet Junior, Constables. Police Office, Manchester.

19 January 1814

R. S. Surtees, the creator of Jorrocks, was inspired by such advertisements. He was also a great enthusiast for *The Times*, and for the personal column in particular.

'What a wonderful institution is *The Times*!', he exclaims in *Plain or Ringlets*. 'It is a perfect modern miracle. It has kept increasing for the last five and twenty years, till it is nearly the size of the table cloth on which it is laid every morning at breakfast time. No one feels fit to confront his fellow men until he has mastered its contents.' The personal column 'contains hints for a hundred novels', while the general announcements include almost every possible requirement:

Houses, horses, estates, cooks, coals, carriages, straw, stockings, steam-boats, candles, canaries, cows, books, bottles, boots, clocks, clothing, chickens, soap, sugar, shipments, towels, trousers, teeth, corsets, crinolines, cottage pianos, bedsteads, brandy, Brighton, microscopes, mangles, and mustard; harmoniums, harrows and hyacinths, umbrellas and rollers.

But the kind of entry he most favoured were the 'Rewards'. 'The pen and ink portrait gallery is very perfect, and often severely like', he wrote. 'It must be very inconvenient to an absconding gentleman to find one hundred pounds reward for his apprehension.' He gives an example: 'He is about 60 years of age; florid complexion; stout made; grey hair (thick bushy whiskers, which he sometimes dyes); walks very erect with a quick short step, and wears a silk hat with flat brim, placed much over his eyes.' 'After that,' comments Surtees, 'we should think the gentleman would very soon give up dyeing his whiskers and have his hat on the back of his head like a lady's bonnet.'

Absconded, George Rochford, from the service of Mr Dixon, City Repository, in Barbican, generally employed in delivering bills. George Rochford, who has absconded with £119 10s in notes and cash, is about 40 years of age, a native of Stokesly, in Yorkshire, about 5ft 6in high, long face, sullen countenance, has an impediment in his speech, a black speck in the middle of his front tooth, rather knock-knee'd, and loose made; supposed to have had on, when he left, a black lapelled coat, black waistcoat, and blue trousers, and lately resided at No 3 Ratcliffe Place, St Luke's. Whoever will apprehend and lodge him in one of His Majesty's gaols will be handsomely rewarded.

10 October 1822

Left his home, on Sunday last, a very tall thin gentleman, name John Jones, about 45 years of age; has a long thin face, and peaked nose, stoops and walks lame, from having tender feet; had on a black coat, light waistcoat and pepper and salt trousers, and boots; supposed to be out of his mind.

30 August 1828

The appeal of such notices to the mind of a writer with a gift for caricature is obvious. The best ones appear at about the time Surtees was writing: evidently the more detailed descriptions brought better results, for earlier examples are much shorter and sparer. An advertisement from 1802 offering a £50 reward for a certain James Parsey, Junior, who had robbed his master, gives very little in the way of a description of the man, though it does offer a few clues about the world in which he lived:

He is 21 years of age, 5 foot 6 high, sallow complexion, dark hair; by trade a glazier; served his time in Bell Alley, Coleman Street, worked lately at Messrs Croucher and Johnson's, glaziers, in Grocers' Alley, lodged in Chimney Sweepers' Alley, Fore Street, and generally was of an evening at the Black Horse, in Aldersgate Street.

The following, likewise, is evocative of a world rather than an individual, though it speaks of a harsher, darker world than any Surtees cared to write about:

Found drowned in a ditch, leading to the Marshes, near the Green Gate, Plaistow, in the Parish of West Ham, Essex, a man, apparently a seafaring man, pitted with small-pox, light brown hair, supposed to be about 50 years old, or upwards; 5ft 5in high; has on a long brown greatcoat, a sailor's jacket and trousers, check shirt and blue striped Guernsey waistcoat. Any person owning the body, may have it by applying at the Workhouse, in the said Parish, on or before Sunday next.

18 December 1805

The Times was indeed becoming a wonderful institution, and the scope of its column of announcements was growing rapidly wider. When, in 1802, peace was declared with the French, the Lord Mayor of London, Mr Eamer, inserted an announcement on April 28th that the formal proclamation was to take place the following day. He begs his fellow citizens:

> that they will afford him their best assistance in his endeavours to preserve good order during the whole period of the Procession, and the Illuminations in the evening. And to this end the Lord Mayor has given strict injunctions to the Peace Officers and their assistants to take care that no injuries are committed upon the persons or property of any of the inhabitants. And has also directed that no Coaches, Carts or other Carriages, be suffered to stand or remain in the principal street, through which the procession is to pass.

As the layout and shape of the newspaper develops, other sites, such as the Court page, or the news columns themselves, are found for announcements of this degree of importance. It is nonetheless interesting to see how, in those early days, matters of state jostle for place with lost and found notices and advertisements for patent medicines. Political announcements, for instance, are often made there or requests such as the following, which casts a dim light on prevailing standards of rectitude in 'a Certain Assembly':

> A Seat in a Certain Assembly. Any person having the power to insure the introduction of an independant gentleman, by resigning, or otherwise, is desired to direct a letter to J.G.J. at No 12 Upper Thornhaugh Street, Bedford Square, which will meet the politest attention, and a personal interview granted.
> *19 June 1807*

'*Douceurs*' of between £500 and £1600 are offered for 'a Place under Government'; and one occasion (12 January 1802) a message to constituents is inserted by the mother of Lord Kensington, an absent Member of Parliament, thanking them for their:

> unanimous choice of him as your representative in Parliament this day; an honour the more flattering, as it has been bestowed upon him without his personal solicitation, and apparently from the same sources of goodwill and regard as marked your attachment to his father, and seated him for so long a course of years as your representative in Parliament.

A more uplifting aspect of our island history is to be seen in the following resolution inserted by the Lord Mayor, Mr Shaw, at the head of the column of personal announcements, on 31 January 1806:

> A Court of Common Council, holden in the Chamber of the Guildhall of the City of London, on Thursday, the 30th day of January, 1806.
>
> Resolved unanimously, that the Freedom of this City be presented to Captain Thomas Masterman Hardy, and a sword of 100 guineas value, as a testimony of the high sense this court entertains of his gallant behaviour on board Lord Nelson's flagship, the Victory, the 21st day of October 1805, at the memorable capture and defeat of the combined fleets of France and Spain, off Trafalgar.

Already, amidst this confusion of quackery, trade, lost and found articles, public proclamations and private tragedies, some of the elements which are to become familiar in the personal column are emerging. The very diversity of these early beginnings foreshadows what the column is eventually to become: more a meeting-place than a market-place and a forum where national quirks and characteristics can be expressed, where lovers can make their rendezvous and lost causes can be proclaimed.

The last word on these bustling, boasting years can perhaps best be left to that giant among pigs, intellectual forebear of the Empress of Blandings:

> Toby, the Sapient Pig, the greatest production of nature. – Whoever has seen his surprising performance are delighted beyond imagination: he is in colour the most beautiful of his race, in symmetry the most perfect, and in temper the most docile; he far exceeds anything ever yet seen for his intelligent performances, it is impossible to form an adequate idea of the surprising sagacity of this animal: in him the power of instinct is so extremely striking that it seems superior to reason in many instances; and to some persons it may even have the appearance of romance, but the curious may form some just idea of his extraordinary capacity from the following particulars: this phenomenon will spell and read, cast accounts, play at cards, tell any person what o'clock it is to a minute by their own watch, also tell the age of anyone in the company, and, what is more astonishing, he will discover a person's thoughts, a thing never heard of before to be exhibited by an animal of the swine race: the performance of this truly surprising pig must be seen to be believed.

6 September 1817

3 *Gaslights and Balloons*

Among the enduring themes that leaven the daily fare of lost and found, wanted and for sale are appeals for help, financial or otherwise, from the desperate and the announcements of those with no other channel to bring their ideas before the public.

In this last category are those aiming to reach a small but widely scattered or otherwise untraceable group, either to persuade it of some common interest, to sell it something, or to ask for its help in other ways – authors in search of specialised information, veterans of battles trying to organise reunions, or holders of a particular belief or viewpoint not readily expressed elsewhere. The column can, in other words, function as a public platform for the desperate and the inspired. It thus has a certain appeal to the lunatic fringe, to faddists, and to inventors. There have been, from time to time, rules to exclude certain forms of sectarian advertising from *The Times*, and the productions of obviously deranged minds are sometimes (though not always) rejected. But inventors – who, however seemingly eccentric, are by no means all deranged – continue to bring their brain-children before the public in this way.

I myself inserted an announcement as recently as June 1985, which was aimed at reaching a small, widely scattered and otherwise untraceable group, and also at bringing my own particular brainchild to the attention of those who might be able to use it.

In the eighteenth century automata earned their keep by being exhibited to the public in fairgrounds and arcades, or, more rarely, were bought as the playthings of rich aristocrats. Today their patrons must be the visual media – film and television. I had created the modern, electronic equivalent of an automaton – a flying model of *Pteranodon ingens* – and had heard that some film company,

43

somewhere, was planning a remake of Conan Doyle's adventure story *The Lost World*, in which extinct animals, particularly pterodactyls, play a starring role. Here, I hoped, was a chance for *Pteranodon* to earn his keep. But how to trace the film company, and at the same time flag down anyone else who might find employment for *Pteranodon*? Where else could I advertise but in the personal column of *The Times*?

Lost World – Film makers requiring flying 15ft pterodactyl for this or similar films, apply Stephen Winkworth.

Alas, this advertisement broke one of the cardinal rules of such announcements. It contained an ambiguity – not evident to me at the time – which resulted in my telephone being swamped with calls from people who claimed either to be able to build 15ft flying pterodactyls 'in a couple of weeks', or to have a friend who had one.

This, however, is a digression, for this chapter is devoted to a single group of advertisers: the inventors of the late eighteenth and early nineteenth century. These inventors are different in one very important and delightful respect from those that were to follow, for they were unaffected by the industrial revolution and were concerned not to improve methods of manufacturing goods nor to foist new weapons of destruction upon the world, but simply to amaze and amuse spectators – and most of their announcements are more akin to those of the theatre, which from the newspaper's earliest years were allotted the top left hand corner of the front page. But the balloonists, wizards of automata and creators of spectacular scientific effects also belong to the history of invention; so, as precursors of those ingenious men whose appeals for credence or financial support crop up regularly in later years, they find their place here.

The first mention of ballooning in *The Times* occurs in April 1785 and it reads rather like a circus broadsheet, except that half-way through its tone changes from the boastful to the apologetic. A good deal of apologising usually accompanied these ballooning announcements. More often than not there was some previous failure of a greater or lesser kind to be explained away, for the balloon was not usually viewed as an object of scientific experiment which could be allowed its share of mishaps as improvements were made and the limits of performance tested, nor was ballooning thought of as a sport or leisure activity of an expensive and slightly risky kind, as it is today. No, ballooning, as this advertisement for the 'British Balloon', which headed the personal column of the day, quite clearly shows, was one of the performing arts and its objective was to put on a visual display, as colourful and stirring as possible.

British Balloon. Lyceum, in the Strand. – Count Zambeccari, Constructor of the superb air balloon above mentioned, returns his most grateful acknowledgements to the numerous, illustrious and respectable persons who were pleased to honour his ascension from Tottenham Court Road, in company with Admiral Sir Edward Vernon, with their presence; and begs leave to assure them he shall ever retain the liveliest sense of their generous favour and indulgence upon the occasion; regretting as one of the most mortifying experiences of his life that, through the violence of the wind, the inflating operation was not only unexpectedly tedious, but insufficient to gratify the spectators, with so ample display of the superior beauty and magnificence of the British Balloon, as would have been the case, had not the weather proved hostile to his endeavours. Count Zambeccari presumes further to add, that a second ascension will shortly take place, the splendour and glory of which, he flatters himself, will more than compensate for the former unavoidable deficiency. In the meantime, and in compliance with the wishes of numbers of Ladies and Gentlemen, who had not an opportunity, either before, or at the ascension, of viewing the scientifically constructed, elegant and much admired aerial vehicle, the public is respectfully informed, that the British Balloon, with improved decorations, is again exhibiting, at the Lyceum on the Strand, from ten o'clock in the morning until the close of the evening. Admittance one shilling. N.B. Any lady or gentleman, inclinable to make one of the party at the next Ascension, may be accommodated by applying as above.

Meanwhile, that rival and more reliable branch of 'invention as show business', the mechanical models, the 'animated figures' of the museums and exhibitions of automata, offered numerous counter-attractions. An advertisement from the Glass Warehouse, Coventry Street, near the Haymarket, in June 1785 is chiefly remarkable for its description of a flying mechanical bird 'very useful for the direction of an air balloon'. The mention of such a device antedates other known similar devices by a hundred years, but since no detailed description is given, one cannot be sure whether some ingenious deviser of automata had in fact made a breakthrough in aerodynamics or whether the 'flying bird' was a derivative of something like Leonardo da Vinci's flying top, in which revolving feather rotors are powered by a tensioned string. There is on display in the Air and Space Museum in Washington a French toy flying bird, made in 1885, whose flapping wings are powered by a rubber band and whose flight is directed by a movable tailplane. Whether the mechanical bird was of this kind or not, its claim to flight was almost certainly genuine – for, as we shall see, the museums of automata boasted a number of flying objects. Flying was very much in vogue, and the personal column shows many more signs of this vogue in its earliest years than it does when manned flight becomes a reality a century later.

In the eyes of the exhibitors, however, the mechanical bird was not the most important object on display. In language reminiscent of the proud claims of the owner of Toby, the Sapient Pig, the Glass Warehouse advertisement describes 'a speaking figure . . . composed by a mechanic'. It is 'about the size of a new-born infant' and it shares with Toby an extraordinary power to speak and read thoughts:

> Those ladies and gentlemen who go to see this figure, may question it promiscuously in any language they think proper, and the figure will answer to every question with that precision, as though it had been prepared for those questions. If agreeable to the company, the figure will put the question.
>
> Any person may speak either with a loud voice, or whisper that no person in the room can hear, and the figure will answer to every question asked; and to prevent communication, the figure will be suspended in the air by a riband, which may be examined or exchanged.
>
> The author has had the honour of showing it to the King and Queen of France, and all the Royal Family; and to that of Portugal, where she was the wonder and admiration of them all.
>
> And at Madrid, she caused so much surprise, that the whole Spanish Institution assembled, and sat together to interrogate her, to all of which questions she answered very well.

All this, preposterous though it is, somehow gives greater credibility to the flying bird which follows, for the inventors of this 'speaking figure' – evidently a fairly elaborate automaton operated by a clever ventriloquist, perhaps concealed beneath a platform – would not have been content to exhibit a fake flying bird (strung from wires, for example), which simply flew and did nothing else. They would have made it sing, lay eggs, peck at spectators, or recite in Latin the passage in Virgil describing the fall of Icarus.

> The mechanical bird. – Who flies in all senses, and is very useful for the direction of an air-balloon; it is the first piece of mechanism that ever was known to fly.

A bold claim, indeed. Maybe the bird was one of the first flapping-wing mechanical toys, powered perhaps by wound string; certainly it was not the first piece of mechanism to fly, for Leonardo's flying top, unlike his man-carrying designs, flew well enough.

The other flying inventions on show the following year were the product of a Mr Enslen, who had thought up a new twist to the idea of ballooning as a visual display. His balloons, though tethered, were gas-filled and fantastically shaped to represent mythological figures. His 'Cabinet of Aerial Figures' is announced on 6 January 1786. Like the inventor of the mechanical bird, he claims to be the first in his field; and there is no reason to doubt him, since the use of gas for balloons (as opposed to hot air) was a recent discovery.

Mr Enslen, a celebrated German naturalist, on the first discovery of the properties of Inflammable Air, thought it might be applied to a less dangerous and more agreeable use, than that of inflating simple balloons. After two years of constant application, numberless experiment, and great expense, he flatters himself to have at last attained the wished-for end, and thinks himself amply rewarded for his labours and researches, by the universal approbation his truly wonderful figures have met with from every person who has seen them. He has discovered a method of preparing a nervous membrane, taken from the bowels of animals, in such a manner that, inflated with air, it instantly assumes the form to which he had adopted it; and the deception is so complete that the astonished beholder thinks he sees an animated being of the fullest proportions, not a mass of air. After having exhibited in Paris these masterpieces of human industry, justly acknowledged to be so by the first liberal and most enlightened artists, Mr Enslen now hopes to gratify the most sanguine expectations of the curious in the metropolis.

The following aerial figures will be inflated and exhibited at the Pantheon:

A winged horse, mounted by a warrior fully armed, representing Pegasus and Perseus. No description can convey a just idea of this wonderful figure and of its masterly execution, though ten feet high, and much larger than life, yet the most delicate proportions have been observed and expressed: the attitude is grand, warlike and graceful. The beauty and elegance of the form, the transparency, the vivid glow of the different colours, everything fills the spectator with delight; but nothing can equal his astonishment, when he is told that the

47

whole weight of the horse and rider is but twenty-eight ounces.

Enslen's advertisement goes on to describe a 'dreadful and enormous Harpy of South America covered with green and red shining scales', a 'colossal figure of Fame', a 'beautiful Mercury' and an 'elegant Nymph with a balloon head-dress eight feet high weighing ten ounces'. Unfortunately his works must soon have disintegrated – 'nervous membrane from the bowels of animals' sounds perishable stuff – and, unless illustrations of them can be found in contemporary posters or magazines, their impression on the art-historical record must be faint.

Another inventor and maker of automata who advertises frequently in the personal column at this time is 'Mr Merlin', who lived at Princes Street, Hanover Square. We know that is where he lived, for apart from announcing his mechanical displays, he advertised in the personal column for a lodger:

Mr Merlin, Princes Street, Hanover Square, well known for his mechanical inventions, being single, and not having occasion for a whole house, would like to accommodate a single gentleman of character, with genteel furnished apartments. He thinks this might prove agreeable to a gentleman of a mechanical and musical turn, who might have an opportunity of observing and gratifying his curiosity in numerous respects. The nobility, gentry and amateurs may be accommodated, as usual, with the following articles, and several new inventions, viz. his patent double bass pianoforte harpsichord, with twenty different stops; also his grand and patent pianoforte, with four unisons, richly finished; and likewise his patent harpsichords, with two unisons and octavo, with various stops. Mr Merlin recently offered ladies and gentlemen a newly invented machine, that will play kettledrums and trumpets, and may be added to any harpsichord; it may be used with or without the harpsichord at pleasure; also undertakes to build mechanical organs, which will imitate vocal and instrumental music, with kettledrums, trumpets, etc.

N.B. His patent piano forte stop may be added to any harpsichord, which, upon trial, will be found to render the same harmonious beyond description . . .

By this time the lodger has been forgotten, and the advertisement rambles on about musical desks with receivers for candles, weighing machines and Mr Merlin's marvellous 'Morpheus sleeping chair, made to form a bed at pleasure for infirm persons'.

Another prominent figure was Maillardet, whose exhibitions are

announced from the turn of the century until about 1810. Among
Maillardet's attractions was 'Cage with birds that fly from one perch
to the other, alternately singing their natural notes, then joining in a
duet; the motion of wings, beaks etc are minutely accurate. On the
top of the cage is a butterfly fluttering.' There is no claim here that
these birds were actually flying in the true sense of the word; no
doubt fine wires or hidden arms were operated to give the illusion.
Maillardet, whose exhibitions were sited at Spring Gardens,
claimed to have received the 'approbation of their Majesties' and
they were altogether more ambitious shows, as well as grander and
(at 2s 6d admission) more expensive than Merlin's.

There were also museums, such as Rackstrow's, which specialised in medical and natural history displays and demonstrations of
'Animal Magnetism'. No scientifically proven phenomenon has
ever been introduced to the world amid such a din of quackery and
showmanship as 'animal magnetism', or hypnotism as we now know
it. 'Equipment portable by coach', announces one charlatan in
1789. There were also serious discussions at the Westminster
Forum. One advertisement reads:

> Animal magnetism. – The following popular question will be
> debated, viz. 'Are the authors of Animal Magnetism en-
> thusiasts who deceive themselves, pretenders who attempt to
> deceive the public, or men of real information who have
> discovered a secret beneficial to mankind?'
>
> Dr Yeldall, and several other eminent professors of animal
> magnetism are expected to attend. (The experiments the
> doctor performed at Capel Court Society will be deemed a
> favour.) Several of the literati have signified to the Managers
> their intention of speaking, particularly a learned foreigner
> who was present when Dr Franklin made his report to the
> French Academy. A debate is therefore expected every way
> worthy of the attendance of the philosopher, man of genius,
> and that polite assemblage of ladies and gentlemen who
> patronise this institution.
>
> *20 October 1789*

A curious sidelight is cast on contemporary attitudes to science
and to mechanical inventions by the following advertisement, which
appeared on 28 January 1793:

> Readings and Philosophical Experiments. No 11 Cork Street.
> On account of the shocking regicide of the unfortunate Louis
> XVIth, there will be no readings this evening. But on Friday
> next, the first of February, the tragedy of P. Corneille,

announced for last Friday, will be read. Between the acts, Mons. Adam will make some experiments in physics, with machines hitherto unknown.

The beheading had taken place on the previous Friday, the 21st. There is no indication of the nature of Monsieur Adam's machines, but by Friday advertisements were already appearing announcing the publication of an account of the execution, with an engraving of another French invention 'the beheading machine – La Guillotine'.

A French balloonist, Monsieur Garnerin, inserts a fine series of advertisements in 1802. This was the year in which, of course, thanks to the temporary peace between England and France, things French were accorded a special degree of interest; besides, Garnerin's experiments were unusually spectacular and successful, though by no means without incident. Such was the stir aroused by Garnerin's performances that *The Times* felt called upon to describe them at some length – thereby initiating the tradition of editorial comment on the outcome of personal column advertisements, a practice which, incestuous as it sounds, almost always produces stories of particularly piquant absurdity and interest.

There was ostensibly nothing specially bizarre about Garnerin's announcement on May 27th that he was planning to ascend from Marlborough Garden to a height of 10,000 feet, except for the method by which he planned to descend – by parachute, for parachutes were still a novelty at this time.

Garnerin is careful to lay emphasis, beforehand, on the need for the right weather:

> Fine weather is absolutely necessary for the experiment of the parachute, both for the gratification of the public, and the safety of the aeronaut. Therefore, in case of a boisterous wind, this experiment will be put off till the 8th; and that the public may not be disappointed, Mr Garnerin, in spite of the wind, will ascend without a parachute, and give them a sight of the most extraordinary aerial voyage ever made in Great Britain.

Numerous trials at the Marlborough and Ranelagh Gardens were necessary, as it turned out, before the weather became suitable for the descent. Meanwhile, excitement mounted. During one of these trials, in June, the wind was so strong that Garnerin found himself carried nearly 60 miles in three-quarters of an hour. *The Times* describes the event with some verve, viewing it more as a social occasion than as a landmark in aeronautics:

RANELAGH BALLOON AND BREAKFAST

Yesterday the Pic Nics gave their grand breakfast at Ranelagh. The company began to assemble about two o'clock; they consisted of the chief part of the Beau Monde remaining in town, amounting to upwards of five hundred. There can be no doubt, had it been earlier in the season, that the spacious premises of Ranelagh would have been scarcely sufficient for the accommodation of all that must have been desirous to partake of the festivities of the day.

The breakfast consisted of all the delicacies of the season. The wines were not only abundant, but of the best quality. Those who came with guinea tickets were admitted to the gallery of the Rotunda to breakfast, others that had half-guinea tickets breakfasted in the Rotunda below, but whose tables were equally well supplied.

About four o'clock the company quitted the breakfast tables, and repaired to the garden to behold the balloon, which was suspended by ropes in a perpendicular direction, ready filled with inflammable air. A scene so novel and grand could not fail to be truly interesting; it was beautifully adorned with small flags, representing the colours of different nations. While the company were admiring the balloon, several gentlemen offered to accompany Mr Garnerin in his aerial voyage, but a Mr Sotheron had been already chosen for that purpose. The wind blew exceedingly strong, and it was considered by many as very likely to prove a dangerous excursion; however, Mr Garnerin, considering his reputation at stake, never varied from his determination. The time at length arrived, and the guns were fired to announce the immediate ascension of his balloon. All the cords were unfastened, and the spectators retired from the plot of ground where the balloon was fixed.

Precisely at five o'clock Mr Garnerin was handed into the gallery of the balloon, and his partner was following him when he was laid hold of by a female, either a relation or his wife, who entreated him with tears to give up his project. The lady however implored in vain, he leaped into the gallery and joined Mr Garnerin who was busied in throwing out a few bags of sand to accelerate the rising of the machine, it being at the same time held by about a dozen men, who were not to quit till a proper signal was given. When it was found that the balloon was in a situation to ascend, the men still keeping hold of it, walked round the ground, which was railed in in order to give Mr Garnerin and Mr Sotheron an opportunity of taking leave of the spectators. Having quitted their hold, the balloon instantly began to ascend in a perpendicular direction, until it rose nearly the height of the trees in the garden; it then began to descend, and was once on the point of being entangled with some of the branches, but Mr Garnerin at the same time with great alertness throwing out two of the sand bags, it again ascended, and cleared the garden amid the plaudits of the spectators. Having risen a considerable height, the wind forced it in a Northeast direction. Mr Garnerin and Mr Sotheron had each in their hand a flag, which they waved as long as they could be perceived, but in the space of ten minutes, at a great distance, they entered a cloud, and it was impossible afterwards to descry them from Ranelagh. At this time the rain was pouring down in torrents. Those who were in town, and had an opportunity to mark its progress, saw it pass over the upper end of St James's Park, where two more sandbags were thrown out. It continued its progress across the Strand, and seemed to be pursuing its course over Islington, in a direction for Hertfordshire.

It was the intention of Mr Garnerin, if the weather turned out pleasant, and his companion was not affected by the different changes of air, to take a long voyage, and not alight till dark. As we know he had not returned to town at twelve o'clock last night, it is likely that they have proceeded so great a distance as to render their reaching London last night impracticable.

The Times lists the nobility and gentry present at the event – a glittering company including the Duke and Duchess of Devonshire and the Earls of Stanhope, Spencer and Shrewsbury. The following day letters are printed from Garnerin and his companion (whose name, it turns out, is not Mr Sotheron but Captain Sowden). The pair had landed near Colchester, and it had been a rough trip. Garnerin declares himself to be 'all over bruises'. Their landing, according to Sowden, 'was rather difficult, owing to the wind being very high. You may conceive what a devil of a rate we came at.' The balloon itself was 'all to pieces'.

It must therefore have been with considerable excitement that readers of *The Times* on the first of July came across another advertisement by Garnerin declaring that his attempt was to be repeated and 'will irrevocably take place at Lord's Cricket Ground, in the New Road, Marylebone, on 3rd of July next at 3 o'clock in the afternoon.' July 3rd was a Saturday, so presumably any cricketers who might have hoped to use the ground had been obliged to give way, for Garnerin's announcement explains that he had obtained the approbation of the magistrates for the attempt. However, once again, he is careful to assure the public that 'the trial of the parachute requires fine weather, yet, if his descent was thereby prevented, he would, nevertheless, perform his Majestic Ascension in his balloon, and moreover pledges himself that nothing on his part shall be wanting to gratify the curiosity of the public.' He goes on to give a long list of the agents from whom tickets for the event can be bought, at prices ranging from 10s 6d downwards.

Garnerin's advertisement was pasted up all over the town and the event drew crowds of staggering proportions – according to *The Times*, the largest ever witnessed in the capital:

> To have formed any idea of the numbers which occupied the Jew's Harp fields, the nursery grounds adjoining, the cricket grounds, and the tops of the houses for some distance round the neighbourhood, would be utterly impossible. Carriages, hackney coaches, and market carts, filled every avenue, and for more than a mile and a half on the New Road, vehicles of every description were standing in rows three deep. The footpaths were also completely blocked up by crowds of pedestrians.

The report goes on to describe Garnerin's preparations for the ascent. The balloon and parachute had been carried to the ground early that morning, in anticipation of the crowds that were to assemble, and the casks of chemicals from which the gas for the balloon was to be produced set up well ahead of time so that by three o'clock the balloon was filled and ready to take off. It then started raining. The weather indeed turned out much worse than it had been for the ascent at Ranelagh Gardens, with an 'extremely boisterous' wind. But 'Mr Garnerin having pledged himself in bills stuck up in various places, that the weather, however bad, should not prevent his ascending with his friend Captain Sowden, no choice remained.'

Poor Garnerin! How he must have hated the English weather! And for that matter poor Sowden, since his leg must have been heartily pulled by his brother officers, for according to *The Times* he 'did not sanction his name being brought forward on this occasion, nor has he any intention of visiting the upper regions again.'

This time the Prince of Wales was there, and he came into the ring where the balloon was being prepared with the Duchess of Devonshire on one arm and Lady Duncannon on the other. After commiserating with Garnerin on the state of the weather, he obligingly signed a piece of paper for the aeronaut declaring that he had witnessed the attempt.

Emboldened by this royal approbation Garnerin determined to set off, despite the storm. Climbing into the basket with his companion, a Mr Brown ('although we have reason to know that his real name was concealed', observes the *Times* reporter), Garnerin gave the signal for the balloon to be released and off they went on another yet more tempestuous journey. They reached Chingford in Essex, this time, in fifteen minutes – an average speed of over 60 m.p.h. They left behind them scenes of chaos and disaster, for pickpockets had run riot among the crowds and a stand had collapsed, killing or injuring several spectators.

Mr Garnerin's name does not appear again in the personal column. Soured, no doubt, by his experience of British weather, but satisfied that his final flight had been graced by a princely witness, he returned shortly afterwards to France. As the novelty of ballooning – and hence its appeal as a public show – began to dwindle, fewer ballooning advertisements appear in the column and there is a rather desperate search for novelty in these latter-day performances. For example, in 1828 the 'veteran aeronaut' Mr Charles Green, who claims to have made his first ascent 'at the coronation of His Gracious Majesty', announces his ninety-ninth – from the bowling green of the Eagle Tavern, City Road. On this occasion, he declares, 'should the evening prove calm', he will ascend on horseback. Incredible as it may seem, this is not to be his first attempt at equestrian ballooning. The horse is quite a veteran aeronaut too, for 'this docile and highly trained animal' has already made two successful flights. Admission is a shilling, and a military band is promised.

More practical uses for 'inflammable air' were also beginning to emerge. In 1804 a series of lectures at the Lyceum Theatre are advertised by one F. Winsor who, 'animated by the life and example of Peter the Great, Emperor of All the Russias', proposes to demonstrate a new form of illumination employing 'inflammable air'. In 1807 a further series of advertisements appears. They are remarkable in every sense. There is an undeniable quality of showmanship about them, yet the voice of the crackpot inventor is there too; they are couched in the language of a grandiose financial enterprise, yet they are full of craziness and jealous remarks about rivals.

By the time these advertisements of 1807 appeared, Winsor was, thanks to a fund which had been set up for his assistance, firmly established in a house of some grandeur at 97 Pall Mall. In 1805, at the invitation of the Prince of Wales, he had provided gas illuminations for the birthday of George III. He then conducted an experiment on a large scale, which consisted of illuminating Pall Mall and the surrounding area by means of gas jets at the top of tall posts. The spreading flame of these lamps suggested the spur of a cock, and the wits christened them 'Cockspur lights'. As a result, the street which runs from Pall Mall into Trafalgar Square has borne the name 'Cockspur Street' ever since.

While this experiment was still in full swing, Winsor inserted the following triumphant, if somewhat crazy, advertisement in the *Times* personal column (his scheme, by the way, had been attacked by Nicholson's *Philosophical Journal*):

Gas Lights. – Whenever a discovery of such unqualified approbation from Royalty, Lords, Commons, Physicians, Chemists, Philosophers, and men of all ranks and understanding, when it excites such general surprise, satisfaction and conviction in every beholder, the inventor may, indeed 'Like patience on a monument' smile on all envious and ignorant opposition. Impressed with this idea, we insert the following from Mr Winsor's reply to Mr Nicholson, just published: "It may, perhaps, be deemed unfortunate by Mr Nicholson and his friends that my discovery is not brought forward under the patronage of some dignified member of an Academy, or scientific institution, but by a mere stranger, rushing like Saul into the sphere of prophets. In this case I can easily console myself with a few lines from one of the wittiest poets of France, being expelled from an Academy, the same as Dr Harvey was excluded from the College when he dared to publish his great discovery of the circulation of the human blood: the same as the first inventors of printing were deemed infernal agents, by the learned fanaticism of priestcraft, and the arrogance of journalists."

Translated from the French – Epigrammatic Question
"Who's Winsor, who dares to invent and to write
Before we can discover, approve or indite?
Who fears not our wise heads, or envious hearts,
Pray is he F.R.S., or Master of Arts?"

Epigrammatic Answer
"He's nobody! He's nothing! Pshaw, only remember,
Not even so much – As Academical member."

No prudent man of finance could have felt assured that here was a national industry in the making; no cautious investor would have given serious consideration to Winsor's advertisements any more than they would have to the announcements of the many isolated seers of invention whose more or less manic appeals and pronouncements crop up from time to time throughout the history of the personal column. Luckily there were some investors who were not so wise. Frederick Winsor (his name is an anglicisation of Friedrich Winzer, for he was born and educated in Germany) was the man who first brought gas lighting to England and, although he ultimately failed as a business man, his faith in the new product and his vision in understanding how portable light and heat could transform the face of the civilised world were something Victorian England never ceased to be grateful for. As with 'animal magnetism', the scientific facts were swathed in clouds of self-aggrandisement, braggadocio and pomp, yet for all the gilt and red plush language the prophecies of this infuriating man turned out to be true. The following is a sample of one of the many appeals he made to investors through the personal column of *The Times* in 1807 and succeeding years:

National Light and Heat Company for the Use of Coke and Gas Lights: to be established with £1,000,000 of capital in 20,000 shares, at £5 costs only, as the other £45 will be deducted from the dividends.

Thousands witnessed, on the 4th of June, the complete success of my experiment on a large scale; for all the lights with and without glasses, dispersed within 2,000 feet of my stove, burnt with equal brilliancy from 8 o'clock in the evening till 7 in the morning. With active assistance, I hope to introduce these pure and sanitary lights in all the streets and houses throughout the realm and colonies. My plan is calculated to insure, in a few years, nearly as much benefit to my subscribers as to their heirs and successors. The first general meeting will be held on the 26th of June, at 12 o'clock, at the Crown and Anchor, Strand, and I entreat the gentleman country bankers to make their returns on or before that day, to ascertain the number of shares sold. Subscriptions are still received, without advances, at Sir N. Bloxham and Co's, Gracechurch Street; Messrs Devoynes and Co, Pall Mall; this office, and several respectable country Banks. The list for the reserve shares, without deposit, continues open; and the illuminations etc are given as usual on Mondays, Wednesdays and Fridays at 8 o'clock, until the meeting. Plans may be had gratis.

Pall Mall, 5 June 1807

P.S. Thanks to the author of the humorous poem, entitled "Debates among the Gods on Gas Lights and the London Smoke, &c" for his present of a dozen copies. I should be happy to thank him in person, if I could identify him among several hundred share subscribers.

N.B. The persons who poured the liquor of asafoetida along the garden wall are known, but their intent was defeated, as much as breaking the transparency with stones. They may bark at their own scents, but they can never bite my Gas Lights.

(The purpose of the asafoetida saboteurs was to discredit Winsor's system by making out that it had an unpleasant smell. As initiates into the darker secrets of Indian cuisine will know, asafoetida is an aromatic gum with a pungently rotten smell.)

Winsor's advertisements continue to appear frequently during the next few years, but by 1912 his enterprise was finished, for he failed in his efforts to produce a practical gasometer. Others stepped in where he left off, and he came out of the business no richer than when he started. However, he was not altogether forgotten, for Charles Dickens, writing in *Household Words* in 1861, points out that, although much abuse was heaped on him for his lack of scientific training and for his over-energetic, not to say unscrupulous, business methods, nevertheless it was hard to see how anyone without his drive and enthusiasm could have done so much to lay the foundations of the gas industry in the face of so much prejudice and caution.

The history of invention is littered with the names of pioneers who have sunk into obscurity, not to mention the many who believed they had hit on original ideas, but whom time has buried. Occasionally such people advertise in the personal column, either with statements of their ideas or seeking financial assistance. It also happens, in times of great industrial confidence, that manufacturers and businessmen advertise for inventors. This is a much rarer event, but there was one such announcement in the middle of the nineteenth century:

To inventors and patentees. – From £1,000 to £2,000 will be given for any chymical or mechanical invention not expensive to manufacture and for producing economically some article of general consumption. – Apply to Mr Donks, King William Street, City.

1 May 1845

Many of the ideas of Frederick Winsor's contemporaries make

bizarre reading. An ingenious idea was hit on by a Mr R. Macpherson who, extrapolating from the well-known buoyant properties of cork, decided the public could be persuaded that a small fragment of this magic substance would act as a talisman against drowning. Named 'The Cork Preservative from Drowning', the device was advertised in 1785 at 10s 6d. 'It can be carried in a handkerchief', reads the announcement, 'and instantly applied to the body, whether naked or clothed, so as to effectually preserve the person from drowning.' Far from being an encumbrance, like a lifebelt, the preservative 'proves no hindrance to motion or action of any kind in or out of the water, and assists in swimming.' A series of 'trials' with the substance are then described, in which various volunteers allowed themselves to be carried with the stream without any motion of their own through the central arch of London Bridge, some lying on their backs, some upright in the water. 'The broken waves only dashed over them, as they do in boats', exclaims the enthusiastic Mr Macpherson.

By contrast, 'Beetham's New Patent Washing Mill', which appeared on the scene in 1790, sounds as though it might still sell well today in areas deprived of mains electricity. It could wash from one to twelve dozen shirts at a time and was claimed to be simple, easy to manage, economical and safe. 'One person will, in an equal space of time, wash as much linen as twelve of the ablest washerwomen, with one fourth of the fire and soap' by using this magnificent machine. It is also capable of dealing with boiling water, unlike the hands of the washerwoman, yet it washes 'so equally and admirably as not to wear the finest muslin . . . and you may wash with it for five shillings, as much linen as must cost one guinea in the common mode of washing.'

'Newly invented folding round hats' are advertised in July 1812 'in consequence of cocked hats being nearly exploded' and, as Mr Hare of the Strand (later immortalised in *Alice Through the Looking Glass*) explains, these hats 'answer most completely, opening and shutting with the same ease as cocked hats, without injuring their shape; their utility and convenience must be obvious to gentlemen who frequent crowded assemblies. (Not injured by rain.)' The advertisement ends with the delightfully mad-sounding sentence 'Be particular to notice 7L.' A hat size? Or, perhaps, a printer's error?

'Portable Water Closets, patronised by the late Emperor and Empress of Russia' are announced by Blades & Palmer in 1814:

Orders for the above useful articles have been executed for all parts of Europe where they have universally given satisfaction.

They are constructed on the best principles, having the peculiar convenience of being removable from one room to another by a single person, with the greatest ease, while at the same time they possess all the utility attached to a fixed water closet, and are totally free from smell.

The 'Anhydrohepseterion', advertised in March 1850, sounds like one of those indispensable inventions which have somehow been allowed to disappear and should be revived. It is 'a vessel for cooking potatoes without water or steam . . . it is impossible to render potatoes wholesome or nutritious by any other process.'

An inventive firm of undertakers in 1820 chose to launch their 'Patent Wrought Iron Coffins' on the world as a tribute to the late departed George III. But there was another motive, of a more disquieting kind, behind the idea:

> Patent Wrought Iron Coffins are actually needful for those who regard the safety of their deceased relations, as more than ten theatres of anatomy are now operating in London, for the supply of which, together with private practitioners in all parts of the kingdom, and the Scotch schools, an amazing number of our dead are dragged from their graves and vaults.

Edward Lille Bridgman, furnishing undertaker, of Goswell Street, was the public benefactor whose invention was to put all this right 'for the same price as wood'. His firm also supplied cast-iron vaults, tombs and tablets – 'much cheaper and more durable than stone'.

Finally, invaluable assistance is offered in 1830 for all those who labour in Grubb Street, in the form of a device which, unique among inventions, provides:

> Consolation to the tremulous writer. – The public may look to this most singular and unique invention with confidence, as an inestimable source of comfort to those who experience any difficulties in the command of the pen, occasioned by tremour in nervous exertion, weakness from age, heat of climate, agitation of spirits, excess or over exertion, injury to the thumb or fingers by sprain or otherwise, even to the loss of part. This happy relief exists in a little instrument, the appearance of which, when in use, escapes observation, is capable of giving firmness, confidence and freedom, and cannot fail to assist the declining powers of a good penman, and would materially improve the performance of a bad one. It is honoured by the patronage and recommendation of Sir Astley Cooper and other highly respectable professional gentlemen. A few minutes' practice will prove its efficacy, and it has this

advantage over all medicine, its power increases by use, and one prescription will last for life. Made in elastic gold, price 25s each. Sold by T. Tucker, 269, corner of the Strand, opposite the Crown and Anchor Tavern.

20 March 1830

4 *The Extraordinary Mr Wilson*

During the years 1841–77, under the editorship of John Delane, *The Times* consolidated the reputation it had earned under Barnes as 'The Thunderer' and grew rapidly in popularity and success. Delane, a powerful man, depicted by Thackeray in the figure of Tom Tower of *The Jupiter*, saw the circulation of his newspaper rise from 23,000 in 1845 to 58,000 in 1855. Simultaneously, there was an enormous increase in the number of advertisements printed. In 1810 there had been on average about 150 per issue. By 1855 there were 2,500 and by 1861 on one occasion the number reached over 4,000 advertisements in a single issue. As always, a small and relatively constant number of these advertisements continued to be of that unclassifiable kind known as 'personal'. These were allotted a special position at the top of the second or third column of the front page, with the most urgent or interesting messages printed whenever possible at the head of the column. Though the numbers of these advertisements did not grow at anything like the rate of growth of the total, their appearance became a permanent feature of the newspaper and on a good day in 1850 there would be two or three romantic assignations, a couple of 'Come home' pleas and a few cryptic communications – whether from secretive businessmen, spies or denizens of the underworld was anyone's guess. There would also be a handful of legal announcements, lost and found notices, and miscellaneous objects for sale. Indeed, it was a period of great richness and variety, and the personal column, together with the notices of births, deaths and marriages, which in 1853 took their place alongside it, was now becoming the focus of steadily growing interest among *Times* readers.

61

One man in particular saw the attractions of this form of communication and explored them to the full. His name is E. J. Wilson and he is the author of more personal column messages than anyone else in the history of the newspaper. This chapter consists of a selection of those messages, of which there were in all over four hundred, published during the years 1851 to 1870.

It was suggested in a *Times* article of 1914 that someone should try writing a novel in the form of personal column advertisements. That novel exists, buried in those middle years of the nineteenth century, and it is the purpose of this chapter to begin the process of disinterring it. Had Wilkie Collins himself written it, it could not have been a darker or more mysterious tale, full of inexplicable and desperate happenings, locked rooms, lost children, wrecked fortunes and mysterious cries for help. The whole novel cannot be given here, and the scraps that have been chosen can give only a fragmentary impression of the maze of possibilities the reader is confronted with. The action is set in London, Bristol, in Ennis, County Clare, at a girls' school in Hertfordshire, in Grenoble, Hamburg, the Abruzzi mountains in Italy and, for a brief but horrible moment, in a castle lost in the marshes of Silesia.

Who was Wilson? From his messages one gathers that he worked for a time for the Customs, but fell out with them, and that his business before and afterwards was connected with importing goods from France and the Indies. He retired to Ennis, County Clare, after the failure of his business in London; while there, he taught French, German and, probably, classics at a local school. Customs records show that an E. J. Wilson continued to hold the post of 'landing waiter' at the Customs in Newcastle in 1860 at a salary of £160 per annum, though by now his interests were largely elsewhere. Landing waiters, who were responsible for examining imported cargo, were quite high in the hierarchy at this time. The post was much sought after and carried some social standing.

Records also show that an E. J. Wilson, Customs official, died at Liverpool in 1879, leaving £200. These tantalisingly scant records are all that remain of Wilson in official files. His claim to have 'introduced the decimal system to H.M. Customs' is belied by the fact that no trace exists of any such system having been employed by them during the nineteenth century.

Beyond this, all one can say is that there was a D. J. Wilson who died at his house, Belvoir, at Six-mile Bridge, near Ennis, County Clare, in 1864, leaving a handsomely furnished house and a prosperous farm, as well as a library of classical and historical works and books of theology, travel, etc. It seems likely that this was a brother or some other close relation, for it would explain E. J.

Wilson's move to Ennis in 1858. Wilson was obviously well read, and gives the impression of being a man of great energy and imagination. Could he be related to any other prominent family of the same name which flourished at this period? The founder of *The Economist*, James Wilson, for example, one of whose daughters married Walter Bagehot; or James Wilson, the Australian politician, who is accused of having introduced the sparrow to that continent and is known to have attempted to naturalise the llama? Or Sir Robert Thomas Wilson, Governor of Gibraltar; or the Wilson who was co-founder of Price's Patent Candles and in later life took to experimental gardening at Wisley; or Sir William James Erasmus Wilson, F.R.S., who brought Cleopatra's needle to England and first popularised the regular use of domestic baths?

All this is in the realm of speculation. What can be more definitely deduced is that many messages not actually signed by Wilson are nonetheless his, as can be seen from their subject, their style and their relation to other messages in the personal column before and after. He delights, in fact, in adopting a Protean variety of pseudonyms – rather in the manner of Clare Quilty, as he pursues the luckless Humbert Humbert from one motel to another in Nabokov's *Lolita*. There are also the names of those he generally writes to, and these are invariably disguised. There is a further bunch of messages to strangers and there are of course messages to Wilson from his regular correspondents, signed invariably not with real names but again with a variety of pseudonyms. The forms of address used include 'To the Equator', 'Indigo Blue', 'Alexis', 'Rouge et Noire' (Wilson, one can surmise, saw himself as a Julien Sorel), 'Battledore and Shuttlecock', 'Hide and Seek' (probably Wilson's ex-wife, who was in trouble with the police and spent these years in hiding), 'Cygne' and 'Egypte'. The latter is frequently used and other pseudonyms, too, have an Egyptian flavour; 'Cheops', for example. The habit of surrounding the signature with two 'X's characterises another series: 'X Tribe X', 'X Cheops X', 'X Blue Eyes X' and 'X Gamins X'. There are oddities such as 'Double fin' and 'Leb! Wohl!', and there are those which imply treachery or subterfuge in the recipient: 'Au simulacre', 'To the Counterfeit' and 'Flybynight'. All Wilson's messages display a certain sense of drama and some have overtones of megalomania, such as 'Alpha the First', 'The Invincible Achilles', 'The Key', 'The Pillar' and 'The Anchor'.

Wilson is much addicted to quotation; he is equally at home in French and German, and is given to making asides in both languages. He has a working knowledge of Latin, a fondness for classical myth, and specialises in the use of metaphor, right from the first message:

To D. – Thanks for your communication. As the clothes are ready, I am ready to wear them. Always the same, the bar of iron. Pray communicate. E.W.

15 February 1851

After that insignificant beginning we hear nothing more of Wilson for a whole year. Then there is a spate of messages:

To Equator – Fortuna audaces juvat – vincit omnia veritas. – E.W.

20 February 1852

(Fortune favours the bold. Truth conquers all)

Aut Caesar aut Nullus. Indigo blue is willing.

23 February 1852

To which the reply is:

Quis est Caesar? Do pray enlighten me. The agonizing week's delay has not been occasioned by J. . . . S.

2 March 1852

Circumspice. Boxmoor. Herts. – E.W.

8 March 1852

Boxmoor, beware! Wilson's daughter, as we later learn, has been sent to a boarding school at Boxmoor, from which she is eventually kidnapped. The school is on a hill. In this, and in the next message inserted the following day, Wilson addresses a business colleague who has offered to help, by paying a visit, for already some danger is threatened to the little girl, 'Alice', who suffers, it seems, from a curious minor deformity, inherited from her father's family. (We learn of this detail later.)

To Equator – Circumspice. – Your great Ship, the Christopher Columbus, when laden with indigo, opium, or the most costly merchandise of the east, never contained so much wealth as stands on that said hill. – E.W.

9 March 1852

Indigo Blue. – Where and how shall I send my address? I, too, have grown cautious at last. Are you as entirely ignorant as you seem? Be careful and candid as to this.

10 March 1852

'Indigo Blue' is another business colleague, whom Wilson does not as yet entirely trust – and with reason. Wilson lost most of his money four years earlier in an unlucky speculation in the City.

Not to Equator. – You might have saved yourself the trouble, and been richer by 5s. Tom is sure to go to the wall without your telling him. The other is particularly happy, the chances being 10 to 1 that he will cross Earth's central line, and then, being as invulnerable as Achilles, he will have nothing to fear. Tom will understand this mystery without trying. – E.W.

11 March 1852

To My Beloved Equator. – When I visited the Great Exhibition I fancied Hampden, though refreshed with the living water from the crystal fountain, frowned at me; I hope our great countryman is now convinced we have not degenerated, and that his impersonation has resumed its accustomed serenity. Ce n'est que le premier pas qui coûte, c'est fait; et c'en est fait d'eux. Vous voyez, la Providence n'est pas toujours avec les forts bataillons. – E.W.

15 March 1852

The Hampden here referred to is not a living man. The reference to 'living water' implies that he is now in paradise; and Wilson means the great seventeenth-century reformer, John Hampden, cousin of Oliver Cromwell. The 'Hampden Clubs', founded in 1811, agitated for the extension of the franchise to all tax-payers; they also focused discontent against any government levy members felt to be unjust. Wilson's business, as an importer, was much affected by Customs levies, and he is planning at this point a method of evading the tax on the import of indigo.

Tuesday – Quite correct. Quietly wrapped up in mystery and silk. I have seen it before mixed with others of different colour. One of the two letters you address answers the question of initials. Homage to truth, to discretion.

1 May 1852

Wilson, who is referring here to a consignment of indigo, has hit on a good phrase – 'wrapped up in mystery and silk'. That the message is his may be inferred from the last sentence, which is much used by him at this period. During the next few months we see him planning a new business venture, based in Grenoble. His enthusiasm at finding and securing the co-operation of this colleague is somewhat overwhelming and gives a clue to his character. Wilson is one of those entrepreneurs who combine great energy with a considerable streak of paranoia:

Wonderful! Thy star in conjunction with mine against the great globe itself! – nor Afric's poisonous vapours, nor Asia's caloric, nor America's life-absorbing ether, nor Europa's invigorating breezes – fortune's sycophants, nor adversity's treason – shall ever loose these sharp hooks of steel with which I cling thee to my heart; – France's terpsichorean votary, Rome's javelined gladiator, and London's belted champion, were never lighter of foot, nor stronger of nerve, than Fortune's spoilt and favourite child. – E.J.W.

7 July 1852

The new venture makes him all the more certain of succeeding despite the efforts of his adversaries in trade. He is thinking here, of course, of the statue of 'Il Commendatore' in Mozart's *Don Giovanni*:

To the counterfeit. – Continue, and fill the coffers of this Leviathan. Like the statue wanting at the celebrated banquet, though absent, I am all the more present. – E.J.W.

24 July 1852

To my Beloved Equator – Circumspice. Praeterea censeo Carthaginem, esse delendam. Serve the Queen; be just, and fear not; let all the ends thou aimst at be thy country's, thy God's and Truth's – then if thou fall'st, thou fall'st a blessed martyr. My country, my beloved country, nothing but my country. – E.J.W.

13 October 1852

The fact that Wilson refers here, as he does in several of his messages, to Cato's famous phrase, used every time he spoke in the Senate, that Carthage must be destroyed no matter what else happens, implies that he has a fixed plan in his mind, overtaking all other matters in importance. He then, by way of general exhortation, goes on to quote Henry VIII's speech to Thomas Cromwell in Shakespeare's play of that title.

Flybynight wants the anchor. It was expected all last week, and will be every night this week. Come or write. Silence added to absence is a cruel and unnecessary torture.

1 November 1852

A la Croix Rouge. – Victoire. C'est fait. Soit. 'Dieu me l'a donnée, et gare à qui la touche.' – E.J.W.

4 November 1852

Circumspice. Corruption falls or I fall. 'Il est trop tard.' – E.J.W.

5 November 1852

He was now trying, at the same time, to regain the money he had lost in the City and to secure the Customs post which was to be important in his future work; and his anxiety for the fate of his daughter is evident from the message of November 4th. The two messages that follow (November 11th and 16th) show once again the obsession with mythology and the grandiosity of vision that are characteristic of his style. He sees himself as the invincible Achilles; his ally 'Tom', of whom more anon, is Alcyone, the kingfisher, and also the Fisher King, who weds the sea. Heady stuff for an importer of indigo and opium!

Flybynight wants the anchor. A kingfisher has stolen the ring of it, and flybynight will founder. – E.J.W.

11 November 1852

Flybynight wants the anchor. – Solution. Invincible Achilles has pinioned great Neptune to the Equator, seized his trident, and with his triumphal car skimmed the boundless expanse of waters to hold communion with the pearl of the great eastern seas. Scandinavia's gate has been regained, and he now steers direct for the Pillars of Hercules, after razing corrupt and perfidious Troy to the ground, he will glide over the purple waves of the tideless sea, and pass in safety between the dreaded whirlpool and the six-headed monster; then, and not till then, the Kingfisher will restore the stolen ring, and honest pride, clothed in humility, and beauty enshrined in youthful loveliness, will be his ultimate rewards. La lutte est la fin. – E.J.W.

16 November 1852

Quelle journée! The proudest day of my life. He looked! Ah! how did he look? Like a man I visited two years ago in N--e. Tu comprendras. – E.J.W.

10 January 1853

The following (January 14th) is from Wilson's ex-wife. The degree of estrangement is clear from the icy quasi-legal language she uses. There is a tug of love developing over the daughter, which Wilson eventually solves by selling the house in Hammersmith, where Mary Crawford, as she is now called, has taken refuge from proceedings that are being instituted against her for fraud.

If E.J.W. did not oppose Mary (alias Emily) Pierce Crawford, daughter of Daniel Mereweather Ford, he would have applied, ere this, at 4 Spring Place, Black Lion Lane, Hammersmith. A wilful error is maintained against all justice, honour and truth to oppose my right. Why not come immediately?

14 January 1853

Trevor Square, Kenilworth, Scarborough. J.E.W., where are you? My daughter! O my daughter! – E.J.W.

1 May 1854

To Hide and Seek – Lutte à mort. Je veux voir ma fille. – E.J.W.

17 May 1854

Poverty and Honour – I'll not touch the money. It's stolen property. – E.J.W.

27 June 1854

La rue de la Tamise. Vendre, vendre, faut il vendre? – Egypte.

16 December 1854

Thames Road, just below Kew Bridge on the north bank, runs out of Spring Grove, not Spring Place, so perhaps the road has been renamed. Wilson finally decides the moment has come to sell, and inserts an advertisement which must rank as one of the best in the 'oracular' tradition of the personal column:

La poire est mure. – Egypte.

29 December 1854

The sale is completed. Wilson has reclaimed property which is rightfully his and confidently announces 'Justice and her scales – come what may!' '*Vogue la galère*' is one of his favourite phrases: 'La Justice et sa balance. Vogue la galère. – Egypte' is followed soon by the request of an intermediary, a 'Mrs B.', writing from St James's Street, who has a scheme to regain certain trusts in his wife's name. Wilson is more concerned about the future of his daughter:

To St James's Street. My ideas have undergone a complete revolution on that subject and I tell you again I'll not touch the money; it's all stolen property. But where's my child? – Egypt

27 June 1855

There then ensues one of those puzzling silences which characterise this curious tale, and when next we hear of Wilson, a year later, it is through the mouth of 'Tom'. But 'Tom' himself, the 'Kingfisher', is a shifting personality, through which the authentic voice of 'E.J.W.' can clearly be heard. With one of those sudden *volte-faces* which Wilkie Collins delighted in, the identity of 'Tom' and Wilson himself seem to cross over. Tom's first message begins innocently enough, almost domestically, but the tone of voice rapidly changes:

Dear Jane – You did not send the dog over to amuse the children. Leonora will easily change. There are light and shade to every picture. When the weird sisters can allow the dark curtain of silence to be withdrawn the combined outward evil influences now operating unopposed will fade away before the light of duty and affection. The fruit of the past has been not only bitter but humiliating. – Tom

24 June 1856

My colours are nailed, not tied to the masthead. – T

19 July 1856

Mystified, not gratified, but pacified. My colours have been rather roughly torn away; but I am trying to steady myself by keeping a sharp lookout upon the windmills, and nailing an old head of Don Quixote at the prow. – Tom

26 July 1856

X.Y.Z.E. – This day's accounts are, I fear, too good to be acted upon. How can you ask me to write when you have most annoyingly taken the key of the escritoire containing your address? With all my anxiety to comply, you know me too well to suppose that I can bring myself to break open your lock, even for this pleasing purpose, without your leave. You will see from my last that this matter now rests with you. Yours ever. – T

29 July 1856

At sea, becalmed, in a chilly fog; confused sounds of distant guns, betokening a sudden engagement with an enemy. My tattered colours are still flying at the masthead. Send me a pilot, that I may clear the shoals and grapple with the foe. – Yours, Tom

20 August 1856

There are a number of messages after this from 'E.J.W.' to 'Hide and Seek', the name he uses for his former wife. 'No,' he declares in March 1857, 'there are some things money cannot do, and all the ill-gotten wealth of London will not purchase my "Egyptienne" ' – by which he means his daughter. Someone writes offering help, signing themselves 'A Christian', but E.J.W. makes this peculiar reply:

To a Christian – You don't know their antecedents. It is not envy. My daughter has two toes joined together. I have not seen her for seven years. – E.J.W.

30 March 1857

To Hide and Seek. Mrs B., late of St James's Street, proposes a legal document, but does not know your hiding place. I will not accept any English legal document. One of the first lawyers in the City of London told me I should always be crossed in all I attempted; and I could not get the competent men to act for me in the Court of Chancery, although the costs were deposited in hard cash. Men, to whom I had advanced ready money at 5 percent, have laughed at me when I talked of recovery by law. My money has been stolen from my pocket book, yet no redress. In short, I am *hors la loi*; but, fortunately, I know it. – E.J.W.

22 May 1857

Ich Dien – I now call upon you. Those who could discover the secret in the most secluded nook in Europe can do anything. Double the signs. Banc Signe, Hungary beyond the Theiss.

30 June 1857

The Hungarian connection eventually has Wilson involved in desperate attempts at recovering his stolen money from the castle to which the rich businessman who defrauded him has retired. The castle is in Silesia, in the middle of a dismal swamp. It is suggested that Alice should be sent to join him there.

X Cheops X. No, no, hands off my child. I am no longer bound by the laws of humanity, and had it been a boy, yes, but I will not risk my little girl amongst the pestilential marshes of Hungary, though there secure against every power. R.Z.X. 666 – Cygne

30 December 1857

X. – Christopher Columbus – O, no language can describe what I have had to endure in endeavouring to earn an honest living in my dear country. Kicked out of my beautiful native city into the vilest – and now wounded in my dearest affections. I was told it would be so, Alec. Boxmoor on the one hand, Decimals by the Right, Eggs by the left. Comprenez vous? Yes, I did it. – Cygne

31 December 1857

X Blue Eyes X. – I protested (in writing), both before and after, against that 'Genug fur Alles' business. The Moravian

March Rose must give 'Auskunft' and guarantee £500. – Tom.
– Cygne

3 May 1858

Wilson is now very short of money. His efforts in Silesia have failed, and he is reduced to teaching to earn a living. At one point he writes 'I must send my little girl round by sea to be tossed on the Atlantic for six days. My poverty, not my will, consents' – using here the words of the apothecary who sells the poison to Romeo with which he commits suicide, in Shakespeare's *Romeo and Juliet*. He finds refuge in Ennis, Ireland. Meanwhile another colleague has died, making the chances for his 'Decimals' system ever being introduced yet smaller.

Decimals to Cheops. – T. C. Jones Esq. died, last year in America. It is exceedingly unfortunate. He and I were the only merchants who thoroughly understood the whole system. Address
E. J. Wilson, Ennis, Ireland

2 August 1858

In the next advertisement Wilson makes some grandiose claims for himself, with which succeeding generations would find it hard to agree. It is, however, clear from what follows that he hopes at last to be able to arrange for his daughter to be brought to him in Ireland.

Decimals to Cheops. – Honest John Bull is pig-headed, but he begins to grasp this business. I claim to rank with Cobden, Bright and Rowland Hill. I go on (Long R---Joey). Address
E. J. Wilson, Ennis, Ireland

2 September 1858

Decimals to Cheops. – I have lost my money and my child. You can guess my feelings. Can a lawyer advise a criminal without rendering himself equally liable? Answer to E. J. Wilson, Ennis, Ireland

7 October 1858

Orion's Boat. Do nothing without a lawyer until I come. Delay does not matter – failure does.

1 February 1859

The idea of 'Orion's Boat' as the code-word for the rescue attempt is typical of the way Wilson's mind works. He is always better at metaphor and myth than at the practical business of everyday life. The 'Orion' myth has many suggestive elements, so it is worth recalling the story. Orion was a hunter who was in love with

71

Menope, daughter of Oenopion. When Oenopion delayed in giving her to him, Orion became drunk and violated her. Oenopion blinded Orion for this, but the sun's rays restored his sight and Orion went on to become the favourite hunting companion of Artemis (Diana). He then got into trouble with Apollo, who loosed a giant scorpion against him and persuaded Diana to chase him into the sea and shoot him. If Orion had had a boat, he might have escaped the scorpion and the arrows of Artemis, and he could have sailed away, instead of being immortalised as a constellation of stars.

To Contre Coup. – To terminate this disgraceful business I had made arrangements to place my daughter at school, at Boxmoor, Herts, but I cannot get her now. Now, what am I to do? The money I relied on in my old age has been alienated – my child lost forever – myself in the most miserable part of the land of misery, with a miserable salary. Write and address E. J. Wilson, Ennis, Ireland.

7 February 1859

There are further messages to 'Orion's Boat', but events seem to move slowly. Meanwhile, Wilson loses pupils when the rumour of his misfortunes reaches parents who have started to read his announcements in *The Times*. He must have realised that this was a risk, but he despises what he is doing – 'the author of the decimal system at Her Majesty's Customs, which pours pure gold every day into the coffers of the nation, earning a miserable subsistence in the worst part of Paddy's land!'

Tribe – You are not to seize my child, even if you can find her. You know how the detectives and police served me, but I intend to have my rights like any other man, or – Vive la Reine. – E. J. Wilson, Ennis, Ireland.

15 March 1859

Caution. – All persons assisting in secreting my daughter, Alice Jane Wilson, 10 years old, are liable to seven years' imprisonment. – E. J. Wilson, Ennis, Ireland.

19 March 1859

The writer of the anonymous letter, from London, is informed by Mr Wilson, Ennis, Ireland, that the money he relied on in his old age has been alienated, both capital and interest; and he will have his daughter sent him by the Limerick steamer.

22 March 1859

Nicht Eine Million. – If an English schoolmistress betrays the

72

most sacred trust a father can confide to her, there is no power in England to right him. So 'Vive la Reine'. – E. J. Wilson, Ennis

12 April 1859

Nicht Zwei Millionen. – £10,000 sterling. (Bah!) In 1848, the commencement of the Golden Age, I would not have changed prospects with the proudest French merchants in London. Durch u. durch verfault. – Ennis

23 April 1859

My dearest Alice – I have not received any communication from you for 18 months. Oh! if you knew what persecution your poor father has had to undergo to try to deprive him of you forever. Address me Mr E. J. Wilson, Ennis, Ireland.

11 July 1859

We learn that 'Contre Coup' is making some ill-defined attempt at restoring some of Wilson's money, and Wilson writes, gleefully, of one creditor who is being squeezed: 'Down upon lovely Apollo! £30 per annum out of his own pocket.' Enormous sums are mentioned: '£250,000 on eggs alone.' (It is clear from later messages that Wilson is an importer of eggs as well as indigo.) These methods 'Contre Coup' is using sound desperate, for as Wilson explains to 'B.C.Z.' he has tried legal, gentleman-like ways without success: so, as he enigmatically puts it, 'Vive les imprimeurs'. Orion's Boat continues to be invoked at intervals for the next year. A message then mentions that 'E.H.W.' has died at Boxmoor, documents are sent for, and Wilson returns to the mainland.

C.C.C. – I must see you. This place is not what I expected (Plants). I have rivals (foreign) earning double as much as I do. You know what happened to my money and papers in the City. – E.W., Bishops Stortford, Herts

24 September 1861

The scene then changes to the Abruzzi mountains in central Italy. Wilson maintains contact through a private enquiry agent, a Mr Pollaky. He awaits the arrival of someone – a woman, a child, it is not clear which – at the Hotel des Ambassadeurs, L'Aquila. Mountain air, and sun, cure many diseases, but principally tuberculosis. Wilson institutes the code-word 'Moribond', which is used in several messages, but a new form of numerical code is also tried out – possibly related to the 'decimal' system of which he has given us inklings earlier:

'05,100' – Moribond. – Abruzzi. – 9th December 1861.

Tempora mutantur et nos mutamur in illis. Ab uno disce omnes. – Ignatius Pollaky

10 December 1861

0'503, ad capiandum vulgus. – She has arrived, but dangerously ill. Forgive. You can have the necessary guarantee on applying to Mr Pollaky, Private Continental Enquiry Office, 14 George Street, Mansion House.

15 January 1862

From this point on, Wilson makes increasing use of the services of the detective, Pollaky, and for six years there is no message in plain English, other than short 'reminders' to agents, signals that messages have been received, and so forth ('X. Eggs. X. – Amazon. – Received 29 October 1862'). The coded messages which appear relevant are those addressed to 'Diplomat'. Certain Wilsonian tags and phrases recur, though the code itself has not been broken, and Wilson's movements during these six years can only be guessed at. A number of 'plaintext' messages start to appear in May 1867, addressed 'E.G.G. (en voyage) Grenoble'. Evidently Wilson's activities as a merchant have recommenced. There is no mention of his daughter at this time, though it is possible that this message may be his:

Why little girl leave old man all alone?

19 March 1867

Money is still a problem, for Wilson complains 'Modern languages? No. My three languages, even this year, have not produced me as much as I have paid to a carpenter for wages.' There are then several messages to 'B.E.N.', who, mystifyingly, is also connected with 'Old Tom'.

B.E.N. (My premier) – What do you intend to do with 'Old Tom' of Grenoble? – E.W.

15 October 1868

B.E.N. (My second) – What is your opinion of Christopher Columbus' egg-trick?

19 October 1868

B.E.N. (My third) – I know that Christopher Columbus' egg-trick was only symbolical, and not real. E.G.G. is, or ought to be, at Southampton. – E.W.

20 October 1868

B.E.N. (Old Tom) – Méfiez vous des veuves. Oh! what a fool I was to kill the goose that laid the golden egg! And such an egg!

Le gamin de Londres. Tom's coffee house. – E.W.

14 November 1868

A long message in French describes Wilson's vision of the fortunate state of the French egg merchants: he sees a rain of gold flakes falling on the Channel, and a little boat sailing after them to catch them as they fall. Everything now seems to depend on the egg business.

E.G.G. (en voyage). – Pitch Decimals to little boys at school; the proper place for them; but pitch yourself in the 'Hôtel du Commerce' at Grenoble; the proper place for you. – E.W.

22 January 1869

E.G.G. (en voyage). K.E.Y. left Southampton on 20th January; Caen 23rd; took tea (avec deux oeufs à la coque) at Austin's Hotel, Paris on 24th; is detained at St Etienne; and calculates on being at Lyons on 4th inst, and Grenoble on the 10th (Hauptverbindungstrassen) – E.W.

3 February 1869

E.G.G. (en famille). – The Jew is strong, the Greek is stronger, the Gipsy is still stronger, but the Counterfeit is strongest of all, having beaten the Gipsy (Horsemonger Lane 1848) – E.W.

22 February 1869

E.G.G. (en famille). – Pitch decimals into the river Isère and let them float down to the Mediterranean, and find their way by Egypt to Arabia whence they came. (Pocket book 1853) – E.J.W.

26 February 1869

E.G.G. (en congé). Like Caractacus when prisoner at Rome, I cannot forget that the 'honourables' whose abilitites, measured by their salaries, must be colossal, envied me my humble cottage in Great Britain. Not the Ides of March but the River March, remember. – E.J.W.

2 March 1869

A telegram from Pollaky addressed to 'Diplomat', with the cryptic words 'He has shaved', marks a change in affairs for Wilson. The telegram is received in November, and later that month another message from Pollaky declares 'A whisper. Empty pocket. As quiet as a mouse.' 'You are a dark shadow on the road of life', says Wilson to 'Bras Pique' that Christmas. A possible Australian windfall is signalled in two bizarre messages, which – even if they have no connection with Wilson, for he is nearing the end of his days as a personal column advertiser and several of his later messages seem ambiguous or wandering – deserve to rank alongside his most manic outpourings:

WOOLOOMOOLOO. – SHOUT

10 May 1870

WOOLOOMOOLOO Shout rapidly and royally. Varmint all vanquished. Impetuous popsey impecunious.

21 Jume 1870

Wooloomoolo is the name of a prison in New South Wales. On the same day there is another message from Pollaky:

Tartarus. – They appeared to be exceedingly jolly in their mourning coaches. – Pollaky, 13 Paddington Green, London W.

Some sort of meeting is then arranged between Wilson and 'S.W.'. Wilson continues to give instructions to 'E.G.G.':

E.G.G. (en voyage). Telegrams of no use whatsoever. Stick to The Times for correspondence. Pass by the Tyrol and the land of William Tell to Grenoble. K.E.Y. is there. – X

26 July 1870

Has 'S.W.' been involved in the kidnap of Alice? Is 'S.W.' the same as 'Hide and Seek'?

S.W. – The German word for 'Baby-farming' is *Engelmacherei* (angel making), a not inappropriate term for this punishable offence. – Pollaky, 13 Paddington Green, London W.

26 July 1870

Blue Eyes. – Bordighera arrived and longs to see you. Write to me, post office, Churton Street. – S.W.

3 August 1870

That is the last definite trace of the 'Mysteries of Wilsono' in the personal column. A strange and sad story of an unbalanced man of great abilities, who lived more for symbol and myth than for reality. But there are four more messages which should be added, for they possibly have a bearing on the story. They are the haunting record of a long-delayed reconciliation between lovers. 'Loyal je serais durant ma vie' is a common enough expression, but it is one Wilson is particularly addicted to and the colour 'green' may refer to Ireland:

I could not speak; it was too sudden.

8 October 1870

Dinna forget! My silence forgie. Whistle at Christmas and I'll come to ye. Loyal je serais durant ma vie.

2 November 1870

The weight of this deep feeling is almost more than I can bear.

21 November 1870

You could not speak. It was too sudden. I am a good rider. Green is my favourite colour. I want money.

23 November 1870

It must be Wilson who is unable to speak, overwhelmed by emotion. Perhaps he and 'S.W.' are planning to return to Ennis, where riding would be the only way of getting about the country-side. Do these last three words invalidate this idyllic interpretation? Surely not. Wilson was the last person to find anything distasteful in such a practical request.

Why did Wilson choose the personal column as a means of communication in preference to all others? Probably he simply liked using it – for, whatever else he may have been, he was obviously a great self-dramatist and no doubt loved the idea of his grandiose schemes and private tragedies being played out in public.

Was Wilson really a wealthy merchant, the pioneer of a 'decimal system', a man living on the grand scale, with powerful enemies, who suffered appalling tragedies in his business and private life; whose daughter was kidnapped; and who was forced to pursue a wrongdoer to a remote castle in Silesia? Were these all the daydreams of a nineteenth-century Walter Mitty? Or was there a criminal factor behind all the counterfeiting, forgery and violent extortion? Surely a Walter Mitty, no matter how elaborate his fantasies, could not have kept such a remarkable detective as Ignatius Pollaky hot on the trail for nine long years?

5 The One-Winged Dove Must Die

During the middle years of the nineteenth century, heyday of the remarkable E. J. Wilson, there appeared for the first time in the personal column lengthy exchanges between lovers, as well as a great profusion of all sorts of desperate messages and *cris de coeur*.

Some of the messages were coded. Others had a weirdly oracular or cryptic sound, although they were written in plain English. Of these the strangest was, perhaps, a series which appeared over a period of several years. The first, on 24 March 1849, announced, in capital letters, NO DOORMAT TONIGHT. The second, on 28 May 1851, DOORMAT TONIGHT; and the last, on 20 March 1852, DOORMAT AND BEANS TONIGHT. That is all. There was much speculation as to what these mysterious announcements meant. Could they signify the absence or presence of a jealous husband? Or perhaps they were invitations to a burglary?

Also in capitals, and equally laconic, is STOP THAT PIANO (5 May 1849, signed 'J.P.') and it may just be that somebody upstairs had installed one of those damned tinkly things, for pianos were all the rage just then. *The Times* was full of the music publishers' advertisements. That very day, for example, there is an advertisement for sheet music:

> The new song, King Clog, by the author of 'There's a good time coming' . . . The most popular of the day, vide the opinion of the press. Apply to Effingham Wilson, 11 Royal Exchange. Price 6d or free on receipt of eight postage stamps. It is the song of the times.

Surely Effingham Wilson could not be E.J.W.? No, let us banish the thought.

Many of the advertisements have that fascinating quality of

seeming inconsequentiality which one finds in snatches of conversation overheard on a bus; the difference is that the emotional charge behind these 'agony' messages is so much greater. For example, it must have been with something of a flourish of the pen that some rascal in June 1843 issued the challenging observation: 'A Newfoundland Dog has Teeth!' Although it is unsigned, no doubt its provenance was all too obvious to the unfortunate person for whom it was intended.

'The Bear has Come to Town' is another of this period which has that faintly sinister, Sibylline quality, not unmixed with absurdity, which is the hallmark of the personal column at full stretch. Careful research has unearthed a probably innocent meaning for this, which will be revealed in due course, but no firm theory exists to explain 'Why Shave?' (unsigned 12 January 1854). One possible proposition is that it is part of the Wilson series, in which 'shave' appears to be used metaphorically in one instance to mean 'pay up'. Can it, or anything else, be linked to 'The Three Pigeons' (unsigned, 27 September 1867)? And were they anything to do with 'Lorelei – The Anthropophagous didn't gobble the partridges' (unsigned, 6 September 1861)?

Chance, or a fine ear for assonance, gave rise to 'Why has not Drosselmayor written to Flibbertigibbet, at Aberdeen?' (unsigned, 14 July 1865), and of course Wilson had dealings with Drosselmayor's fellowcountrymen, while 'Flybynight', who is firmly within the canon, is not far from 'Flibbertigibbet'. And for that matter, was it Wilson, or some unlucky minion or delegate of his, who on 4 October 1854 uttered the reproachful cry 'Schlag auf schlag! Schloch!' ('Blow upon blow!' The exact etymology of 'schloch' is unclear, but it is certainly not a term of endearment.)

We know now that it was indeed the irrepressible Wilson who came up with that masterpiece of the mysterious 'La poire est mure – Egypte'; and we know it had something to do with selling a property in Thames Street, Chiswick. There is, however, no explanation short of the supernatural as to who has continued to insert at intervals over the past two centuries the single word 'Excelsior!' Apart from the fact that it is the motto of New York State and the title of a resounding poem by Longfellow (in which the oracular mood is coincidentally very much to the fore), and that this poem was later subjected to hilarious embellishments by the pen of James Thurber, there is nothing to go on at all; nevertheless, it is undeniably the case that the word has continued to appear from time to time, all by itself, at the considerable expense of some person or persons unknown for as long as the agony column has been in existence.

Another apparent enigma, which admits of a less than supernatural explanation, is a mysterious single word insertion which
appears for many consecutive days in May 1865. 'SILENCE' in
capital letters, and nothing else. This is followed a few weeks later
by 'Silence where?', then by 'Silence in the Metropolis' and, finally,
'Silence where? Why, "Silence in the Metropolis". Silence on the
Railway is good, but "Silence in the Metropolis", remember, is
excessively better.' Just as one imagines that some sort of sense is
emerging (here, clearly, is another public-spirited announcement
by the author of 'STOP THAT PIANO' and 'WHY SHAVE'), the
thing turns, apparently, into a book advertisement: 'Silence – Read
"Carry's Confession" ', followed by 'Silence – Ask for it in any of
the circulating libraries in London'. The prosaic answer seems to be
that here was yet another author or publisher trying to push a book.
The personal column has been used for this purpose again and again
– within recent memory indeed, Jilly Cooper (or her publisher) has
been known to insert advertisements purporting to emanate from
the headmistresses of girls' schools stating that any girl found reading her books will be expelled forthwith. So! No, not so. One
reads further, and comes across 'Silence. I have read "Carry's
Confession". I think I understand.' There then follows a 'romantic
exchange', from which it is obvious that two people are making
various arrangements to meet, that mutual reproaches are being
exchanged ('Silence – There is no such thing as shame!'),
reconciliations negotiated, and typical personal column messages,
of the sort which mean nothing to an outsider, are the order of the
day ('Y. Silence is kind if the R. – is never to return.') As is the rule
with the personal column, the reader has been led well and truly
round the mulberry bush, up the garden path and back again.

Misunderstandings of this sort sometimes had more serious
repercussions. The Liberal parliamentarian Sir John Hanmer was
so perturbed by an advertisement he saw in *The Times* in 1869 that
he wrote to the editor, Delane, demanding an explanation. The
advertisement read:

The bird has come to town. Call immediately; important.
22 February 1869

Would Delane, he wrote, please give full particulars of the person
who inserted it, for the purposes of justice and the defeat of a
conspiracy? Delane replied that the announcement was handed in
on a piece of blue paper, torn at the edges. It was written in black
ink and, apart from the words quoted, bore no clue to the identity of
the advertiser other than: 'Please insert the following in the Agony
Column of *The Times*. I enclose envelope for receipt and do not

know whether stamps would do or must be Post Office order. Do please excuse mistake if any.' He offered to show this mysterious missive to Hanmer, but declared that he could not hand over the original to him: it was not the practice of *The Times* to give up a manuscript. Hanmer did not reply; however, a staff member, Mowbray Morris, later reported that following tactful enquiries Hanmer appeared, without actually saying so, to be quite satisfied and to have abandoned the matter.

In all likelihood the bird was a close relative, in emotional terms, of the Bear. (Both 'the Bear', by the way, and 'the Newfoundland Dog' seem to have escaped official notice.) But to do Hanmer justice it should be remembered that Fenian conspiracies were being hatched at this time, and the previous month two other avine advertisements, whose meaning could scarcely have been so harmless, had been inserted by a private agent – a rival to Pollaky – operating from a dark alley on the fringes of the Temple:

> O.K. The Three Jackdaws have arrived. Private Enquiry Office, Devereux Court.
>
> *1 January 1869*

> O.K. The three jackdaws have new feathers, blacker than before. C. Nicholls.
>
> *8 January 1869*

> O.K. One of the three jackdaws is unwell. C. Nicholls.
>
> *22 January 1869*

The last truly oracular announcement of this period was repeated, with relentless monotony, every day of the last week of January 1870:

> Not in these boots. H.R.

Whereas the value of such utterances lies precisely in their portentous meaninglessness, the combination of emotional meaning, staccato utterance and an absurdly inconsequential final sentence makes the following one of the most prized of personal column messages:

> Nil Desperandum. – Pray write immediately and tell me what H--- said, and what you answered or promised. You tell me nothing. What you ask is impossible. I told you I could not come again in the way you propose. If you wish it as much as I do, it must be the old plan. Write. I am worse than you are. Settle something. What a bore hats are.
>
> *5 January 1863*

The piece is evocative as well as funny; it tells a fragment of a story and establishes a mood. But there are other mini-sagas as good or better. The following gives a glimpse of a family tragedy, a hint of a character sketch, a distinct tone of voice and a change of continents, in thirty words:

> Your order, Sir, is rather cool, like yourself, and your adopted country; nevertheless, it shall be obeyed. Your mother is dead – died on the 6th of April 1844, of cholera.
>
> *20 March 1846*

What deep wells of isolation and repressed longing lay behind these startled words:

> Birthday Drawing Room. – Why did you address me so publicly? You overwhelmed me with terror.
>
> *27 May 1854*

A precocious schoolboy addresses the somewhat older object of his affections:

> Queen of Hearts. When is our pic-nic to come off? My holidays are nearly over and I shall not ask my masters for more, unless you write and tell me you wish it. After I left school I was down in Norfolk three times, but you were not visible. Since I saw you I have learn't something by heart, and if I get your direction I will let you know it.
>
> *5 June 1857*

The aftermath of a visit that went wrong – there is no love lost here:

> The black velvet dress, which was sent back by rail and coach in a very compressed parcel slightly covered with brown paper, and unaccompanied by any letter, has arrived as safely as under the circumstances was possible.
>
> *24 February 1857*

And what was the story behind Punch and Judy at Mentone on the Riviera? Was Dr Punch a despised lover as well as a medical man, and was Judy his new mistress? Or is there a more sinister interpretation?

> Mentone. – Dear Kate, if you go to Mentone, as now proposed, look out for Dr Punch. Judy will be with him. Best avoid.
>
> *25 January 1869*

In the same month a fantastic reward was offered for a piece of paper:

One Million Pounds Reward – Will be given for a certified copy of the baptism of Robert Jennings, son of Robert and Ann Jennings; believed to have been baptized at St Giles in the Fields, London in 1704. Address Robert Read, Woodman Street, York Road, Leeds.

27 January 1869

There are two explanations for this, neither greatly to the credit of the advertiser. Either Robert Read wanted the certified copy of baptism in a great hurry, and hoped some gullible clerk would rush to search it out and send it to him in the foolish expectation of this vast sum, whereupon he would easily be fobbed off with some excuse, or Robert Read was a confidence trickster.

The agony column was undoubtedly used for such unscrupulous purposes at this time. It probably always has been a means of communication not only between lovers, but between all those whose business is unfit to pass through the normal channels. An ingenious Mr Fynn managed to make a good business for several years out of advertising for young governesses to accompany him and two boys on a tour of the East: they would be asked to send a £70 deposit to Hamburg as security, and when they arrived Fynn would take advantage both of their money and of their reputations. The girls frequently ended up working in the red light district of Hamburg. Fynn was eventually exposed and run to earth by Sir Robert Carden, who revealed that these unwitting white slaves were engaged by means of advertisements in *The Times*.

The advantages to blackmailers of using such a means of communication are obvious, and the column is littered with advertisements starting 'to my anonymous correspondent' and either denying or in most cases acceding to the requests made. A few perhaps are more innocent than they sound. The difficulty of being certain in such cases is illustrated by a series of communications in April, May and June 1858 signed 'Tichborn' or 'Tichborne'. These look exactly as though they might have emanated from the 'Tichborne claimant', the vanished heir whose case was later to become a *cause célèbre*. Was he attempting to blackmail Sophia?

Sophia W---m. – 'Ti ho scritto tante volte inutilmente' [I have written to you so often in vain] What is to be done? Do you wish the letters etc to be published or not? Answer quickly, for time presses. Shall I be more explicit? Yours, Tichborn.

15 April 1858

Sophia W---m. – In looking over the Mss., Jerrold discovered the Missing Slip written at the hotel, Plymouth; also 'il mio tiranno'. All is now ready but the dedication. Which do you think? Father or son? – Tichborne.

6 May 1858

Alas for such conjectures, a study of the case reveals that the claimant at this date was either at the bottom of the ocean, off Rio, or practising butchery in Wagga Wagga.

There is however a curious link between the personal column and the Tichborne case. The first advertisements for the missing heir, who had 'sailed from the port of Rio de Janeiro in the ship *La Balla'*, were placed there by Lady Tichborne; moreover it was from *The Times* that Lady Tichborne obtained the name of the detective agency in Sidney which eventually unearthed the claimant, who was at the time, as all the world was later to learn, working in his butcher's shop in New South Wales. The agency advertised under the name 'Missing Friends' and a typical advertisement in February 1865 offers to make personal inquiries for missing friends through correspondents resident 'in all the chief towns in the United States, America, Canada, Australia and the other British Colonies'.

The advertisements to Sophia signed Tichborne must remain mysterious: could they have been inserted by Roger Tichborne's brother, the eccentric and spendthrift eleventh baronet, who before going bankrupt for £40,000 spent much of his fortune on attempting to construct a geometrically perfect sphere and the rest on a luxury yacht in which he claimed to be about to set off in search of the missing heir? The possibilities branch out: was the yacht at Plymouth, was there some elegant book of verses to be dedicated, or was he referring to the naming of the yacht?

Stranger still, and very much in Sherlock Holmes territory, is the following, which the great detective must surely have clipped out for his cuttings book:

Serpent. Dove. – Bedford. – Geranium. – Just received, First Signal, unknown to the rest. Write it me, and let me answer you. Quite right so far. Annie dear, good night. M.T., South Norwood – Glove Size.

2 October 1861

There is another by the same hand (and with Holmesian logic one may deduce that it is a hand which takes a size nine in gloves) over a year later:

Hydra. – Guarda. – Gorilla Hand. – What has become of this? Though apparently forsaken early, the interest I felt in it remains undiminished. Still M.T.P.O. Nine, South Norwood.

27 November 1862

Is it too much to imagine from the single word 'Guarda' some link with the Fenian movement? With tantalising slowness the plot thickens, until, nearly five years later, we come across:

Time and time over time forever flown, Mimi! Serpent, Dove and Geranium still never. – Montre

23 April 1867

The following little exchange tells the story of a typically Victorian situation:

Spurs and Skirts. Page 296, lines 10, 11, 12. Garibaldi. Pio Nono.

18 December 1862

Spurs and Skirts. Page 154, Lines 14, 15. Anita. Pope Joan.

19 December 1862

Spurs and Skirts. – The father of E-- W-- informs Garibaldi Pio Nono that all is discovered, and any attempts to renew the correspondence is futile, Spurs and Skirts and The Times being forbidden at S--- Lodge.

20 December 1862

Spurs and Skirts was a romantic journal and the passages referred to concern an assignation leading to an elopement. Why Garibaldi, why Pio Nono? Garibaldi, whose army of volunteers had that year marched on Rome but been defeated at Aspromonte, was the romantic hero of the day. Pio Nono (Pius IX) was the Pope whom Garibaldi was hoping to defeat, thereby annexing the Papal States to the newly united kingdom of Italy. Garibaldi's wife's name was Anita, so Anita (Pope Joan) is the feminine reply to 'Garibaldi's' invitation and one might suspect from the choice of pseudonyms that S--- Lodge, the citadel under siege, is of firmly Catholic persuasion and that E--- W--- is a spirited girl in her teens making every effort to break loose from the bonds of a strict and religious upbringing, while her father, whose action is so radical and prompt, sounds the typical authoritarian paterfamilias. At S--- Lodge, one may safely infer, there would be no nipping down to the village shop for clandestine copies of *Spurs and Skirts*.

In contrast to these attempts at repression, a fashion was beginning to become established for doing the Victorian equivalent of 'letting it all hang out'. Those who did so with most effect were generally female:

To A----. – If humanity has not entirely fled from your breast return 'ere it is too late to the heartbroken, distracted wife you have forsaken – 'ere the expression of those soft eyes that won you be lost in the bewildered stare of insanity – 'ere they may gaze even on you and know you not; write, tell her, oh! tell her, where you are, that she may follow you – her own, her all – and die.

29 May 1850

As with so much of the artistic expression of the Victorian era, one does not have to go along with the sentiment – let alone the logic, of which the focal point seems often to be that death is preferable to earthly fulfilment – to appreciate the quality of the piece. Certainly it is vastly preferable to the fudge-sweet baby-talk of the modern St Valentine's Day equivalent. Nevertheless, one cannot help feeling a pang of sympathy for 'A----', who was obviously not up to coping with the distinctly unstable volcano of passion concealed beneath those soft eyes that won him.

A much sparer though perhaps even more affecting *oeuvre* appears two months earlier:

The one-winged Dove must die, unless the Crane returns to be a shield against her enemies.

There is a sequel to this, and it bears out everything one might have suspected about the effects of these declarations on their intended recipients. It takes the form of two advertisements the following November, from Somerset and then from Kent: 'The Mate of the Dove must take wing from England forever, unless a material change takes place', followed by 'The Mate of the Dove bids a final farewell Adieu to the British Isles, although such a resolution cannot be accomplished without poignant grief'. There is something about the phrasing of both sentences which gives rise to the gravest doubts about 'the Mate's' emotional sincerity. Those heavy final clauses are such a giveaway. The sigh of relief at the end of the last message is almost audible.

Two years later an advertisement redresses the balance on behalf of suffering womanhood:

It is enough: one man alone upon earth have I found noble. Away from me forever. Cold heart and mean spirit, you have lost what millions – empires – could not have bought, but which a single word, trustfully and nobly spoken, might have made your own to all eternity. Yet are you forgiven; depart in peace; I rest in my Redeemer.

1 September 1858

The incidence of 'mates' generally failing to live up to expectations and deserting their 'doves' was particularly high at this time. It must have been an unpleasant shock to a certain J.P.L. to see himself identified by his initials on the front page of the newspaper in July 1852, and no doubt he was overcome with the same yearning for anonymity as the gentleman with a hundred pounds on his head whom Surtees supposed would have given up dyeing his whiskers:

> To J.P.L., who left London, June 26th 1852. – The cruel step has involved utter misery to those left behind – alone, unprotected, in strange apartments, placed in a situation no virtuous woman should be. The furniture has all been sold. The results will prove how far the step taken was justifiable. It is condemned by God and man. To prevent further publicity and misery, immediate communication is necessary. – D.J.L.

One could hardly suppose either that the reaction of 'William', on reading the following biblically inspired taradiddle, would have been to leap onto the first available homeward bound train:

> William, thou wilt go to sea – thou shalt go, but O return and first receive the blessings of a heart-broken father, of a broken-hearted mother! O my son William, my son, my son William! Would God I had died for thee, O William my son, my son!
>
> *15 July 1851*

He must have thanked his lucky stars they hadn't christened him Absalom.

How seriously was this sort of emotional blackmail taken by Victorian readers? Death, the ultimate threat, was bandied about pretty freely by advertisers.

> For the love of God do not persist; it will kill me if you do. You have acted under a misapprehension. I do not attribute fault to you; your absence was first discovered by my going up to tell you so, and be reconciled to you. I will arrange everything to your satisfaction. Your father is entirely prostrated; little he thought what was in your mind when you spoke to him that evening. In mercy write at once and end this misery: delay and it will come too late to save your wretched mother. Come at once, and you shall never hear an angry word; or write. Anything but leave us as we are.
>
> *11 August 1858*

Piling on the agony, though, was not necessarily the best way of resolving a situation whose roots probably lay in overcharged emotion in the first place. By the time the runaway had summoned up the courage to break free, the last thing he or she would have wanted to be reminded of would have been all that *sturm und drang* back home. And how could any self-respecting girl face a climb-down of these proportions?

> To M.L.L. – M.L.L., you have chosen your own lot: may it be a happy one! and if it be so I would not have you think of the desolate heart you leave behind; but oh! my child, if sorrow should ever overtake you, if you should find, when too late, that you have been leaning on a broken reed, then my Maria, come back to her whose heart has ever cherished you; she will always be ready to receive you.
>
> *3 February 1853*

No, a certain lightness of touch is needed to make such messages work:

> To Nolly. – 'The Minstrel Boy' who left Gr-- a I--n unknown to his friends about three weeks since, was dressed in a rusty black surtout coat, common cloth waistcoat, trousers marked with ink, and an old Caen hat. No ear for music. Pray return to your disconsolate friends. All will be forgiven, and Charlie will give up the front room.
>
> *2 October 1851*

'Muv' had the right idea too:

> Dear Fitzy, yr. presence is Required Immediately. Delay not a moment. The little birds, nutmegs, silver beaks etc. greet you. – Muv.
>
> *20 April 1846*

Fitzy, if he had any sense, was back in a flash.

Another advertiser complains about the public airing of his initials:

> DO NOT parade my initials! All other points remaining unanswered, this is to intimate to you an impending calamity, which it is more than doubtful cannot be warded off. You can learn full particulars by applying to those kind gentlemen who, being friends of both parties, are anxious to make you acquainted with this distressing affair. – S., June. W. H--y . . ., W. D. W.
>
> *7 July 1858*

Another danger of using initials was of course that they were liable to be misconstrued, or even taken advantage of:

A and E. – You do me an injustice to say that I am tampering with you. Your kind notes were duly acknowledged. The first was destroyed 'unopened'. The other was returned. N.B. Those vowels 'A.E.' may be adopted by a third rival party for the purpose of misleading through falsehood, but the true vowels 'U' and 'I', being relatives, will not be deceived by capital letters or capital hoaxers. The wise only accept as true evidence handwriting, signature and seal.

26 May 1860

Many messages express regret at failing to fulfil appointments, or disappointment at not finding the other party at an agreed rendezvous. Love by the medium of the personal column was fraught with difficulty, and dejection is often the prevailing mood:

No body, no body. – Again drifted on the uncertain sands of time in silent doubt. Yours received. – P.M., Saturday, 5 o'clock Feb 13th.

1 March 1869

It must have been an infuriatingly difficult way of corresponding, this business of entrusting carefully worded dispatches intended for the eyes of only one person to the public columns of a newspaper – and go-betweens, however respectable-sounding, were not to be relied upon either:

C.R.S. – Your long wished-for note, dated Sunday only, and written near Exeter, was received at my proper address in London, a few days after I left it. I immediately acknowledged, as it desired, in The Times, informing you that your previous letter, under cover to the Rev. Dr., had not been forwarded by me to him. I requested you to write again fully, and to address (to my proper names) 'Poste Restante, St Martin's le Grand, London.' I have caused enquiries to be made there several times since, but nothing from you has been there. Pray, therefore, write directly to that address. I know of no other, and 'E.M.' puzzles me. If you have sent a letter to any other address, inform me of that address thus, and it may be got and sent to me by a better friend than the Rev. Dr. was, and who knows our views and will act in every way to forward them. – R.S.

30 November 1854

The fortitude of R.S. and C.R.S. in continuing to attempt to communicate is admirable. How they must have longed for some short cut to all this elaboration. Yet these rigmaroles had their own fascination. The content of love letters in code was often quite mundane, but the fun was in sending and receiving coded letters, and fooling everyone in the process. However, if the recipient was not prepared to enter into the spirit of the game, the whole thing became a fiasco:

> Lapin. – En effet une correspondance devient impossible, quand on brûle les lettres sans les lire, afin de pouvoir à son aise accuser celui qui les écrit. (Correspondence really becomes impossible, when one burns letters without reading them, so as to be able to accuse their writer at leisure.)
>
> *29 October 1868*

One need not imagine that the author of this advertisement was actually a native of France: many lovers' messages at this time were in French – whether for the sake of elegant affectation, or simply to preserve their contents from the eyes of the servants. There was, for instance, 'Puisque' or 'Poichè' as he signed himself when he was in French or Italian mood, whose messages show that he was, or fancied himself to be, an artist. His mistress and model, Annie, is variously addressed as 'Sera' or 'Soir'.

> Sera! Carissima mia modella! Non ho piu felicità: come vivere senza te? Ancor vi giuro eterno efede. – Vostro Poichè.
>
> (My dearest model! My happiness is at an end: how can I live without you? Once more I swear eternal faithfulness.)
>
> *4 November 1854*

'Poichè' adopts a number of poetic variants of 'Sera' to address his Annie: Soir de Claude Lorraine, and Chef d'Oeuvre du Peintre Divin being among them (the 'divine painter' is renowned for painting his masterpieces in the evening with the colours of the sunset sky). She is also 'Uccelletta, uccellina' (little bird), and, more mysteriously, G.P.S.P.O.A.

> G.P.S.P.O.A. – Tacete anima mia. Dove, dove siete? Cosi mi lasciare! Ascolta, donna mia, respondi: carissima mia respondi! – Il Cavaliere del Pennacchio Bianco.
>
> (You keep silent, my soul. Where, where are you? To leave me thus! Listen, my lady, reply: my dearest, reply! The Knight of the White Feather.)
>
> *16 November 1854*

'The Knight of the White Feather' sounds as though it might provide a clue to Puisque's identity. Could there be a link with Garibaldi?

He was living safely in Sardinia at this time but was shortly to return to the fray. G.P.S.P.O.A.: how about 'Garibaldi! Popolo Sardo, popolo oltremare! Arriva!' (Garabaldi – people of Sardinia and people across the sea – arrives!) – rather on the same lines as V.E.R.D.I. which became the chant of pro-Garibaldi opera goers because it spelled 'Vittorio Emmanuele Re d'Italia'? This thrilling line of thought was dashed when further reading revealed that the 'drop' for communications between the two was in fact Great Portland Street Post Office: pigeon-hole 'A'. In any case, 'Poichè's' Italian is lamentable. Even E. F. Benson's Lucia, who so loved to show off her limited knowledge of that 'language of art and romance', would not have done quite so badly as this:

> Uccelletta, uccellina! Alma mia dove sia? La tua canta, la tua canta dolce si tace! Alma mia, anima mia respondi!

> (Little bird, little bird! My heart where are you? Your song, your sweet song is silent. My heart, my soul, answer!)
>
> *13 April 1856*

Poichè/Puisque eventually suffers the fate of so many personal column advertisers, as a message of June 1856 signed 'Sempré il Stesso' makes clear. 'Sempré il Stesso!' Really! He means 'Ever the same', but he has put a French acute accent on the final 'e' and, as Lucia could have told him, it is always '*lo*' or '*gli*' before 's' impure'. He asks plaintively whether a note bearing his adopted name, which had recently appeared, really came from his Soir de Claude Lorraine. He doubts it, and attributes it 'ou à quelque desir de me tendre une piège, ou à une coincidence incroyable et presqu' impossible.' His answer is two inches down on the same page. This is, by the way, something of a bumper day for the personal column – eight messages, at least one of them from Wilson, before descending to 'Lost: a Black and Tan bitch'. But here is Puisque's answer:

> Puisque. – A reply so headed, in this morning's paper, is not mine. I have not replied at all until now, and shall not do so again in this manner. Some mistake, or curiosity, or worse perhaps. Write to me, name in full, Post Office, giving an address: I will reply, giving you one, and then there can be no more mistakes. Do this at once. Grief and anxiety are rapidly doing their work. My idol is indeed a rare combination of tenderness, talent, and every virtue. Love and admiration still contend, represented now by two sweet cherubs. – Ever your own.
>
> *21 June 1856*

Two sweet cherubs, *perbacco*! Are we to assume that Soir had produced a couple of little Soirées as a tribute to her union with her artist friend? Serial romances, such as these, conducted in this semi-public manner, were perhaps not to be taken too seriously and they provided readers of *The Times* with an agreeable sense of continuing titillation, like a sort of proto-Perils-of-Pauline. They were moreover something to discuss with friends – part of the bric-à-brac of daily gossip. Tongues must have wagged over Sera's revelation.

Things did not go too well for the romance and a last, slightly incoherent message from Puisque, suggesting a macabre version of the traditional Victorian 'final solution' for an unhappy romance, appeared in January of the following year. His Italian is wilder than ever, though some kind friend must have told him about 'S impure':

> Sepolto vivo. – Se tu m'abandonne son'io risoluto di tutto lasciare. Veramente si giura che si m'ama solomente com'uno fratello lo credo non basta a me. Se tu nonne vieni nell'estate io partiro. Son'io nell' estremità della miseria, poco manco ch'io non morissi. Solo vivo per te. – S lo S.

> (Buried alive. – If you abandon me I am resolved to leave everything. Truly I swear that if you love me only as a brother I believe it will not be enough for me. If you don't come off it in the summer I shall leave. I am in an extremity of misery and I am little short of dying. I live only for you.)

> *24 January 1857*

Yet romantic exchanges could be remarkably simple:

> Out of town, spirits, hope.

> *24 November 1854*

> Why?

> *25 November 1854*

> Unrequited love.

> *27 November 1854*

> Unrequited love – be more explicit.

> *28 November 1854*

> It is not unrequited love.

> *30 November 1854*

The speed of developments of the above affair says much for the efficiency of mid-nineteenth century postal services, and for the ease of inserting announcements in the paper; they could be accepted up till six in the evening for publication the following day.

More sympathetic than the above were two lovers, Pole Star and the Bear, who were always writing things like 'Can what I hear be true?', 'I hardly dare to hope' or 'God bless you, I can think of nothing else!' One of the Bear's happier inspirations was:

> Pole Star. – Bear as I am, I do rejoice in some of the qualities of that animal, and still hope to hold you in my paws, as ever. – W
> *10 April 1854*

The correspondence continues, though at rare intervals, for some years, and from the context it is almost certain that the mysterious message 'The Bear has Come to Town' referred to earlier is this particular bear, and nothing more sinister.

The Victorians could, of course, be revoltingly cloying and it would be hard to get a higher reading on the cringe-meter than:

> Penny Land to Will. – 'Papa! Pockey hankey hi!' Would you not like to see little Gussie again?
> *6 December 1866*

Mercifully, this sort of thing is very rare and there is surprisingly little sugariness. However, there are, on occasion, hearts and flowers:

> Heartsease. Pray be calm. Do not be too eager. All will yet be right. Do you agree to meet and part no more. Some are foes – find a friend. The flowers in the conservatory, I suppose, bloomed last week. Do not part with anything. Do write. – Valc.
> *17 June 1858*

> Heartsease. On the brow of the vale. Received with thanks. Agreed as desired, if not too long delayed. Foes I never feared. Friends are sometimes treacherous. I have not forgotten the conservatory. As ever – W.
> *19 June 1858*

When flowers are invoked, the favourite is the rose, and the thorns are never left out of the imagery. Earlier that year a man whose rose has evidently done a bunk, after using her thorns to good effect, twice implores her to write:

> Can the rose be drooping whose thorns wounded the hands that would have tended it? That rose is now, alas! beyond the reach of those hands and yet they fear mischance. But write at

once or advertise more particularly, and a letter will be sent by 'Appletree'.

10 March 1858

A weed on which a rose has flung fragrance cares nothing for a few scratches. An advertisement, stating that a letter has been sent to it, in its own real name, at the General Post Office, would delight it. Its assumed name is Anti-Chesterfield.

13 March 1858

Meanwhile, back in the real world, who else was advertising in the personal column? That day in June 1856, when 'Sera' revealed the existence of the two little cherubs, gives a fair cross-section of events. It was, as I have already mentioned, a good day for the personal column (Wilson, in the character of 'Tom', is in fine metaphorical form with the weird sisters and the curtain of silence):

First in the column is 'A', cheerfully saying 'yes' to 'B's' questions number 1,2,3,4,5,7, etc and 'no' to 'B's' '6', '13', and so on. In more open-handed mood, J.S. offers to send assistance to M.P., and helpfully suggests 'state your position to your aunt, who, I am sure, will aid you'. 'G---E E---S' is earnestly entreated to return to his relations, when all will be forgiven. E.B., less informative even than 'A', simply says 'Yes', but adds 'certainly'. Then there is a long and very important-sounding message to 'Manchester' about 'the public documents on the great question in which we are both engaged'. It goes on 'Prices do not fluctuate much (especially cotton) because the annexation question (which chiefly affects us), though complicated (look at Marcy's note), may probably be finished, if a proper mediator can be found.' There are fifteen lines in this manner, and since research has not elucidated exactly what it all refers to no more will be quoted here; however, general experience indicates that the more important personal column advertisers sound, the more trivial and inflated they turn out to be. 'The states affairs', for instance, which the advertiser tells his correspondent he is much distracted with at present, are probably nothing to do with the United States but refer to one of the local councils of the Channel Islands, which are called 'the States'; 'Marcy' has probably nothing to do with William Learned Marcy, the Secretary of State under Pierce who handled the Gadsden Purchase, but is the name of a local boat-owner who sometimes imported clothes from France. The message is not signed, but ends 'weasel is not caught twice in the same trap'.

'Weasel', though, is curious and, going on for a moment with this wild weasel chase, there are other advertisements which seem to link up with this clue. During the previous April two 'weasels' put their heads above ground and, for a moment, sniffed the air of Hampstead Heath.

Hampstead Heath enclosure. Look out! The weasel is not asleep!

1 April 1856

To which there is a reply:

Hampstead Heath enclosure. I am glad to hear the Weasel is not asleep, as traps are laid for him.

3 April 1856

An April Fool's Day joke? If so, it is very nearly the only one in the history of the personal column. No, clearly there is a serious point at issue:

Hampstead Heath enclosure. Wake up and petition Parliament.

21 June 1856

Several attempts were made by Maryon Wilson, Lord of the Manor of Hampstead, to develop the heath for residential purposes. The attempts failed, owing to the opposition of copyholders, and Wilson was refused permission to build.

That is very nearly all there is to say about the personal column of 24 June 1856. There are some enjoyable lost-and-founds, and some 'Rewards', though none outstanding. They range from 'A small black and tan rough terrier bitch, very gray about the head', with an address in Shoreditch and no reward, to, at the other end of the social scale:

Lost, in the Brompton neighbourhood, a small gray cockatoo, marked with yellow on the breast. Very tame. To be brought to Eden Lodge, Kensington Gore.

There was a one pound reward for him. A couple of years earlier another parrot, evidently immune to vertigo, had sought sanctuary in or on a cathedral:

Parrot found. On the Dome of St Paul's, July 16th. Full description of size, age, colour and sayings, to be sent by letter to F.C.P., 4 Trafalgar Square.

On the subject of birds, and flight in general, there are several announcements in the 1860s for what sounds like a rather entertaining gentlemen's dining club – 'The Buzwings'. They sound a silly and amiable lot, and their chief delight was to make fun of that most absurd notion – that man could ever learn to fly. 'To Stray

Buzwings! Hark the Lark at Heaven's Gate Sings!', declares their announcement of 9 July 1868, heralding their 'Summer Lark – Banquet at 8.00 p.m., rising of the Larks at 9.30, neats at 1.00 a.m.' The following year there was:

A grand inauguration of the apiary. October swarms will occur as per notices. Postulants will hive and buzz as directed in September circulars. For honey certificates apply to past grands; for flight see further advertisements.

They met at the Star and Garter Hotel, Richmond, and when that was burned down in January 1870, 'A Grand Flitting of the Order' was decreed. Then on January 7th, Jaharah Singh, P.B., announced that he would lecture (D.V.) at the 'Buzwing Hall' on 'The Buzwing Theory of Flight'.

Other clubs went in for singing, or amateur theatricals. The following exchange, interpreted by Alice Clay as referring to the breaking off of a matrimonial engagment, more probably refers to a leading lady, torn between two rival theatrical companies or clubs – the 'Charades' and 'another company'. There is certainly something flirtatious going on as well, and there is a Victorian nudge and a wink in the name 'Spoonini', who is presumably the Charades' male lead. It all sounds frivolous and skittish enough.

Spoonini is anxious to hear of Daisy's whereabouts. The Charades pause for a reply.

27 December 1855

Daisy feels inexpressibly flattered by Spoonini's tender enquiries, but having found a more perfect hero in a new Company, she begs gratefully to decline any renewal of the old engagement.

2 January 1856

The role of Alice Clay, like that of any commentator on such material, including the present one, could only be to select and lay before her readers those items which seemed to her curious, amusing or remarkable and make suggestions, where appropriate, as to their possible meaning. The true meaning of the following messages, if she had guessed at it, would certainly have shocked her profoundly, as it would have shocked the management of *The Times*:

S to L, the 2 R's and W. – Charles Urquhart Newport Tilney has not suffered from the eels.

10 September 1861

Let us hope no worldly-wise critic ragged her, no outraged moralist attacked her for her blindness to initials. Probably she thought the following referred to the hazards of travel over the Swiss Alps, but the topography is undoubtedly human and the dangerous mountain is that of Aphrodite, not Mont Blanc:

> AIXA – The horseman dangerously ill. Search pass leading to mountain. Pollaky's Private Inquiry Office, 13 Paddington Green, London W.
>
> *27 October 1869*

> AIXA – The horseman slightly better. Pollaky's Private Inquiry Office, 13 Paddington Green, London W.
>
> *1 November 1869*

> AIXA – The horseman is dismounted, and left in the cold. Pollaky's Private Inquiry Office, 13 Paddington Green, London W.
>
> *12 November 1869*

Pollaky's detective agency, through whom the above advertisements were placed, brought a lot of business to the column during these years. E. J. Wilson, as noted earlier, uses him and the name Pollaky must have impressed itself on any *Times* reader with an inquiring mind, who happened to glance at the columns during the latter half of the nineteenth century. Pollaky's name appears far more frequently than that of any of his rivals, such as C. Nicholls of Devereux Court, and he busies himself with all kinds of matters from lost relatives to stolen jewellery. Sometimes his concerns are of a more enigmatic nature:

> Monsignor – Many roads lead to Rome, but how to return? The way is crooked, even for – Pollaky.
>
> *31 July 1868*

That Pollaky cast his net widely is evident – we read of him investigating the fall of a girl from a pleasure steamer on the Rhine; a diplomat in Copenhagen, the passport office in Madrid and the Swiss consul in Rome all come into his messages. Altogether, Pollaky was a remarkable figure. He also made sure everyone knew it, and may well have put in the following to impress prospective clients with his abilities:

> Marquise – 'Broken reed' will trouble you no more. – Pollaky's Private Inquiry Office, 13 Paddington Green, London W.
>
> *14 August 1867*

'Xantippe'. – Although possessing a thorough knowledge of

eight languages I cannot deduct sense from your epistle. –
Ignatius Pollaky, Private Inquiry Office, 13 Paddington Green,
London W.

1 October 1869

Xantippe, by the way, was a pseudonym preferred by governesses
and schoolmistresses. She was Socrates' wife – a fearsome lady by
all accounts. A housekeeper advertising in 1850 to 'widowers and
single gentlemen' who, presumably, were not looking for a wife,
makes convenient adjectival use of the name in her alphabetical
self-portrait:

> She is agreeable, becoming, careful, desirable, English,
> facetious, generous, honest, industrious, judicious, keen,
> lively, merry, natty, obedient, philosophic, quiet, regular,
> sociable, tasteful, useful, vivacious, womanish, xantippish,
> youthful, zealous, &c.

After that catalogue, what could she have meant by '&c'?

The origin of many family names can be found in the change of
name announcements in the personal column. There were two main
reasons for changing a name: legal, as in the case of an inheritance;
and aesthetic, where the original name was judged for some reason
ungainly or undesirable. There are several examples of unfortunate
names which were dispensed with in this manner and they provided
an amusing topic of conversation among devotees of the column,
whose malicious gossip would ensure that the name lived on, if not
in legal fact, at least in after-dinner stories, to the intense embarrassment of the very person who had been so anxious to expunge
it from memory for all time.

In 1862 a successful innkeeper, with the unlovely name of Joshua
Bug, moved from Epsom to Wakefield in Yorkshire and decided at
the same time to take the opportunity of the move to disinfest
himself of his irritating surname and substitute something
altogether grander and more in keeping with his newfound prosperity. What he wanted was a name right at the opposite end of the
scale, a name of distinction and irreproachable connections:

> I, Norfolk Howard, heretofore called and known by the name
> of Joshua Bug, late of Epsom, in the county of Surrey, now of
> Wakefield in the county of York, and landlord of the Swan
> Tavern in the same county, do hereby give notice, that on the
> 20th day of this present month of June, for and on behalf of
> myself and heirs, lawfully begotten, I did wholly abandon the
> use of the surname BUG and assumed, took and used, and am
> determined at all times hereafter, in all writings, actions,

dealings, matters and things, and upon all occasions whatsoever, to be distinguished, to subscribe, to be called and known
by the name of NORFOLK HOWARD only. I further refer all
whom it may concern to the deed poll under my hand and seal,
declaring that I choose to renounce the use of the surname of
Bug, and that I assume in lieu thereof the above surnames of
Norfolk Howard, and also declaring my determination, upon
all occasions whatsoever, to be called and distinguished
exclusively by the said surnames of Norfolk Howard, duly
enrolled by me in the High Court of Chancery. Dated this 23d
day of June 1862.

NORFOLK HOWARD
(Late Joshua Bug)   *26 June 1862*

This elaborate legal jargon, enshrining the absurdly pretentious
new name, had the very opposite of the effect intended. Far from
being forgotten, thanks to the malice of the wits, the name Joshua
Bug stuck to Norfolk Howard like a tick to a dog, and in polite
society it became the fashion to refer (Oh Joshua!) to bed-bugs as
'Norfolk Howards'.

Five years later, heedless of his calling, a Dr Coughlan blithely
changes his name to Colon.

Following this, there can be no alternative but to go further down
the path of insanity. Often the seeming lunacy of personal column
advertisers is a result of trying to convey something to a particular
person while concealing it from others by the skilful use of curious
metaphors or unlikely allusions. Increasingly, towards the middle
of the nineteenth century, they use ciphers or codes: a complex
subject which will be dealt with in the following chapter. Sometimes, however, the oddness is of a more alarming kind. Two
examples from the mid-nineteenth century will suffice to demonstrate symptoms which may perhaps be of greater interest to the
student of psychology than to the general reader. The first has a
rather stylish quality and one might imagine it to be the work of a
biblically minded social reformer, were it not for its mystical tone:

> Fat oxen – starving people. – The fat oxen are gone from their
> glass palace, and are eaten by the rich; the starving people
> remain in their over-crowded fever dens, and are being eaten
> by disease. Fat oxen. Starving people.
>
> *12 January 1866*

The second shows all the signs of a febrile mind – the obsession with
numbers, the vagueness and the overwhelming sense of self-
importance:

99

I have been for nearly 21 years investigating the value of shape in relation to value in different branches of economic science, and on the 11th of June current I finally solved the problem, discovering simultaneously the square of the circle, the key of the pyramid of Cheops and the value of the number seven. The problem is of vast importance, and I wish, through the columns of The Times, to prove the date of my 'instantia crucis' and its truth on the base of the world's evidence in a series of seven letters. – William Harvey, 10 Albert Terrace, Albert Gate, London.

18 June 1867

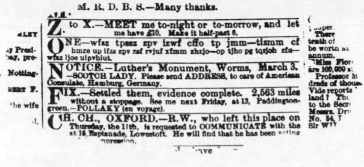

6 *The Collinson Cryptograms*

Sir Charles Wheatstone, who with Sir W. F. Cooke was a pioneer of the electric telegraph, lived during the middle years of the nineteenth century by the Thames, near Hammersmith Bridge. He was a small, tubby, bespectacled man and he had many interests beyond his work as Professor of Natural Philosophy at King's College, London. The son of a musical instrument maker, he is credited with the invention of the concertina, as well as with more serious contributions to science, including the method of measuring electrical resistance which still bears his name – the 'Wheatstone bridge'.

A close friend of his, a chemist and Fellow of the Royal Society, named Lyon Playfair, also lived near the Thames, though on the Surrey side. Lyon, who combined extraordinary scientific brilliance with great organizational ability, was one of the leading men behind the Great Exhibition of 1851 and also helped to found the Royal College of Science and the Science Museum. He became Postmaster-General under Gladstone, and later Chairman and Deputy Speaker of the House of Commons. Lyon, who was made Baron of St Andrews in 1884, was also, as it happened, a small rotund man and a wearer of spectacles. Indeed these two eminent gentlemen were so alike that Lady Wheatstone more than once confused the two and addressed Sir Lyon as her husband.

The two men shared a curious hobby – the unravelling of those coded messages which during the middle years of the nineteenth century so often appeared in the personal columns of newspapers. They used to stroll by the river on Sunday mornings with copies of the week's codes and puzzle out their meaning; although many of the messages were very short (a great disadvantage when trying to decipher an unknown code), they were hardly ever defeated. The moral they drew from this was that the codes in use at that time were too easy to break to be secure in wartime. This led in turn to their joint invention of the cipher Sir Lyon was eventually to offer to the Admiralty, which still bears his name – the Playfair Cipher.

The earliest coded messages of any length appeared in *The Times* in 1821. The code is an odd-looking assortment of asterisks and letters, and may be decipherable, but it appeared too early to catch the attention of Wheatstone or Playfair, or of that other great decoder of the age, Charles Babbage. I was unable to make head nor tail of it, but I had better admit at the outset that I am a mere beginner at this kind of thing. In the hope that others may find it entertaining to solve, it is given in the Appendix.

The term 'code' conceals two distinct systems of disguise: ciphers and codes proper.

Ciphers involve a simple substitution: 'B' for 'A', 'C' for 'B', for instance, and so on – or 'boe tp po', as a cryptographer would say. There are of course many variants of this, and a slightly different form of encipherment is to write the message out according to a prearranged pattern, and then read it off.

In the second kind (the true 'code') whole words, or even whole messages, are substituted by an agreed combination of letters, numbers and/or symbols. This involves both parties being issued with a code book, a sort of phrase or word dictionary, which has to be consulted to discover, for instance, that the phrase 'this involves' has to be coded into 'ZD12', the phrase 'both parties' as 'B7Q', while 'being' is the single letter 'J', 'issued' is P23, 'with' is '9', 'a' is '3' and 'code book' is F2Y – so the opening phrase of the sentence becomes ZD12 B7Q J P23 9 3 F2Y.

A true code is almost impossible to break, unless one has the all-important code book, bound of course in lead, so that it can be conveniently thrown into the sea in emergencies, and, in war novels, bargained for by enemy agents or left in railway compartments by foreign countesses. Codes can sometimes be broken even without the book, if there is enough material to go on.

The first kind – fortunately by far the commonest in the personal column – is no more than a brain teaser and can almost always be broken eventually, provided there is enough there to be analysable. This is where the personal column advertiser sometimes beats the Babbages, Wheatstones and Playfairs: the messages are often too short, and sometimes a given advertiser will only insert one message and will never be heard of again.

There is one remarkable instance in which Wheatstone and Playfair together were able to puzzle out the meaning of a single short sentence, which appeared several times early in 1852. It read as follows:

Tig tjvhw it tig jfhiiwola og tig psgvw. – F.D.N.

The method of reasoning they adopted in working out what this meant is interesting. First, they noticed that it contained the word 'tig' repeated three times. This told them several things. For a start it meant that the method of encipherment was constant throughout the sentence: it was not a cipher of the complex kind that employs a change of rules with every word or letter. Secondly, the frequency of 'tig' argued in favour of it being a common word. The concept of frequency is at the cornerstone of the art of code-breaking – there are tables of frequency for the most commonly used letters of the alphabet and word frequency tables, too. As code-breaking is an art as well as a science (informed guesses and intuitive leaps are very much a part of the technique), the two men decided to try substituting the word 'the' for 'tig'. This started a further train of thought – for whereas the 't' seemed to have remained unchanged, 'h' is one behind the 'i' in the alphabet and 'e' is two steps behind the 'g' of 'tig':

```
        E
    H   F
T   I   G
```

Following suit with the next word is not so promising:

```
            S
        E   T
    T   F   U
I   U   G   V
T   J   V   H   W
```

'Tites' is not a word. But one of the watchwords of cryptography is 'follow through', so, despite this initially discouraging result, they continued to apply the technique to the remaining letters. It was soon apparent that the central 't' of the second word ('v' in the code) was a 'blind', deliberately put in to throw cryptographers off the track – and possibly to avoid a suit for libel in the event of the conundrum being solved, for here is the result of the complete process:

```
                                              S
                                          E   T
                                      I   F   U
                                  R   J   G   V
                              E   S   K   H   W
                          F   F   T   L   I   X
                      F   G   G   U   M   J   Y
                  E   G   H   H   V   N   K   Z
  THE   TIMES   IS   THE   J F H I I W O L A

                      S
                  S   T
              E   T   U
          R   F   U   V
  OF   THE   P S G V W
```

Amused at this result, Playfair then inserted an advertisement himself, addresssed to 'F.D.N.', repeating the message '*The Times is the Jefferies of the Press*' in plain English. This appeared on 3 March 1852. The following morning the editor, Delane, got in touch with Playfair through the box number he had given. He was extremely angry, but when Playfair explained that all he had done was decipher the code and let 'F.D.N.' know his secret had been 'rumbled', there was nothing more he could do. As to the identity of 'F.D.N.' and the nature of his grudge against *The Times*, nothing could be discovered.

Many of the ciphers used are much easier than that. Words, for instance, are simply spelled backwards:

TO C.A. – I dluoc ton og ot eht hcnual fo Cressy. I deen ton yas woh hcum ti detnioppasid dna dessertsid em ot ssim gniees ruoy ecaf, hguoht I dluoc ton evah nekops ot ym Eisle. Dog evreserp uoy. A raey txen yadsendeW ecnis ew detrap. Etirw noos, sa erofeb. Yllo.

26 July 1853

Had this message not been written in sdrawkcab language, nobody would have bothered to read it; far from concealing the banal affair of Olly and Elsie it served only to advertise it. It can be assumed, however, that Olly and Elsie were in earnest: they might not have been very good cryptographers, but they probably thought they were concealing their messages, rather than setting conundrums for their friends to solve, as became the fashion after the First World War. Lovers were genuinely anxious to find secret methods of communication and it is easy to see why *The Times*, whose innocent appearance on the breakfast table was unlikely to arouse the suspicion of jealous husbands or wives, often served as the ideal Trojan horse. Business men occasionally employed the technique too, as did political conspirators such as 'I Carbonari'. This Italian secret society, which was in revolt against Austrian-Spanish rule, in one famous instance became so confused about a coded message inserted for them in the Dundee Exchange that they were forced to show their hand to the extent of publicly advertising themselves:

Todd oder Todt? Schreibe welcher. – I Carbonari

(Todd or dead? Write and say which.)

On the whole, however, the intellectual challenge of solving the coded messages was more interesting than the results, which proved in most cases to be messages making or cancelling romantic appointments. The appeal of this kind of puzzle is not dissimilar to the crossword puzzle, which had not yet been invented and was not incorporated into *The Times* until 1 February 1930. Thus the messages that did appear in code attracted a good deal of attention from readers with inquiring minds.

Charles Babbage, who was incomparably better at this kind of exercise than anyone else alive at the time, was regularly employed by the legal profession on divorce cases in which lovers' messages were written in code. His understanding of the links between cryptography and mathematics is one more example of the originality of the man who was the first to appreciate the possibility of devising machines to solve mathematical problems – the earliest computers. Babbage's reputation as a cryptographer led him into strange avenues, such as Sherlock Holmes would have delighted to explore – though many of the texts he was invited to unravel turned out to be erotic in the extreme, which would hardly have suited that confirmed mysogynist. His solutions to these codes often involved highly complex mathematical equations and he was far in advance of any other practitioner of the science of cryptography. Unfortunately, he never published the results. Babbage's great weakness was his failure to complete the tasks he worked on. The most notorious example of this failure concerned the two elaborate computing 'engines' he devised, consisting of banks of cogged wheels. Neither was ever completed.

Often Babbage would annotate simple coded messages with a few scornful words. These annotations have been preserved in his papers. Two messages in January and February 1854 which attracted his disfavour were:

J.M.M. has received it. Wndr, wpng nd wrshp flw

against which he wrote 'vowels omitted'; and

> Carnage. – JP and JL to Thetr Oupea Tmi L touh Ill. – H. Y. T., or send all further applications respecting the A. of H. to the D. of P.

of which he remarks 'amateurish tergiversation of all the laws of cyphers.'

He noted without comment:

> Q.L.B. – Gszmph ixvrevw hzuvob – zoo szh yvvm olmt ztl rm zmhdvi gl gsv gdl jfvhgrlmh.
>
> *14 November 1854*

> L'abbandonata. – Bmfyboesf spdigpsu sfqpufe efbe. J tbx zpv zftufsebz. Npbuf wbjomz tfbsdife ufo zfbst.
>
> *18 December 1855*

Babbage was vastly experienced in reading codes from all kinds of sources and all walks of life, from parlourmaids to secret agents, and he must have been struck immediately by certain tell-tale combinations such as 'gsv' in the first of these two pieces and 'zpv' in the second. Both are in ciphers of great simplicity. The first employs a reversed alphabet; and the second is simply 'b' for 'a'. Its message however is intriguing – a drowning (for love, of course) in a castle moat.

Also for beginners is a series of advertisements starting with the word 'One', which appeared in 1868 and 1869.

> One – nx – hr hkk; cn mns khjd sn kdaud xds. Gnv knmf mnshbd vntkc xnt vzms udx jhmc sgntfgsr.
>
> *29 October 1868*

It is 'xnt' which is the give-away here – not 'the' (there is no 'the' in the message), but 'you'. There are also two mistakes – the sender has forgotten to change the 'a' of 'kdaud' to a 'z', and has left out the 'q' which should come before the final letter of 'udx'.

The same type of cipher had appeared a few years before, both in the 'Abbandonata' message referred to above and in one addressed to 'A.C.' It is just possible that the same people are involved. There is a triangle of two lovers and a sick person.

The theme here is somewhat grisly:

> To A.C. – Cpof up gjstu kpjou ublfo pvu zftufsebz. Dimpspgpsn – sfhjnft bmpof qsfwfoufe nf gvmgjmmjoh nz qspnjtf up zpv. – Nzptpujt.
>
> *3 May 1865*

The removal of a bone and the use of chloroform clearly suggest an operation. What was the promise? Not merely to meet at an agreed rendezvous. Is it a surgeon who writes, or a relative of the patient? The uneasy suggestion of a medical murder cannot be ruled out.

But let us continue with 'One', whose spelling, by the way, is getting a little shaky:

> One. – Hpu 2 opuft – tpssa zpv xfsf tp jmm – ipof rvjuf xfmm opx – mpoh xfz po kpvsofx – wfsz hudi cfuufs ljoe ufpvhiut gffm mpofmz.
>
> *4 January 1869*

And what was this childish rigmarole which appeared at the end of the week?

> To S.H.H. – Susammume tuto yuyou fufruromom allul.
>
> *9 January 1869*

The meaning is obvious enough – it is playground babble language for 'same to you from all'. It is also apparent, from the next message, that it was directed at the inserter of 'One', whose code had, presumably, been broken and who would have recognised the initials 'S.H.H.' But nearly three weeks elapse before the next message:

> One – hpu exp gppmt uijt ujnf yuyou tuare fuas guotuther. S.S.H.
>
> *27 January 1869*

This is just the sort of mixture of cipher and nonsense that Babbage deplored. The first half is clear enough ('One got two fools this time'), but the second half is not a cipher. It must be guessed at – 'you two are fools together', perhaps.

The one-sided correspondence continues, without throwing any light on this odd interruption:

> One – wfsz tpssz zpv izwf cffo tp jmm – tizmm cf hmze up ifsz zpv zsf rvjuf xfmm zhzo op tjho pg tzpsjoh zfu – wfsz ljoe uipvhiut.
>
> *23 March 1869*

Syoring? There has been a curious misreading of handwriting here: what is meant of course is 'tqsjoh', the 'tqsjoh' in which a young man's fancy lightly turns to thoughts of 'mpwf'.

> One – hpu opuf tibmm cf bu uif qmbdf obnfe po uif uxfouzzjstu pg uijt npoui – up tbwf ujnd nffu bt tppo zpv dbo – xsjnf.
>
> *9 April 1869*

The last word, which translates as 'wrime', must be shorthand for 'wire me'.

The correspondence continues with appointments made and remade in September, until trouble strikes:

> One – Sghmfr bzmmns qdlzhm zr sgdx vdgd. Bzmmns bnld sn okzbd mzldc. Zkk hr chrbnudqdc. Sqtrs mn nmd. Jhme sgntfgsr zmc vhrgdr.
>
> *1 October 1869*

All is discovered! The perennial cry of clandestine lovers in the personal column.

At this point, a number of other messages in more complex ciphers start to appear. These are not only more complex, but betray rather more élan and passion than 'One'. Two new names and personalities emerge: 'Umbrella' and 'Curly Feather', alias 'Bicycle'. Names Freud would have relished.

> Aqmlj hmd louch ault lgj tjlljq vwjq qjeyg tmwj xjhmiu ljttvir fdqjth ciu lqdj, viqefldqju avlg vtmwj ueqtvir im oljjf lgil ivrgl.
>
> *5 October 1869*

(Wrote you today will the letter iver reach love beyond telling purely and true inraptured with love darling no sleep that night.)

Once again the mistake 'i' for 'e' in 'ever' has occurred before encoding; perhaps, given the stilted language, the author was not English. 'Umbrella's' code is much simpler – the alphabet has been displaced two steps instead of one:

> Skzpcjjy. – Bcyp Dyllw, kccr wmsp bgqrpyarcb dpgclb zcyclcyrf rfc ugjjmu zw rfc jyic. Pmu slbcp rfc qrypq. Amkkml qcy zpccxcq. Dcyrfcpucgefr. Wmspq Zgawajc.
>
> *11 October 1869*

Rowing under the stars by the willow tree sounds rather out of 'One's' league. Indeed there is a message from 'One' the following day, typically terse and unromantic:

> One – vhkk ldds nm lnmczx mdws – he xnt khjd – kds ld jmnv – cn mns qdlzhm hm okzbd mzldc – ldds vgdqd xnt khjd.
>
> *12 October 1869*

The reply can only be guessed at, but it rather looks as though 'Bicycle' might have put a spoke in 'One's' wheel. Here is the last message from that quarter:

One – Xnt rzx xnt vhkk bmld he H khjd; vghbg knnjr zr he xnt che mns bzqd; he rn oqzx cn mns sqntakd xntqrdke.

15 October 1869

It is bad enough getting a brush-off over the telephone; receiving one in code must be an even more depressing experience. However, the romance between 'Umbrella/Fanny' and 'Bicycle/Curly Feather' fares no better:

Vncsfmmb. Efbs gbooz ep xsjuf epou lopx xibuup nblf pg zpvs tjmfodf zpvss cjdzjmf.

25 October 1869

'Bicycle's' ciphering goes somewhat astray at the end – the effects no doubt of distraction at his disappointment. There is a last plea in December, this time in plain English:

Curly feather. – Wet or dry, must I never see you any more? – Disconsolate Umbrella.

18 December 1869

And the reply is suitably enigmatic, in the best personal column tradition:

Curly Feather cannot tell.

30 December 1869

In April the following year there appeared a message in what is probably a 'Vigenère' cipher – for the translation of the letters changes progressively throughout the message, though the displacement is only by one or two letters each time:

Frankenstein. – Wjshg grws ikwh uja afv rp dnm eg ddwuqvv cobyhhtt hxtq ko jgspco lp ddut rh thkaatt rt twqqschh qn lv tliodvvug x iqs wjf stfrgcw vxli grt tdhfwa dpz oguwgs wq nh ubig ihtf wtvvv nh K xlnm qgwht hlxf bqvxr obxfw fbunjqi swu snfqvz rh mrxf lp zrws oguwgsv.

8 April 1870

(Three, four, five, six, yes to all. Be cautious anywhere even in German in case of seizure or stoppage, omit signature W for the present, twig for safety any letter to me, safe here, trust me. I will never give you up – never, darling. Put plenty of love in your letters.)

The 'monster' was clearly enjoying a spot of jwxasw, but msxpbs was probably at the root of the whole business.

Charles Babbage, who was never a man to give up easily, spent the whole month of February 1846 on a brain-teaser his nephew sent him – noting in his diary that he finished it at 1.30 a.m. He soon decided that the cipher was based on a code word or words. He knew the message probably ended 'ever your affectionate nephew' and began 'dear uncle', since the groupings of letters fitted these obvious phrases. Much of the time he devoted to the problem was spent trying to find key words. 'Somerset' seemed to fit the dedication, but did not work for the rest. Concluding that the other key was a multiple word, consisting of a group of five letters and three letters, he went through a lengthy list of possibilities, trying each in turn: birthday, death-bed, water rat, handy cap, house dog, under cut, heavy-wet, witch elm, small pox, money bag, hedgehog, brick bat, tithe pig, tight fit, apple pie, night cap, opera box, *vingt-une*, pussy cat, bull's eye, pearl ash, *faux pas*, and finally, with success, the Greek word for 'nonsense' – *cacoethes*. Three pages of mathematical tables were then used to solve the problem from these keys.

A problem of particular interest to Babbage the mathematician was posed by the following numerical cipher which appeared in the personal column in 1853:

FLO 1821 82374 29 30 84511. 185270 924 184 182 82460. 8842 31 8599120 31 8355 7239241 8218. 726 85400 021.

21 September 1853

Underneath this Babbage notes: '1st Obs: Every letter cannot be represented by two figures, because if it were each word would contain an even number of figures. 2nd Obs.: If all letters were represented by two figures then the words 29, 30, in line 1 and 31 in line 2 must each be in the English language, viz "a" and "I". Therefore either the cipher is not in English or one at least of these words, 29, 30, and 31 contains *two* letters.' This was fairly elementary. What follows is not. After several pages of calculation Babbage notes a possible key-word – 'Florence', to see if this fits the results of his calculations. Fortunately this time he does not need to try any other key-words. He proceeds directly to '726 85400 021: God bless you'. How he arrives at this is beyond the scope of this book; however, after some further lines of reasoning and mathematics he produces a table for the solution of these messages. This table, which shows that each number may represent several different letters, is as follows:

0	1	2	3	4	5	6	7	8	9
y	u	o	i	e	a	d	k	h	f
s	t	n	m	r	l		g	w	p
x							c	b	
								v	
								I	

Equipped with this, the messages become relatively easy to read. That just quoted translates as: 'Thou voice of my heart. Thanks for the two words. When it happens it will comfort both. God bless you.'

The rest of the correspondence is rather more affecting than that of 'One'. The entry for 29 September 1853, for instance, reads 'How I love you. My heart is pining for you. Come and meet me. Thou voice of my ---' But here the message must be interrupted: there is a problem over the last word. In the original, the numbers are 8454, which translates as 'bear'. One of the disadvantages of conducting a romantic correspondence in code is the ever-present danger of such unlooked-for zoological intrusions.

The next message is clear enough.

> FLO – Thou voice of my heart! Berlin, Tuesday. I leave next Monday, and shall press you to my heart on Saturday. God bless you.
>
> *29 November 1853*

What happens after that is worth describing in some detail. Two nearly identical messages appear, on December 21st and 23rd. Here is the first:

> FLO. – 1821 82374 29 30 84541 8 53 02 522450. 8 3300 021 3244 1852 4844. 8 5227 51 0214 9371144 48440. 8 0426 021 52 326352 08585 12 8459 42116 021 88354 505449 59144 632244. 31 8355 7449 021 8543 526 021 3101 95270 1851 31 5430 544 42126 021 726 85400 021.
>
> *21 December 1853*

The second is slightly longer. There is an additional 184 5501 850 84227 8 449451 31 at the beginning 'the last was wrong I repeat it'. There is also 828 8 62 5284 021 ('how I do love you') at the end. Other than this, it has two corrections: 42116 is changed to 42126, and 31 to 30. Neither of these corrections would have been significant to the recipient. The sense is not in doubt – 'wrap round you' and 'fancy that my arms are around you' can easily be guessed despite the minor errors in the original version. Why then did 'FLO' bother to put in the whole message again with these minor improvements in accuracy? The answer is that it was not 'FLO' who inserted it at all. It was Charles Babbage who put the advertisement of December 23rd in *The Times*. By doing so and by adding the opening phrase, which is not used in any of the other messages, and the final phrase, which is, he demonstrates to 'FLO', that he has broken the cipher. The effects of this action are apparent from the message that followed:

FLO. – I fear, dearest, that our cipher is discovered: write at once to your friend 'Indian Shawl' (P.O.) Buckingham, Bucks.

6 January 1854

The way these three brilliant men used their intellectual powers to interfere with clandestine romantic affairs is questionable. It was all very clever, but it must have been extremely irritating to those concerned. At least Babbage restricted his interference to this gentle, scholarly joke, demonstrating not only that he could read the 'FLO' codes but knew the rules of the code better than the advertiser. A rather more ruthless practical joke was perpetrated by Wheatstone and Playfair on the author of a series of advertisements in 1853, most of which are headed 'Kensington'. The one given below inaugurates a new code system, as the first sentence in plain English makes clear, though an instruction to the printer has crept in too:

To be inserted July 1st. – Some of the signs are not in type; send figures instead. Nb wziormt blfi ovggvl nfxs xlmhlovw nv kivkzirmt gl uloold nb nlgsvih olevw ivnzrmh. Ovg fh vevi pvvk rm ervd gszg yovhhvw hzerlfi gl dsln blf wriixg nv – gsvm dv nzb rmwvev xzoxfozgv fklm szkkrmvhh gvnklizo – vgivmzo. Nb hrhgvi rh hzwob wrhgivhhvw, bsv hvmwh svi olev. Nb yrignwzb rh gsv vovevmgs lu zftfhg. Yv mlg wrbzkklrmgvw ru gsv urihg hslfow mlg zodzbh yirmt gsv ovggvl zh rg rh wruurxfos gl tvg gsvn rm gsv vczxg wzb. R mvevi hzw nb nlgsvi zugvi ovzermt blf, mlg vevm rm wvzgs zh gsv xluurm dzh xolhvw yvuliv R ziirevw. Dirgv gl nv zh lugvm zh lugv, zh blf xzm zh rgrh nb lmob kovzhfiv*R szev blfi kvmxro *.

1 July 1853

As will no doubt be immediately apparent to those skilled in such matters, this is in reality a very simple code making use of the alphabet backwards. The mention of the funeral and of the coffin that was closed before the writer arrived is noteworthy, as is the curious signature – 'I have your pencil'. That the code was easily broken, is evident from the next advertisement, four days later, in the same cipher system, but in French. This decodes to:

July 1st. – Tout est compris! Ecrivez moi en chiffre et rendez moi mon crayon!

On August 1st the correspondence resumes, still in the old code, though it is clear that a new code is planned:

Nb wvzivhg z., blfi olmot vckvxgvw ovggvi zg ozhg ziirevw rgsrmp blf dviv dilmt rm kilnrhrmt blfi hrhgvi gl dirgv hl

hvowln. Kizb ivnvnyvi dszg blf kilnrhvw nv dsvm blf tl gl gsv
hvz. Blf ulitlg gl hvmw nv urtfivh uli dliwh wl hl vhkyxrzoob uli
gsv hnzoo lmvh zmw gslhv dsrxs lxxfi hlhg lugvm, rwrw mlg
hvmw gsvyllph. Xfnnrmth rhx xovevi dllp, rdrhs rdviv drgs blf
gl ivzw gltvgsvi. Nb hrhgvi rh yvggvi hsv rh orermt zg Xsvhsfmg
zg kivhvmg, yfg gsv slfh droo yv pvkg lm. Rvckvxg gl tlgl
Hxlgozmw rmz dvvp, yfg dirgv zh Yvuliv. *Rh dvoo. Rtzev srn
dszg blf hvmgzmw vmervwsrn rollp ulidziw gl gsv vovemgs –
TLW yovhh blf – blfi ldm.

1 August 1853

'Figures for words' evidently refers to the cipher the author is
planning to introduce. Possibly 'the books' are to provide the key to
a code he is intending to use. There has presumably been a misprint
in the sentence 'Cummings is a clever *dllp*' – the gastronome may
once again prefer an aberrant reading, substituting an 'x' for the 'd',
but it seems more probable that there is a letter missing and
Cummings was a crook. Some care has been taken to avoid giving
away too many clues by joining up words and by never allowing the
letter 'I' to stand on its own – in contrast to the previous
advertisement, where there are several capital 'R's, pinpointing
that letter infallibly. The capital letter 'I' is the Achilles' heel of
the amateur cryptographer – nothing gives the secret away more
quickly.

A few days later the new cipher system was inaugurated, as
follows:

Kensington. – Ftmf ftq nqzf ar qhqdk ymze yuzp etagxpng rax
xlqp uz lme qpgomfuaz mzp az tue pqefuzmfuaz uz xurg ue azq
ar ftq ymjuye itust tme nqqz arfqz dqbqmfup ngf itnot omzzaf
nq mpyuffqp iiftagf grmzl dgefduofuaze.

13 August 1853

Alas for the young lovers, the combined forces of Playfair,
Wheatstone, and Babbage were against them, and within four days
a teasing answer was printed in the same code:

Kensington. – Kagd okbtqd ue ympq agf, ngf egot saap ymjuye
etagxp nq iduffqz uz bxmuz qzsxvet, ftmf mxx nqzqruf.

(Kensington. – Your cipher is made out, but such good maxims
should be written in plain English, that all might benefit.)

The alphabet has merely been shifted half-way along, to start at 'm'.
And to drive the point home, the following was inserted the next
day:

113

To Kensington. – That the bent of every man's mind should be followed in his education and destination in life is one of the maxims which has often been repeated, but which cannot be admitted without many restrictions.

Probably the writer, whom Playfair assures us in his autobiography was a young student from Oxford on a reading party at Perth, failed to see these indications that it was all up for the codes until too late. The next day a long message appeared, which in translation reads:

My Darling A., need I say how delighted I was to receive your letter and dear remembrance on my mother's birthday. I beg you not to think I wrote under any irritation, but I fear my letters being read by others, so I confined myself to facts and events. I am now at Amulrie near Dunkeld, Perthshire, but you had better write as before. I did not blame you for adhering to your promise, but for making it. If you knew the joy and gladness your letters bring me you would forgive any hastiness. God bless you for all the kindness and love they manifest. I am down here reading amid beautiful scenery. I will collect the ferns. How shall I send them? Give McG my love and tell her I don't agree with her about her conduct – I have not seen our dear friend. Your letter did not arrive until the 13th. So I could not send this before. Write soon, so that I may answer on the first if possible. As ever, your own.

19 August 1853

The suspicion that all was not well must have grown, and back issues of *The Times* were hastily consulted in the library at Amulrie. The suspicion became a certainty, and a warning note was despatched to *The Times*, which appeared on the 23rd in plain English:

To A. – I fear our cipher is detected and known. Do Not Write again at present: I will endeavour to send you a fresh one. W.M. 'Le beau temps viendra'.

A further blow to the plans of the young lovers was received two days later, when the following sinister message appeared:

To Kensington, (m,n,o, etc). – Ftq gzpqdeuszqp tme ragzp agf kagd okbtqd mzp Ftue rad kagd squpmzoq. – M Sdqqw in Manchester.

(The last word before the signature contains an error.)

Earlier that year there had been a series of plain English

advertisements signed with an extraordinary word in dog-Greek;
Aleekephaleskepasteer. There is almost certainly a link, of a kind
only the most adept of crossword-solvers could forge, between this
and 'Greek in Manchester' – for on examination of these earlier
messages, it is apparent that the same people are involved. As for
the word itself, which is sometimes written as one, and sometimes
divided into 'Aleekephales – kepasteer', it sounds like the incan-
tation of a satanist. 'Kephales' is head, the prefix 'Alee' perhaps
means 'wandering', and 'kepasteer' is probably a misreading of
'kerasteer' (capital 'r' in Greek is 'P'). Kerasteer means 'horned'.
Either someone is being cuckolded, or there is a pre-Christian
reference to a horned God. In any case, it is the sort of preposterous
word an Oxford undergraduate of that date would have relished.

Aleekephaleskepasteer must wait. The summer is before him.
7 May 1853

Aleekephaleskepasteer, compare the will with the copy in
Doctor's commons.

10 May 1853

Were it my heart alone, let it break – others' lot and misery are
involved in 'Aleekephaleskepasteer'.

9 May 1853

The funeral was a private one. 'Aleekephaleskepasteer'.
11 May 1853

Aleekephaleskepasteer. – Your guardian is now in London,
but leaves for Genoa on the 18th proximo.

12 May 1853

This means of correspondence is both *expensive* and *mysterious*. I can neither afford the one, and I hate the other.
'Aleekephaleskepasteer'.

13 May 1853

Aleekephaleskepasteer. See Mr Melton at once; tell him all.
14 May 1853

All is explained. I have been to Regent Street and seen Mr
Melton. Aleekephaleskepasteer.

16 May 1853

But let us return to events in Perthshire, the following August.
With great determination the Oxford undergraduate, whose name
we learn later was Charlie, continues his efforts, and on September
1st he writes, still in the old code, to say 'Our last cypher has been

read so I must change it. It was in *The Times* a fortnight ago'. He asks where he can write *poste restante* – somewhere where she can ride out alone and collect the cypher key unobserved. The very same day yet another message is published from a member of what was now becoming a growing band of eager readers:

> Cryptograph. – W.M. – 'Le beau temps viendra' would greatly oblige one whom he has already obliged by *Forwarding* his *Address* to the same direction as before.

The author of this was probably one of the commercial purveyors of codes who occasionally advertised at this time. (For example, F. Wilkins, of the 'Submarine and Telegraph Wire-rope Works, Wapping' advertises, 'for a very moderate sum', a 'new system of secret correspondence, exceedingly simple in application and impossible to read without the proper key'.) Realising that his earlier code had been blown, he was hoping to do a little more business. He was too late. The next week a final message from 'A' put paid to the romance. It read:

> Dear Charlie, write no more, our cypher is discovered.

Babbage, Wheatstone and Playfair were not the only ones to threaten the peace of lovers who adopted these 'secret' codes in the personal columns of newspapers. Relatives, suspecting that something was up, often went to great pains to find out what was going on. The strict father who forbad those two scarcely comparable publications, *The Times* and *Spurs and Skirts*, to the inhabitants of S --- Lodge is one example. But there is also the sad case of Cinderella, or 'Cenerentola' as her Italophile lover calls her:

> Cenerentola. – N bnxm yt ywd nk dtz hfs wjfi ymnx fsi fr rtxy fscntzx yt mjfw ymf esi, bmjs dtz wjyzws, fsi mtb qtsldtz wjrfns, mjwj. It bwnyf f kjb qnsjx jfwqnsl, uqjfxj. N mfaj gjja ajwd kfw kwtr mfuud xnshj dtz bjsy fbfd.

There is a misprint here, such as Babbage would have delighted in correcting, in the word 'jfwqnsl', which translates as 'earling'. Touching as this endearment might seem to those particularly attracted by pretty ears, it is obvious that the first letter of the coded word should have been 'i', for the cipher is a simple five-place alphabetical shift. Babbage, however, seems not to have noticed the 'Cenerentola' series. It did not last long. Another message appeared on 11 February 1853:

> Cenerentola. – Zsyng rd mjfwy nx xnhp mjav n ywnji yt kwfrj fs jcugfifynts ktw dtz, gzy hfssty. Xnqjshj nx xfkjxy nk ymt, ywzj

hfzxj nx sty xzxkjhyji; nk ny nx, fgg xytwpjx bngg gj xnkyji yt ymj gtyytr. It dtz wjrjrgjw tzw htzxnsx knwxy uwtutxnynts. Ymnsp tk ny.

Again, there are a few misprints, mainly 'g's for 'q's. But the translation appeared four days later:

Cenerentola. – Until my heart is sick have I tried to frame an explanation for you, but cannot. Silence is safest if the true cause is not suspected; if it is, all stories will be sifted to the bottom. Do remember our cousin's first proposition. Think of it. – N pstb Dtz.

The last three words, meaning 'I know you', show that someone is on to Cenerentola, for the above is what Babbage calls a 'marplot' advertisement. It is not long before a final dismissive note in plain English finishes the business for good:

Cenerentola. – What nonsense! Your cousin's proposition is absurd. I have given an explanation – the true one – which has perfectly satisfied both parties – a thing which silence could never have effected. So no more such absurdity.

The popular fashion for corresponding in code was aided not a little by the ever-present example of a regular series of advertisements which appeared on the first day of every month from March 1850 to March 1855. They appear to have baffled everyone at the time:

No. One. – Slmpi. F.npi. C. qgnl. mkqn. Fugli. lokg. pil. S. nigl. F nmkl B.qglp. F. hkom. C. qknp. SF. il Capn. A.F. ngli. rkpg. C. kpn. F.pil. ogq. kmol. hnpo.hlom. hqcn. lokg. C. on. F.pll. Elder.F. hqik.hpmh. qmkl. pil. S. pang. F.orph.rhmn. E. nolp. F. lgoq. mqho. olhi. C.hgo. F. lqkg. S. pgqm. – J. de W.

The literary journal *Notes and Queries* published a number of observations on these strange coded messages in *The Times*. A correspondent signing him or herself 'W.T.M.' in 1855 boasts that he or she has solved them all, and with a flourish of a Latin tag announces 'the mystery solved becomes the ridiculous mouse'. This did not satisfy C. Mansfield Ingleby, who wrote back 'will your correspondents who think themselves so sharp at deciphering have the kindness to give me the key to the celebrated· "Slmpi" advertisements in *The Times*, signed "J. de W."'? They have quite floored me.' Other readers agreed. Babbage makes no mention of them and does not appear to have been concerned about solving them. It seems likely that he, and Playfair and Wheatstone too, for that matter, had become aware that these were codes based on a code book and, after having found out their subject, decided to say nothing more about them.

A hundred and thirty years later Donald McCormick, in a delightful small book entitled *Love in Code* (Eyre Methuen, 1980), remarks 'There could hardly be a greater test of lovers' patience, devotion and stamina than this lengthy item' and goes on to cite the entry for 1 January 1853. The publishers of the book reproduce the message of 2 April 1852 on the back of the jacket, with a Cupid postman perched on a butterfly at one corner and a hand bearing a bunch of flowers with the message 'ever yours' at the other.

This advertisement formed the subject of a competition staged by *The Times* Diary shortly before the book was published. A prize was offered for the first reader to decipher this amorous conundrum. But, as the Diary explains, 71½N by 101W led solvers to the coast of Prince of Wales Land, in McClintock Channel, in the northwest territories of Canada – a rather chilly venue for any kind of secret affair. The jacket of *Love in Code* is, in short, another exhibit for those collections of bibliographic curiosities which include chapters printed upside down, authors' names misspelled on the title page, and deadly mushrooms described as choice eating. (No *schadenfreude* intended.)

The story behind the 'Slmpi' cryptograms is moving, and oddly parallels that other famous tale about the personal column already described: the story of Peter Fleming's adventures in Brazil in search of Colonel Fawcett.

What is not so generally known is that eighty years earlier another expedition also set off in search of a lost explorer, also failed to find him, and also used *The Times* as a communications link (though in a different sense) with a similar lack of success. The evidence is all there in the newspaper – not in its news pages, but in the personal column, and it is printed in code.

The *Times* Diary competition did not settle the authorship or meaning of the 'Slmpi' cryptogram, but the winner, Judge Brian Galpin, certainly pointed in the right direction: towards the frozen wastes of arctic Canada, and the search for the Northwest Passage.

When Sir John Franklin started to explore the 'shores of the Polar Sea' in 1819 the Northwest Passage was not exactly a new idea. Henry Hudson and William Baffin had both had a try in the seventeenth century, giving their names in the process to sizeable chunks of geography. Although it was becoming clearly apparent by the early nineteenth century that there was not going to be any great commercial advantage in discovering the passage, several expeditions were mounted throughout the first half of the century, among them Franklin's famous and tragic expedition of 1845. Franklin set out in two ships , the *Erebus* and the *Terror*, with 128 men. Nothing was heard of the expedition for over three years. The first of over forty search parties was then sent out. In October 1849 news arrived that an Eskimo had seen the vessels the previous March, stuck in the ice.

The race to discover what had happened to Franklin was on a far grander scale than the race in the 1930s to discover what had happened to Fawcett. There was serious scientific and geographical work to be done, and to encourage the efforts of explorers the Government put up a prize of £20,000.

First off was a party consisting of Robert J. Le M. McClure and Captain Richard Collinson, in the *Investigator* and the *Enterprise* respectively. Anticipating that he would be away for a long time, Collinson made arrangements with his family for the regular transmission of news. These arrangements were predicated on the well-founded assumption that, while large areas of the globe were not, in the 1850s, blessed with anything resembling a postal service, the myriad tentacles of trade would ensure that an Englishman in the remotest log hut in the wildest part of the globe could count on being able, somehow, to lay his hands on occasional copies of *The Times*. Collinson therefore devised a code system, and arranged for his family to insert advertisements in the personal column on the first day of every month. The exact system of code used by Collinson was not worked out for many years. He explains in his journals, however, that it was based on 'the ordinary signal book of the Royal Navy' and that it involved substituting letters for numbers. An article in *Notes and Queries* in 1947, by R. J. Cyriax, shows precisely how the system worked. The code book used was, in fact, Captain Marryat's signal book, intended for the mercantile marine, but issued to the Navy.

Cyriax translates the first letters of the message for 1st October 1851 – 'F.Qgli. lngk S. mnn F. Olhi. E. qkpn S. niql' – as 'Captain Penny arrived from Baffin Bay early in September'. Occasionally words would appear in the advertisements that were not in the code book. 'Exhibition', for instance, referring to the Great Exhibition of 1851, was not a topic foreseen by Marryat's code, and had to be written out in full in the advertisement of 1 May 1851.

It was an ingenious and seamanlike solution to the problem of communication over great distances at a time when secrecy was important. There were many expeditions and search parties either in the planning stage or already under way, and there was a good deal of rivalry between them. Collinson depended on his family to let him know of any news of these other claimants to the Government prize. Through these advertisements he also planned to keep in touch with family events. It was therefore vital that no one, either on his own ship or on any of the rival vessels, should be able to read the messages.

McClure and Collinson set off together, heading south. It should be explained that these expeditions were made from the western side of the passage: Parry had tried the eastern route in 1820, reaching Viscount Melville Sound. The two ships were thus forced to sail round the tip of South America. The *Enterprise* lost sight of the *Investigator* near Cape Horn, and the two ships did not meet again. Collinson in the *Enterprise* made slower progress than McClure and was a fortnight too late in reaching Point Barrow, which was by then beginning to feel the grip of winter. The ice was too thick and he was forced to turn back, to overwinter in Hong Kong.

The *Enterprise* returned to the attack the following spring, but made slow progress and by the winter was firmly stuck in the ice. She remained stuck for three more winters. It was beyond even the legendary penetrative powers of *The Times* to reach a ship stuck in ice north of Alaska in 1851, so for three years those coded advertisements – rather like Peter Fleming's despatches from Brazil in reverse (for they were being sent from the explorer to *The Times* and from a hot country to a cooler) – failed to reach their target. Meanwhile the *Investigator*, also stationary, had sent out an overland expedition, which eventually reached Viscount Melville Sound, thereby proving the existence of the passage. However, McClure and the party from the *Investigator* did not obtain any evidence of what had happened to Franklin. It was left to a later expedition, under the aegis of Lady Franklin, to discover that *Erebus* and *Terror* had been frozen in the ice off Victoria Island, that Franklin had died in 1847, and that his men had almost certainly perished in an attempted journey south over the frozen wastes of Boothia Peninsula.

McClure returned to claim the prize, but the full amount was not awarded: he was given £5,000, with a similar amount to be divided among the officers and crew. The strait off Banks Island to the west of the north magnetic pole was named McClure Strait in his honour. Fifty years later Amundsen successfully made the passage by sea and in 1969 the s.s. *Manhattan*, an icebreaking oil tanker, made the first commercial use of the route.

The *Enterprise* escaped from the ice in 1854, and made her way back by a circuitous eastern route. It was not until Collinson reached Bango Wangie, in the Straits of Bali, south of Java, that he first benefited from his invention. He found four advertisements waiting for him, giving the latest news of his friends – 'an evidence of the diffusion of that renowned paper which would have been gratifying and perhaps surprising to its managers had they known of it'. On the whole, he felt justified in his assumption that '*The Times* was a publication more likely to be met with all over the world than any other document, public or private.'

So far as I am aware, no one, with the possible exception of Collinson himself and R. J. Cyriax, has ever translated the sixty coded messages. It would be a lengthy and laborious exercise, and Cyriax's comment that they contain 'no details not to be found in standard works about Arctic expeditions, hence they are disappointing' is discouraging. Perhaps some later biographer of Collinson will retrace a passage through their syllabic ice-floes, for surely they must shed light on his family affairs, as well as on contemporary rumours about all those expeditions in search of Franklin and the Northwest Passage.

The search for Franklin, like the search for Fawcett, sparked off quite a literary industry, though nothing written on Franklin quite parallels the extraordinary imaginative transformation achieved in Evelyn Waugh's *A Handful of Dust*. There is, however, a pictorial echo of the search which in its way is quite as remarkable. Inspired by explorers' reports of the novelties of nature in polar regions, the artist Frederick E. Church set off in 1859, accompanied by his friend the Rev. Louis Noble, in a chartered schooner with the intention of sailing north of Labrador to paint the 'supernatural splendours' of the polar seas. It was on this journey that he produced the series of gouache drawings and oil sketches on which his famous painting *Icebergs* was based. After being lost for a hundred years, the painting re-emerged from the obscurity of a boys' home in Manchester and was sold at Sotheby Parke Bernet in 1979. It is a startlingly powerful, austerely realistic work and at the auction fetched the record price of two and a half million dollars.

Though they do not refer to the Collinson cryptograms, Babbage, Wheatstone and Playfair could hardly have been unaware of them and no doubt they would have been asked their opinion at some point, though it seems they said nothing to divulge Collinson's secret. The codes were certainly the centre of much interest and curiosity. Their form would have been familiar to Playfair, who had some knowledge of naval and military codes; and Wheatstone's interest in such matters led to his devising a new military code that would be easier to use and harder to break than anything he or Playfair had so far come across. The secret of this code lay in the use of a 'key word', and the rearrangement of the alphabet into a square of five letters by five (omitting the letter 'J'). To encode a message the key word is written first, five letters to a line, and the remaining letters of the alphabet below it:

P	L	A	Y	F
I	R	B	C	D
E	G	H	K	M
N	O	Q	S	T
U	V	W	X	Z

The message is then divided into two-letter groups and a process of substitution is followed, depending on where the letters appear in the table, according to certain pre-set principles of geometrical symmetry. All this was explained by Playfair to the Foreign Office in an attempt to get them to adopt it. The Under-Secretary complained that he found it far too complicated. Playfair's rebuttal that he could teach any four boys from the nearest elementary school how to use it in under a quarter of an hour was met with scepticism – 'That's very possible, but you could never teach it to attachés.' For the time being it was laid aside, to be dusted off long after the death of its inventors and given official approval for standard Naval use. Attachés, clearly, were judged to have grown cleverer in the intervening years.

Messages in the Playfair cipher can be broken eventually if there is enough material to go on. Nonetheless the cipher – it bears Playfair's name because it was he who presented it to the Foreign Office, though Wheatstone invented it – was much in advance of anything in use at the time. In the Appendix I have listed a number of coded messages which have never, so far as I am aware, been interpreted. Some of these, in particular the FIDES series, interested Babbage, but he does not record whether he finally succeeded in deciphering them.

Among those messages in newspaper personal columns which are least likely ever to yield up their mysteries are those written in 'metaphor' or 'jargon' code, where words have been switched either on metaphorical grounds – or according to some undiscoverable key, when no logical connection is involved. Probably the DOOR-MAT series (described at the beginning of Chapter 5) is an example of this: 'doormat' representing an act of love or burglary and 'beans' something very romantic or very criminal. In the following advertisement, 'acorns' appears to have some such meaning. Why should they be looked for *quietly*? And what on earth are 'types'?

The evergreen oak might fade and fall, but for the strong

obliging arms of the Ivy which, once grown, can never be removed alive. Types will appear tomorrow, and acorns may be quietly looked for in a few days.

10 June 1857

Although we shall never be sure what was meant by the above, it has a certain elegance and is the kind of personal column advertisement one would be glad to puzzle over any day before breakfast. Like some forms of modern art, one does not have to understand it to enjoy it. The same could be said of:

K – Pott. Sploce. Lak. The Mutability.

8 October 1859

or:

If you have 14 light fawn, have 54 crimson, give 28 red 29 ruby 14 rose 7 purple (6 green without 4 green without 4 fawn) to EN, 20 ruby.

10 May 1867

This, however, may prove a conundrum for art historians:

Quien sabe? 1. Pictures. 'Look at the Cat' – The Serpent and the Stork. 'Civet'. 'Moses Scourged'. The Binding of the Dragon. 'A Shark's Mouth'. 'The Dog Barks'. 'The Wolf and the Lamb'. 'I introduce an old acquaintance.' – Major Ker-Callander.

9 June 1864

Not quite picture titles, but suggestive of them. J. S. Copley's *Watson and the Shark* could be number six. Who knows? Perhaps the initials of the artists' names spelled some cheerful word – 'bandboxes', for instance, or 'muffin man'. The Major was doubtlessly setting a weekend quiz for his friends. Darker or more abstruse explanations seem out of place.

The same could not be said of the many coded advertisements inserted by Ignatius Pollaky, the Sherlock Holmes of Paddington Green. He was not setting puzzles for the amusement of country house parties. His clients, one can be sure, generally meant business; whether commercial, litigious or altogether *sub rosa*. Concealment was part of his stock-in-trade – so, with the increasing popularity of ciphers, it is not surprising to find that he leads the way in adopting some of the more impenetrable techniques. 'Passe-partout' is addressed in a series of numerical coded advertisements in 1863; the relevant dates are June 25th, 29th and July 3rd and 18th, but they look unlikely to yield to number-crunching methods – the material is too thin. A similar code is used a year later (the business in this case seems to concern the British Museum):

> Cop. 78.543.0.. 124.05.39.0.70. Br. Mus. trapax. 8,109.. 00 – 054 – dedi vorp – subject to 174 053 sine qua non. 53.24.781 – 0 – 0 – 134. – Pollaky's Private Inquiry Office, 13 Paddington Green, London W.
>
> *10 June 1864*

No dictionary is able to reveal the nature of a 'dedi vorp', but it sounds like something one would rather not meet in a corner of the North Library at dusk. The runes have been cast upon 'Cop', the Coptic scholar; and if he does not come across with the '174 053', a 'dedi vorp' is likely to be following him silently out of the Reading Room one evening across the twilit streets of Bloomsbury . . .

Fortunately, 'Cop' has a friend in the lovely and talented occupant of seat SR7 in the Reading Room, and she is full of helpful suggestions:

> Get the Paddington Dandy to visit the country, and put up at the A--- hotel. He will find the French cuisine to his taste, and at his leisure be able to solve the enigmas of 59 and 60. All is discovered by a friend of the innocent, who forgets not her S-R-7 friend, but can do nothing alone.
>
> *17 June 1864*

Codes dropped out altogether after the siege of Paris, but they were allowed to return after the First World War. Once again one has the impression of a wave of fashion seizing advertisers, for in the 1920s they go to even greater lengths to outdo each other with mysterious and important-sounding messages. This time round, however, there is little or nothing concealed behind the cloak of mystery. The 'Bright Young People', and their jovial uncles, used codes as a parlour game and there is even a diagrammatic cryptogram:

> *8 May 1922*

Keen Sherlock Holmes fans will easily recognise this. It is a 'pig-pen' cipher, like that used in the story of *The Dancing Men*. The same kind of cipher was used by the secret society 'I

Carbonari', to whom I have referred earlier in this chapter. Holmes was able to decipher the dancing men symbols by using the 'method of frequencies'. The commonest letter ('e') was easy; after that he had a good deal of luck on his side and made a number of those 'stabs in the dark' which, though a useful weapon in the hands of any cryptographer, always seem so much more effortless when a fictional 'master detective' is at work. He also had a good deal more material to work with. However, he did not need to resort to guesses as to the logical processes by which the alphabet was built up, as we shall have to in this case.

Given that the symbols used here are of two kinds, some made of lines drawn at right angles to the page and the others at 45°, it is likely that two simple geometrical patterns have been used – a noughts-and-crosses frame ⌗ and a diagonal cross ✕. Such a cipher is known as the Rosicrucian system. The letters of the alphabet have been arranged within these two symbols in some logical pattern – always supposing that, as seems likely in the context of the personal column in 1922, the puzzle is intended to have a logical solution. The commonest symbol is certainly the square, so that must be 'e'. If one arranges the letters of the alphabet in sequence starting at the top left hand corner of the noughts and crosses frame and continuing twice round it before going on to the diagonal cross – assuming that a dot indicates 'second time round' – the following result is obtained:

```
AJ  BK  CL      ST
MD  NE  OF  YZ      UV
PG  HQ  IR      WX
```

The first word of the message thus becomes, promisingly enough, 'Marry'. But this hopeful trail dies out, and nonsense follows.

Sherlock Holmes, please help.

7 A Hunting Ground of the Unusual

'There is one rather obvious line of investigation.' He took down the great book in which, day by day, he filed the agony columns of the various London journals. 'Dear me!' said he, turning over the pages, 'what a chorus of groans, cries and bleatings! What a rag-bag of singular happenings! But surely the most valuable hunting ground that ever was given to a student of the unusual!'

In *The Adventure of the Red Circle*, from *His Last Bow* published in 1917, Sherlock Holmes is puzzled by the odd actions of a reclusive lodger in the top floor of a rooming house near the British Museum. The lodger's desire for secrecy is extreme. Messages printed in pencil on scraps of paper are left for the landlady, Mrs Warren, with requests for such things as soap and matches. Meals are left on a tray and only collected when the landlady has gone down the stairs. In fact the lodger's communications with the outside world are virtually non-existent. The *Daily Gazette* is however delivered every day with breakfast. Obviously, Holmes deduces, this is the sole means of contact. He goes through his cuttings book, and Conan Doyle gives us the benefit of some marvellously realistic imitation 'Agony Column' entries, interlaced with the acid comments of the great detective:

'Lady with a black boa at Princes Skating Club' – that we may pass. 'Surely Jimmy will not break his mother's heart' – that appears to be irrelevant. 'If the lady who fainted on the Brixton bus' – she does not interest me. 'Every day my heart longs – ' Bleat, Watson – unmitigated bleat! Ah, this is a little more possible. Listen to this: 'Be patient. Will find some sure means

126

of communication. Meanwhile this column. G.' That is two days after Mrs Warren's lodger arrived. It sounds plausible, does it not? . . . Let us see if we can pick up the trace again. Yes, here we are – three days later. 'Am making successful arrangements. Patience and prudence. The clouds will pass. G.' Nothing for a week after that. Then comes something much more definite: 'The path is clearing. If I find chance signal message remember code agreed – one A, two B, and so on. You will hear soon. G.'

The very next morning another advertisement from 'G' appears. It reads: 'High red house with white stone facings. Third floor, second window left. After dusk. G.'

Holmes and Watson are there when signalling begins and are at first puzzled by the coded message which is flashed by lantern from the empty flat across the street. But the explanation for the curious pattern of letters soon becomes clear: it is a word in Italian – '*Attenta*'. The story concerns the flight of a Neapolitan couple living in New York from the secret 'Red Circle' gang – an offshoot, naturally enough, of the Carbonari.

There can be no doubt that throughout the Sherlock Holmes stories Conan Doyle drew heavily on the personal column as a device in the unfolding of his plots and as a source of inspiration in general. The evidence is all there in the stories. But there is another sense, beyond the actual use of the personal column as an element in the plot, in which the writer's imagination has been fired by it. For, as Peter Fleming points out, the column conveys a feeling of 'infinite possibility' in the mind of the regular reader; it offers a cross-section of a vastly intricate world, made up of millions of intersecting human lives, all either passively co-existing or interacting, whether on a commercial, romantic or criminal level. Every day some chance fraction of those dealings will be evidenced in a few printed words, often terse and enigmatic, and those printed slivers, like a microtome of a tumour, give the reader a diagnostic vision of the whole purulent metropolis and its outlying limbs – this was the source of its continuing attraction for Dr Doyle. The day to day listing of articles, legal statements, places, names and dates is a sort of spoil-heap of trivial fact: a hunting-ground not only for detectives but for the literary imagination. As Holmes himself remarks, 'life is infinitely stranger than anything which the mind of man could invent. We would not dare to conceive the things which are really mere commonplaces of existence.' The key to the fascination of the column is that it achieves the effect of, as Holmes put it, lifting the lid off London. 'If we could fly out of that window hand in hand, hover over this great city, gently remove the roofs, and peep in at the queer things which are going on, the strange coincidences, the plannings, the cross-purposes, the wonderful chains of events, working through generations, and leading to the most outré results, it would make all fiction with its conventionalities and foreseen conclusions most stale and un-profitable.'

The special place occupied by Holmes and Watson in the Valhalla of old fictional favourites is won not so much by the ingenuity or dramatic power of Conan Doyle's plots, as by the way the stories build up in the mind a lovable, familiar yet always delightfully mysterious world, in which evil barely emerges long enough from the fog for the famous pair to recognise, track down and destroy it. The world is seen to be at the same time a place of comforting certainties – Holmes's briar-root and Watson's Jezail bullet-wound, the reliability of hansom cabs and the infallibility of logical deductions – as well as one of staggering bizarreness, where striped bell-pulls become poisonous snakes and lamp-shades suddenly emit clouds of brain-bending poison from darkest Ubangi. The personal column is just such a world, or rather it is a window onto it. Lost dogs and second-hand bicycles rub shoulders with madness, mystery and murder. Conan Doyle's childhood and youth coincided with a period of particular richness in the column. It came of age – first earning its distinct demarcation and title on the front page the year before the publication of Conan Doyle's first Sherlock Holmes story, *A Study in Scarlet*.

During the years that followed, the real personal column dwindled; meanwhile its fictional counterpart – we find it not only in Conan Doyle but in the works of all those writers who followed in his footsteps – grew stronger, became in fact a stock property of fiction and most of all of detective fiction. Margery Allingham uses it in *Sweet Danger*; Agatha Christie in *A Murder is Announced*; Edgar Wallace trots it out shamelessly time after time; Ernest Bramah uses it in *The Game Played in the Dark*; and Earl Derr Biggers (who later went on to write the Charlie Chan mysteries) in *Agony Column*.

Naturally, a student of the personal column, with these facts in mind, will tend to note those advertisements which seem most closely to foreshadow their later fictional use. For reasons I shall explain more fully later in this chapter, this approach can scarcely give an adequate impression of the curious interrelation between fact and fiction. Moreover, many crucial codes, including Ignatius Pollaky's 'Paean' and 'Diplomat' ciphers have not yet been fully unlocked.

Passing on, however, to some obvious-seeming parallels, let us begin with the story of the *Three Garridebs* by Conan Doyle. The plot revolves around the preposterous offer of a gentleman from America named John Garrideb to share an estate of several million dollars with any two other surviving men of this name. One Garrideb has been found: an eccentric collector who never leaves his museum-like rooms near the Edgware Road. John Garrideb, it turns out, is the alias of a desperado named 'Killer' Evans, who urgently needs to gain access to Garrideb's rooms in order to get at the counterfeiting machinery left there by the previous tenant, Rodger Prescott of Chicago. Evans, alias Garrideb, invents a story about the will of the deceased millionaire, Alexander Hamilton Garrideb, of Topeka, pretends to 'find' another Garrideb a suitable distance away and sends the one and only real Garrideb off in search of his fictitious namesake. Evans then gets a false 'classified' advertisement printed, with details of a Garrideb in Birmingham who manufactures agricultural machinery (in spite of having lived in England for nearly a decade, he spells 'plow' in the American way – thereby confirming Holmes's suspicions). For it is already evident that Evans is a fake. 'Your obvious way', Holmes says to him, 'is to advertise in the agony columns.' Evans says he already has. Holmes lets this pass, but he knows better. Later, he remarks to Watson 'There have been no advertisements in the agony columns. You know I miss nothing there. They are my favourite covert for putting up a bird, and I would never have overlooked such a cock pheasant as that.' What Holmes is referring to here are those legal advertisements which appear from time to time asking for people of a particular surname to apply at a solicitor's office:

Toosey. – Should this meet the eye of anyone of this name, they are requested to communicate with Mr G. Wingate, 8½ Angel Court, London E.C. Solicitor.

14 February 1901

Such notices should be distinguished from those specifically seeking for replies from the relatives of a person who has died intestate. The latter are frequent; the former much rarer. At this period, around the turn of the century, there is but a handful of them. In March 1903, for example, the solicitors à Beckett Terrell & Co of 10 Ironmonger Lane state that any person by the name of St Amour may benefit by applying to them. Undoubtedly Conan Doyle would have seen such notices, and wondered what story underlay them. The example of Toosey appears only a few weeks before the first of a series of advertisements inserted by Conan Doyle himself in the personal column of *The Times*. It therefore seems reasonable to suppose that he was reading the column with even more attention than he usually devoted to it. (Conan Doyle's own advertisement, which was repeated in May and June, was for the loan of officers' letters dealing with certain Boer War battles, a subject he was researching at this time for a book.)

The first Sherlock Holmes story to be published, on 22 February 1886, was *A Study in Scarlet*. In this, the very first crime Holmes encounters – he learns about it from Gregson of the Yard – concerns a man found dead at 3 Lauriston Gardens, Brixton. There is a wedding ring with the body. What is Holmes's first action on taking stock of this state of affairs? It is of course to advertise in the 'agony columns' of the evening papers for the owner of the ring – using Watson's name, a presumption for which he later apologises:

In Brixton Road this morning. A plain gold wedding ring, found in the roadway between White Hart Tavern and Holland Grove. Apply Dr Watson, 221b, Baker Street, between eight and nine this evening.

The advertisement is answered by an old lady who later makes her escape from the four wheeler on the rear of which Holmes is precariously perched. She turns out in fact to be a young man, cleverly disguised. (*The Daily Telegraph*, by the way, commenting on the 'Brixton Mystery', assumes that the Carbonari, among others, may well have something to do with it all.)

Some dawning indication of just how central a theme the agony column is to become in the life of Sherlock Holmes may be gathered from the way it enters *The Sign of Four*. After some purely domestic demonstrations of Holmes's powers, in which he analyses Watson's boots and watch, a client is introduced by Mrs Hudson. Mary Morstan is a petite blonde and, on grounds slighter by far than those which enabled Holmes to tell him he had just sent a wire from Wigmore Street Post Office, Watson starts to ruminate on Miss Morstan's spiritual qualities – always a danger signal in an unmarried man. Hinting quite lubriciously at 'an experience of women which extends over many nations and three separate continents', the Doctor remarks that he has never 'looked upon a face which gave a clearer promise of a refined and sensitive nature'. The drift of the story is becoming apparent. To confirm the reader's suspicions, the very first thing the fair Miss Morstan does, as soon as she meets the two men, is to start talking about classified advertisements in the newspapers. Her inverted commas have scarcely had time to blink open and closed a couple of times before she proceeds to this most central of themes. First there is the advertisement for her father, who has disappeared after returning from India. Then there is this advertisement in *The Times* personal column, which appeared on 4 May 1882, asking for the address of Miss Mary Morstan and stating that it would be to her advantage to come forward. As no address is given, she audaciously inserts another advertisement herself – making a total score of three advertisements to date – actually publishing her own name and address in the column. She has no hesitation about admitting any of this.

The immediate result is the arrival that very same day of a small cardboard box containing a very large and lustrous pearl. Watson, of course, is electrified. What is his reaction? We have to wait until the end of the story to find out, but considering the rate at which classified advertisements have been winging backwards and forwards during the intervening pages, it is not hard to predict the outcome: to borrow that favourite final sentence of the old romantic novelists, 'reader, he marries her'. She becomes, in short, Mrs Watson, and from that day forth never, so far as the record shows, feels any temptation to advertise in the personal column again.

The general trend of things grows clearer. There would be little point in producing parallels to Holmes's advertisement in the evening papers for the owner of the wedding ring – there are far too many, and none of them quite reproduce the original wording. It is, however, worth checking the archives for signs of advertisements bearing on the theme of lustrous pearls and wronged heiresses. What does the famous column have to offer on 4 May 1882?

Have seen your attorney and letters. Cannot act without hearing from you again. Write or send for William. Very urgent.

Crossland: Nova Scotia. Mr James Crossland, who left England for Nova Scotia in December last, is requested to communicate with the undersigned on important matters of business. – Barker, Sons and Yeoman, Solicitors, Huddersfield.

Next of Kin. – Davies, otherwise Eamonson: the next of kin of Elizabeth Mary Davies otherwise Eamonson, late of No 1 Lawn Villas, Verulam Road, St Albans, in the county of Hertford . . .

It is not worth going on. There is a great deal about 'Pursuant to a Judgement in the High Court' and 'Bank of England Unclaimed Stock', and so forth. But at the foot of the column there is an advertisement for the services of Ignatius Pollaky, Detective, 13 Paddington Green. And, turning back the pages a couple of days, another message from Pollaky leaps out that is as chilling as it is significant:

> Eleanor d'Ereillo, aged nineteen, on a plain slab of white marble (with no other inscription). Does anyone know where the above is to be found? Ignatius Pollaky, Private Enquiry Office, 13 Paddington Green,W.

2 May 1882

The Sign of Four contains more material relevant to our theme. It happens at one point in the story that the great treasures of Agra, in the custody of a certain Mr Jonathan Small, a one-legged sailor, together with a pigmy assassin from the Andaman Islands, are on board a steam yacht, *The Aurora*, property of Captain Mordecai Smith, which is moored at a wharf somewhere on the Thames. How are Holmes and Watson to find this ensemble? Watson has the obvious solution: 'Could we advertise, then, asking for information from wharfingers?' he asks. But Holmes promptly steps on this display of initiative, explaining that it would give the game away. Instead, he sets his 'Baker Street Irregulars' on the task. When their efforts fail, Holmes himself sets off down the river, with an abstracted air, leaving Watson to brood. Casting his eye over the *Evening Standard*, searching for fresh news of the affair, Watson is surprised, not to say chagrined, to come across the following:

> Lost. – Whereas Mordecai Smith, boatman, and his son Jim, left Smith's wharf at or about three o'clock last Tuesday morning in the steam launch *Aurora*, black with two red stripes, funnel black with a white band, the sum of five pounds will be paid to anyone who can give information to Mrs Smith, at Smith's Wharf, or at 221b, Baker Street, as to the whereabouts of the said Mordecai Smith and the launch *Aurora*.

Holmes at least, on this occasion, has the good grace not to use Watson's name, however few scruples he may have entertained about stealing his idea.

Holmes and Watson are positively addicted to the column, and hardly manage to have an adventure without it. In *The Red-Headed League* a fake personal column advertisement in the *Morning Chronicle* keeps a pawnbroker out of his shop while a bank is broken into and in *A Case of Identity* Mary Sutherland advertises in the personal column for her missing fiancé, Hosmer Angel. In *The Five Orange Pips* the column is not mentioned, but the letter received by John Openshaw with such terrifying consequences is stylistically straight from the column: 'K.K.K. – Put the papers on the Sundial.' In *The Adventure of the Blue Carbuncle*, the whole story turns on a *Times* personal column advertisement for the missing gem, for which the reward of £1,000 was 'not a twentieth of the market price'. When Peterson, the commissionaire, presents Holmes with the carbuncle, which his wife has found in the crop of a goose, the detective's first thought is to advertise for the criminal who stole it:

Found at the corner of Goodge Street, a goose and a black felt hat. Mr Henry Baker can have the same by applying at 6.30 this evening at 221b Baker Street.

Peterson is instructed to put this advertisement in the *Globe*, *Star*, *Pall Mall*, *St James's*, *Evening News*, *Standard*, *Echo*, and any others that occur to him. As it turns out, the man who duly appears that same evening in answer to the advertisements is not the criminal: but this is a minor hitch, and Holmes is soon on the right track.

Holmes's almost slavish dependence on the personal column is never more apparent than in *The Adventure of the Engineer's Thumb*. When Watson seeks him out with the news that he has a patient in need of forensic counselling, the doctor lets slip a telling phrase: 'Sherlock Holmes was, as I expected, lounging about his sitting room in his dressing gown, reading the agony column of *The Times*, and smoking his before breakfast pipe.' (It is that word 'expected' which says so much.) After the engineer has unburdened himself for several pages – recounting in graphic detail his horrifying hairbreadth escape from a death-dealing hydraulic press in the midst of Eyford the previous night and ending pathetically 'I put myself in your hands, and shall do exactly what you advise' – Holmes, after a few moments' silent reflection, makes straight for his book of agony column cuttings. Some readers have felt that he perhaps shows a certain want of restraint in thus openly indulging his vice at this critical emotional juncture, but no matter. This is what he finds:

Lost, on the 9th inst., Mr Jeremiah Hayling, aged twenty-six, a hydraulic engineer. Left his lodgings at ten o'clock at night, and has not been heard of since.

This advertisement, Holmes explains, 'probably represents the last time the Colonel needed to have his machine overhauled', which, in the circumstances and in view of the engineer's somewhat over-wrought state, was hardly the most tactful conversational gambit. But Holmes, as can now be appreciated, could not help himself.

Similarly, in pursuing the curious circumstances surrounding the termination of the Lord St Simon marriage, the pair can hardly wait to bury their noses in the personal column of the *Morning Post*, where the forthcoming marriage is announced. It reads as follows:

> A marriage has been announced, and will, if rumour is correct, very shortly take place, between Lord Robert St Simon, second son of the Duke of Balmoral, and Miss Hatty Doran, the only daughter of Aloysius Doran Esq, of San Francisco, California, U.S.A.

In *The Adventure of the Copper Beeches* a more sombre note is struck and the very soul of the personal column is touched on in the opening sentence of this charming story, the heroine of which is that sweet female presence most familiar to the devotee of the column – a governess.

' "To the man who loves art for its own sake," remarked Sherlock Holmes, tossing aside the advertisement sheet of *The Daily Telegraph*, "it is frequently in its least important and lowliest manifestations that the keenest pleasure is to be derived." ' Holmes is referring here to the column as vernacular art. He is thinking of those brief, untutored outbursts that express its rawest power. As Holmes and Watson sit in the gas-light that foggy Spring morning in Baker Street it is clear that thoughts such as these are on the minds of both men. 'Sherlock Holmes had been silent all morning', continues this deeply reflective introduction to the main story, 'dipping continuously into the advertisement columns of a succession of papers.' But Holmes's search has not been successful: no bears have come to town, no pianos have stopped for him that day. 'At last, having apparently given up his search, he emerged in no very sweet temper to lecture me upon my literary shortcomings.' Alas, poor Watson! How could his prosaic, workmanlike accounts hope to compare with the urgently poetic compression to which personal column advertisements so frequently attain? Both men settle down with a heavy heart to solving the puzzle about Mr Rucastle, who had engaged the lovely Violet Hunter to sit in the window of his house in an electric blue dress with a fixed grin on her face – a commonplace conundrum compared to the labyrinthine mysteries of Pollaky and the soaring heights of the One-Winged Dove.

The *Memoirs* add many more examples to the file of the agony column in active fictional service. The plot of *The Stockbrokers Clerk* revolves around an advertisement, though the advertisement itself is not quoted, and *The Gloria Scott* illustrates Holmes's close knowledge of the 'jargon' type of code so beloved by masters of 'personalese'. The story opens with the message which struck Justice of the Peace Trevor dead with horror:

> The supply of game for London is going steadily up. Head-keeper Hudson, we believe, has now been told to receive all orders for fly-paper and for preservation of your hen-pheasant's life.

This has at first the appearance of one of those 'jargon' codes in which 'game' stands for 'infantry' and 'Hudson' stands for 'Gladstone', 'hen-pheasant' for 'Field Marshal', and so on. No devotee of the personal column would be misled into believing that this message was 'absurd and trivial' as Trevor's son Victor supposes. But, as Holmes points out, if it is actually a 'jargon' code, it would be impossible to work out the meaning 'which would be arbitrary and could not be deduced in any way'. Holmes is loath to accept defeat, and tries all sorts of recombinations of the words, running them backwards, omitting every other word, and so forth. Eventually he finds that by simply reading every third word only, the message becomes:

> The game is up. Hudson has told all. Fly for your life.

The Greek Interpreter shows Mycroft in his Babbage persona, sending off one of those 'marplots' which so delighted the great mathematician, in an effort to trace Paul Kratides:

> Anybody supplying any information as to the whereabouts of a Greek gentleman named Paul Kratides, from Athens, who is unable to speak English, will be rewarded. A similar reward paid to anyone giving information about a Greek lady whose first name is Sophy. X 2473.

Mycroft, unlike Babbage, was never a stylist.

The result of this advertisement, which is answered by a Mr J. Davenport, is that the unfortunate interpreter is again picked up and driven to the wilds of Beckenham, where he is attacked and nearly suffocated.

In *The Naval Treaty*, the story which immediately follows *The Greek Interpreter* in *The Memoirs*, Holmes dispatches advertisements to the personal column of every evening newspaper in London in order to elicit the number of the cab which dropped a passenger (presumably the thief) at the Foreign Office on the evening the vital papers disappeared. It is not answered and Holmes reacts, unsurprisingly, by blinding Watson with a lot of abstruse talk about the classification of skeletal measurements as developed by the criminologist Alphonse Bertillon.

The great detective then abandons his favourite vice until well after his return from the Reichenbach Falls. However, when he starts advertising for muscular harpooners from the docks, under the pseudonym of Captain Basil, in *The Adventures of Black Peter*, it is clear that, far from being cured of his predilection by his harrowing experiences in Switzerland and his wanderings in Tibet, he has taken it to new extremes. He does so under the guise of organising an Arctic expedition.

There is in this story another example of the way fact and fiction appear to 'bootstrap' one another, leaping temporal barriers. Much is made of the various mystifying initials inscribed on a number of objects found in the vicinity of the murdered man, Peter Carey. There is a tobacco pouch of coarse sealskin with a leather thong, containing half an ounce of strong ship's tobacco – or 'naval shag', as it used to be called. Then there is a notebook bearing the initials J.H.N., the date 1883 and on the second page C.P.R. – and so on. Consulting the archives, it will be seen that *The Times* personal column has during the year 1883 a number of so far undeciphered messages in code headed 'J.H.N.' Looking back only a few years there is the well-known 'C.P.R.' series of numerical codes, whose complexity is unparalleled. Obviously, therefore, Holmes's dismissal of these initials, which have crept in under the threshold of Conan Doyle's subconscious mind, as standing for 'Canadian Pacific Railway', is nothing but what cryptographers refer to as a 'blind' – a misleading signal designed to discourage further efforts at decoding. This point is reinforced by the way Holmes, later in the story, dismisses the initials 'P.C.' – which are also those of the harpooner Patrick Cairns – as mere coincidence! The chances of these two identical initials occurring three times over, in Peter Carey, Patrick Cairns and, of course, 'Personal Column' are, if my calculator batteries do not fail me, 11,881,376 to 1 against. Conan Doyle's subconscious is trying to tell us something his conscious mind will not allow him to reveal.

From this point on Holmes's use of classified advertising never quite deserts him, until at the very end, changing circumstances dictate his abandonment of the method. In *The Adventure of the Golden Pince-Nez*, for example, he does not actually send any personal column messages, but whimsically draws up the specifications of the wanted lady in the form of an advertisement:

Wanted, woman of good address, attired like a lady. She has a remarkably thick nose, with eyes which are set close upon either side of it. She has a puckered forehead, a peering expression, and probably rounded shoulders. There are indications that she has had recourse to an optician at least twice during the last few months. As her glasses are of remarkable strength, and as opticians are not very numerous, there should be no difficulty in tracing her.

In *The Adventure of Wysteria Lodge* we are presented once more with a 'crypto-personalese' message, this time on ordinary cream laid paper in a woman's hand:

Our own colours, green and white. Green open, white shut. Main stair, first corridor, seventh right, green baize. God-speed. D.

If there should be any doubt about the stylistic affinities of this message, one need only look at:

If you have 14 light fawn, have 54 crimson, give 28 red, 29 ruby, 14 rose, 7 purple (6 green without 4 green without 4 fawn) to EN, 20 ruby.

10 May 1867

and of course that last desperate message to E. J. Wilson:

You could not speak. It was too sudden. I am a good rider. Green is my favourite colour. I want money.

23 November 1870

His Last Bow is indeed an orgy of personal column material. We have already, at the start of this chapter, noted the use in *The Adventure of the Red Circle*. As for *The Adventure of the Bruce Partington Plans*, all one can say is that Conan Doyle must have been at the paste-pot again. No less than five personal column advertisements are cited, all signed Pierrot and it is by means of an advertisement inserted by Holmes that Oberstein is brought to the lure, settling his fate for the next fifteen years.

The final story in *His Last Bow* (the title story) again deals with spies and coded messages: subjects close to the heart of any agony column freak. There is even a 'crypto-personalese' message, in the shape of one of those unbreakable 'jargon' codes in which words are substituted by prior agreement between the parties:

Will come tonight and bring new sparking plugs. (*Key*:) If he talks of a radiator it is a battleship, of an oil pump a cruiser, and so on. Sparking plugs are naval signals.

However, the passage which really gives us a glimpse of the author's heart reads as follows (the German spy Von Bork is talking):

. . . even our special war tax of fifty million, which one would think made our purpose as clear as if we had advertised it on the front page of *The Times* has not roused these people [the British] from their slumbers.

The stories in this, the last collection to be published before the First World War, show the author's two main preoccupations at this date: first the coming conflict, with the enormous growth in the power of the machinery of war and the ever greater sophistication of cryptography in the services of espionage; and secondly, the personal column of *The Times*, which was for the author the primary symbol of that England which was itself so terse and laconic and yet so intimate, so finely educated and yet so simple and honest in the face of those evil forces of repression which threatened its liberty and delight in self-expression. Many scholars have seen Holmes's last words to Watson, in which he speaks of 'an east wind, such a wind as never blew on England yet . . . God's own wind nonetheless and a cleaner, better stronger land will lie in the sunshine when the storm has cleared . . .', as a metaphor for the coming war, and there can be no gainsaying this, particularly in the light of the importance of metaphors in cryptography and of the metaphorical element in Von Bork's 'jargon' code. But no one has hitherto commented on the significance of the next sentence – the final sentence in the book: 'I have a cheque for five hundred pounds which should be cashed early, for the drawer is quite capable of stopping it if he can.' In August 1914, the month in which *His Last Bow* is set, the personal column carried the following announcement:

Lost. Certificate of 500 pounds face value in Electric Telecommunications and Signals Company Ltd, in name of V. Buerk. Company have stopped any possible transfer.

The last volume of stories, *The Case Book of Sherlock Holmes*, was published well after the end of the war. It was a changed world, and many of the old customs of secrecy and restraint, which so deeply informed the personal column of Holmes's heyday, were swept aside. New technologies – motoring, aviation and the telephone – were altering the old ways. In one last supreme effort Holmes exercises his special powers to solve the enigma of *The Three Garridebs* (which, as we have already seen, revolved around a personal column advertisement) and the notes exchanged between Fitzroy Macpherson and his fiancée Maude Bellamy in *The Lion's Mane* are a debased version of the sort of message the personal column is full of in the 1920s. Nevertheless, the end is clearly near. Its coming is signalled when, in the last story of all, Watson hears Holmes's distant voice from the telephone of Little

Purlington: 'Most singular, most remarkable! I much fear my dear Watson, that there is no return train tonight . . .' – the far-off words of a man who was never to insert a classified advertisement again.

The key passage in the works, to which I now come, occurs in the first chapter of *The Valley of Fear*. Holmes receives a mysterious letter in cipher – a jumble of numbers containing the name 'Douglas' and the twice repeated place-name 'Birlstone'. The letter is from Moriarty's 'pilot-fish', the one weak link in the chain leading to that mysterious, aloof figure who controls the workings of the underworld from the inner sanctum of a chair professor of mathematics' private study. The clue which so neatly unlocks so many mysteries is to be found first in the name of the professor's 'pilot-fish'. It is not a real name but a pseudonym, behind which lies 'a shifty and evasive personality'. Students of the works of Conan Doyle have in the past made much of the fact that the pilot-fish's pseudonym is the same as the name of a place from which a certain person came to a certain lonely farmhouse on Exmoor, thereby interrupting the work of a great poet. This may be so – but it has nothing whatever to do with the extraordinary events unfolded in the story of *The Valley of Fear*, nor can it explain why Porlock's first name should be 'Fred'.

Holmes supplies the element which enables us to interpret the clue hidden in the name. It is the 'pilot-fish'. Permute 'fish', 'Porlock', 'pilot' and Fred; take out the 'i' of 'Pilot' to give 'plot', add it to 'Fred' to give fried', change an 'r' to an 'l' to allow for oriental mispronunciation – and suddenly the chips are down and everything is clear as the newsprint of a classified front page lightly soaked in No.3 Sesame Oil. 'Fried Pollock' is the 'fish' the 'plot' demands: (pollock, or pollack, a darker and more lustrous relative of the cod with a long lower jaw – *Pollachius virens*, to give it its Latin name. *Pollachius*: have we not heard that name before? Anglicise it, as no doubt his forebears did, and you have none other than that dark and lustrous long-jawed fellow, the Pole, the Paddington dandy, Ignatius Pollaky himself.

Further clues follow thick and fast. It would be beyond the scope of this short chapter to reveal the identity of the great mathematical mind which lurked behind the little Polish investigator. Conan Doyle's choice of the curiously named town of Vermissa (search for *that* in your atlas) as the scene of much of the action in this story gives another clue, as do the numbers of the Lodges of the infamous band of 'Scowrers': Vermissa Lodge, I should remind readers, is Lodge 341, while Chicago is 29 and the Division Master of the Ancient Order of Freemen who writes from Lodge 249 is named

Windle. *Verb. sap.*, or preferably *intelligenti sufficit interlege*, to use a couple of tags much favoured in the Diogenes Club.

The cipher itself need not occupy us long. It is of the 'nearly unguessable' variety which depends for its key on the use of a book in the possession of both parties. As Holmes remarks:

There are many ciphers which I would read as easily as I do the apocrypha of the agony column: such crude devices amuse the intelligence without fatiguing it. But this is different.

There is no clue to the title of the vital book, but Holmes hopes to receive one in a separate letter. His hopes are dashed when the next post brings a letter from Porlock, regretting that he cannot send the key. For several pages thereafter Conan Doyle describes the thought processes which enabled Holmes to guess at the key book and work out how to apply the cryptogram to it – processes which must indeed have been familiar to the author. The almost unintelligible, jumbled message which finally emerges is very different from the usually facile, crystal clear results Holmes obtains in less crucial stories. There is something oddly familiar in its style. It is in fact a typical decoded personal column message. One can imagine the young Dr Doyle occupying the long hours while he waited in his consulting room for the next patient by deciphering such messages, and his growing fascination as they gradually fitted together to form. . . . But I must not anticipate.

There – is – danger – may – come – very – soon – one. – Douglas – rich – country – now – at – Birlstone – House – Birlstone – confidence – is – pressing.

A queer, scrambling way of expressing his message indeed, Watson! With a few minor, irrelevant changes, the message is identical to one that may be decoded, by precisely the same processes, from the Pollaky series in the personal column late in the year 1868.

From this point, it is a straight run to the complete decipherment of the Holmes cryptograms, which are to be found in that series of hitherto mystifying communications from Pollaky to an unknown client covering the ten years prior to the writing of *Study in Scarlet* – the Paean and Diplomat ciphers. That client, at whose identity I have already hinted, is of course the holder of a chair of mathematics at a certain university. The man in question, whose knowledge of astrophysics was so far in advance of his time, was clearly no friend of Babbage. Indeed his efforts to cut off Babbage's funds for the construction of those early computing machines, and his cleverly devised acts of sabotage which prevented either one of them from ever functioning, made him the bitterest, indeed virtually the only enemy of that mild, eccentric bachelor. His last and meanest action, before starting on the journey to Switzerland from which he never returned, was to mount an elaborate campaign to prove that it was Babbage who was behind the disgraceful episode in which the busts of Aristotle, Voltaire and Diderot that face each other across the lofty drawing room of the Diogenes Club were adorned with red paint, thereby hoping to expel his rival not only from the Diogenes itself but from its innermost circle of savants, the Rerum Naturae (in real life 'The Lucretians'). Fortunately for the history of science, indeed for the survival of democracy itself, the attempt failed. The Athenaeum still stands, a bastion for great and lonely minds; the last traces of red have long since faded from those august noses which look down upon slumbering bishops and palaeontologists, and the Lucretians still meet and dine together at rare intervals, unmindful of the rift in their ranks which nearly a century ago threatened to unseat the very foundations of civilised society. But the name of one former member has forever been expunged from their records.

Finally, a word about the Christian name of the great detective. The importance of Pollaky has now been established beyond doubt. His fundamental role in the creation of the Holmesian canon has been explained, though not, for reasons of space, elaborated to the full extent possible. A thorough computer analysis of the coded series will be necessary before that can be done. Meanwhile, now that Pollaky has been identified as Moriarty's pilot-fish, Porlock, is it not abundantly clear how Arthur Ignatius Conan Doyle's mind worked when choosing the name 'Sherlock'? We know he toyed with 'Sherrinford' (there was a Sherrinford in his medical class) and he could not resist giving a hint, in the Christian name of the great detective, of his principal source for the stories. The progression is indisputable: Sherrinford, Pollaky, Porlock – Sherlock!

8 The Finest Hour and the Lowest Ebb

A particular charm of the personal column is that it is such a patchwork of unpredictable and variegated emotions. As sometimes happens in real life, but much more rarely in fiction, the humorous and the tragic are harshly juxtaposed. The impatient historian may be tempted to overlook this odd corner of the newspaper world, but its insights into real human preoccupations are not easily obtained elsewhere. Surprisingly, in the midst of its individualistic, kaleidoscopic reflections of concerns that are for the most part petty and ephemeral, it does at times betray changes of national mood.

In so far as this book has an historical thread, that thread has branched off into the study of codes on the one hand and detective fiction on the other. Returning therefore from our labyrinthine probings of the arcana of the Holmesian myth, we find that the central thread has been left at about 1870. This is a significant date, because it marks a disruption in the normal disorderly flow of advertisements in *The Times* personal column from which the front page never quite recovers. The year 1870 is also, in one sense, the column's finest hour.

From October 1870 onwards the front page of *The Times* becomes increasingly full of advertisements such as the following:

Monsieur Maurice Hourdequin est prié d'envoyer son addresse a sa soeur, 25 Gensing Station Road, St Leonards on Sea, Sussex.

12 October 1870

Monsieur Robert Mitchell, rédacteur en chef du *Constitutional* est prisonnier dans la fortresse de Cosel (Silésie). Il prie ses amis de lui écrire par voie télégraphique seulement.

13 October 1870

Pour Paris. – 9, Rue Suresne – Nort Peat. V. Thornton S. Kerdiffstoun H. 'Cadmus' Aux Indes Occidentales. Trois enfants, toute notre famille, parfaite santé. – Rothschild, Londres, tient 50 livres, à l'ordre de G. sur sa nôte de leur maison à Paris. Toutes vos lettres reçues. 'Au revoir, Victor'. – R.H.B.

30 November 1870

Two or three such messages per week appeared in October; rather more in November; but by December 10th they had grown to ten a day, and a week later to three-quarters of a column. By the end of the year 1870, a column and a half of advertisements headed '*Pour Paris*' were crammed onto the front page of *The Times* every day, and the old personal column of lovers' rendezvous and lost dogs had been crowded out altogether. The German siege of Paris was at its height.

The siege lasted from 19 September 1870 until the end of January 1871, by which time famine had gripped the city. Efforts at communication with the outside world took many forms – there was Gambetta's dramatic departure in a balloon, and pigeons were regularly used to carry messages to and fro. The idea of using advertisements in *The Times* to communicate with relatives and friends in England came early in the siege, though the technique of conveying the messages by pigeon in and out of the beleaguered capital took some time to develop and at first few messages could be carried at a time. It is said that by the end of the siege a regular channel of communication had been opened up between Paris and London, by means of microscopically reduced copies of the front page of *The Times*, prepared on special thin paper for transmission to Bordeaux and thence by carrier pigeon to Paris, where they would be enlarged by magic lantern and messengers despatched to all the addresses given in the advertisements.

The spectacle of all this deadly earnest activity seems to have had a dampening effect on regular users of the old 'Agony Column' and, although dignified a few years later by its own title for the first time, the column goes into something of a decline. It is significant that Alice Clay's book on the subject, although published in 1881, contains no advertisement later than autumn 1870. The last message from E. J. Wilson, by this time disillusioned, impoverished, deprived of job, pension and the affections of the daughter he loved, is earlier that same year. Even Pollaky's activities appear to decline, though he manages a piece of skilful self-advertisement at the height of the siege of Paris:

> Pollaky. – The young French lady, mysteriously missing from the neighbourhood of Park Lane, and advertised for in The Times of last week, is happily found (though not locked up in a cellar à la Tinsley). – Pollaky's Private Inquiry Office, 13 Paddington Green, London W.
>
> *12 December 1870*

In 1887, *The Times* was offered a series of letters condoning the recent anti-British massacres in Phoenix Park, Dublin. These letters bore the signature of the Irish M.P., Charles Stewart Parnell. To establish their authenticity, the newspaper advertised anonymously in its own columns offering to buy collections of political autographs. On the basis of a graphologist's advice, the editor, George Buckle, decided to go ahead and publish the first of the 'Parnell Letters'. Its appearance caused a furore. Parnell was exonerated by a Government Commission; the letters were pronounced forgeries; and the £200,000 legal costs eventually paid by the newspaper resulted in its declaring its first deficit – a financial blow from which it never really recovered.

The starch of Victorian morality begins to seep into the column. There are more and more advertisements for 'good plain cooks', and the shrinkage of the personal column itself is accompanied by a great growth of classified advertising, mainly for servants. In the year the personal column won its official heading 'Personal &c' there are over sixty different categories of domestic servant in the classified pages, including 'Under Nurse', 'Nurse to gentleman', 'Lady's maid (useful)', 'Cook Housekeeper (thorough)', and 'Housemaid where man-servant is kept'.

There is much offering for sale of 'advowsons' (the right of presenting a nominee to a vacant ecclesiastical benefice). There was a rumour abroad that the system of advowsons was shortly to be abandoned by the Church of England, hence the sudden rush. Legal notices fill the columns, together with appeals from charitable organisations of a borderline nature such as 'The Institution for Affections of the Speech' ('an old friend of the Institution has kindly guaranteed £25 in prizes to competitors forming the greatest number of English dictionary words from the word "stammering"'). Then there is a sudden outbreak of 'multiplepoinding' – a legal proceeding of medieval ferocity practised against defaulting debtors. One sees also in the late nineteenth century an increasing frequency of surname changes. Hyphenated names grow more fashionable. At the height of this fashion (1903) there is even a four-barreller: on February 19th Norman Bennett becomes Norman Robert-Ottiwell-Gifford-Bennett (disproving the claim of the Twisleton-Wykeham-Fiennes clan to have explored the Ultima Thule of nomenclature). And there are many followers in the tracks of Joshua Bug.

In May 1899 a Mrs Sophia Lydia Coffin announces that henceforth she is to be known as Mrs Sophia Lydia Lyddingsen. Among other unfortunate names there is a Mr Grime who changes his name to Graham in July 1912; a bank manager from Durham named Herbert Edward Goose, who must have had a hard time of it clamping down on overdrafts and changed his name to Durand; and a grocer from Walsall who might have walked straight out of the pages of *Diary of a Nobody*, along with Cummings and Gowing, for his name, which he wisely changed to Smith, was Shutt.

There is also a minor fashion for adding 'e' to the ends of surnames, an Edwardian affectation, like the doubling of initial 'f's'. (The pseudonym 'ffolkes' was deliberately chosen by the cartoonist Michael Davies as a celebration of such absurdities.) A certain Harold Millington Sing (was he a relative of the dramatist?) changes his surname on 3 October 1900 to Synge, and on 9 February 1904 a plain old Mr Swinburn adds a final 'e', not in imitation of the spelling used by the poet, you understand, but 'the latter being used by ancestors of my father the Rev. Frederick Thomas Swinburn D.D.' Several people, in the aftermath of the scandal of Oscar Wilde, change to other less notorious appellations, but one wonders whether it was wise of the manager of a bedding works in Cardiff to change his name on 11 March 1909 from Wilde to Wilde-Leech, which sounds bloodthirsty, to say the least.

Several of the name changes seem ill advised. One can imagine how urgent must have been the necessity in October 1913 for Walter Horschitz of Great Tower Street, in the City of London, to assume and henceforth upon all occasions sign and use and be called and known by anything but the name 'Horschitz', yet surely he was a little timid in his choice of a new name, which was 'Walter Horschitz Horst'? (There is a want of determined follow-through here.) And was it wise of an entire family to change their name in 1902 to 'Baller', or of Mr Nainby on 5 February 1903 to change his to 'Nainby-Manby'? (This, by the way, is not the origin of the adjective 'Namby-pamby', which was Pope's nickname for the effeminate poetaster Ambrose Phillips.)

There are also one or two advertisements that show how strongly passions can rise when clubland jokes miscarry. Pamphlets are on offer at 2s from an Oxford graduate and Old Etonian explaining why he has been wrongly expelled from his club, and there is trouble brewing at the Junior United Services:

> Warning. – Whereas reports have lately been circulated to the effect that Major Henry Johnson was obliged to resign his membership of the Junior United Services Club, which reports are absolutely false, this is to give notice, that Major Johnson will take immediate action against any person or persons to whom such statements can be traced, and will pay a reward of £50 to any person giving such information as will lead to successful proceedings. All communications to be addressed to J. Balfour Allen, Esq, Solicitor, 5 Furnival's Inn, E.C.
>
> *10 July 1897*

Expulsion from a club, even a cycling club, was a serious matter:

> Mr Cunliffe expelled from the Cyclists' Touring Club. Reasons legible in 'A Sell for Cyclists' (2/3 post free) obtainable of J.I.M. Co, Brighton.
>
> *15 April 1903*

Mr Cunliffe, as later advertisements explain, was expelled from the club 'for holding divergent views to it on truth, honour, honesty and sportsmanship'.

Cycling, a new craze, held all sorts of hidden dangers. The Royal Society for the Prevention of Cruelty to Animals warns in June 1901:

> A Humane Appeal to Bicyclists. – Bicyclists are earnestly desired to be on guard against over-taxing the strength of their dogs when running with bicycles at high speed. Some dogs would rather die than stop when following their masters, and this has actually happened without the knowledge of the owners at the time.

But by 1914 cycling has begun to lose some of its glamour:

> Weary push cyclist offers good home to motor cycle.
>
> *4 February 1914*

In late Victorian and Edwardian times private passion is never allowed to mar the solemnity of the column. Although the mood changes markedly with the approach of the First World War, for the present the only emotion permitted is of a strictly public-spirited kind. One result of this is the appearance in print of a number of marvellously bad poems of a patriotic nature. The best, or worst, are by Jane H. Oakley, writing from Wilbury Lawn, Hove ('late West Brighton', she is careful to specify). The personal column provides a platform for Ms Oakley, whose works are not elsewhere recorded except in *Broad Arrow* and a few other 'service' rags. It must have cost her a lot of money to see her creations in print in this way. I shall refrain from inflicting all of them upon the reader. A few verses from 'Our Glorious Queen Bee' will give the idea:

> 'Tis the noble Flag of Empire
> That dominates the sea;
> The ensign of Britannia
> Belongs to our 'Queen Bee'.
>
> Proud mistress of the ocean,
> And many an inland sea;
> The Universe, her apiary,
> Beloved by all is she!
>
> Swarming millions fill her hives,
> Vast cities by her owned,
> She sits in stately Majesty
> The wisest Queen enthroned.
>
> She counts her ships by thousands,
> Her sailors brave the sea
> To bring home golden honey
> For our 'Glorious Queen Bee'.
>
> *30 January 1899*

'Welcome to the Gordons' (February 6th) also contains some stirring lines, though the poet has a tendency to cram in too many syllables when carried away by the action. 'Australia United' (14 February), to which she has added the note 'Australian papers please copy', is also a resounding piece; and when she speaks of 'wars intestine' one must charitably assume that it is the printer rather than Australian cooking that is at fault.

For Ms Oakley, all men are gallant or brave, all women weak and fair; if in doubt, she starts a line 'Hail! All Hail!' and adds plenty of exclamation marks to carry the action along. It is not quite McGonagal; she has more self-discipline.

Another poet in public-spirited mood provides an invaluable mnemonic:

One hundred lines do make a foot,
One hundred drams a pound.
('Three lines an inch – Six drams an Ounce'
Most useful will be found.)
                                          2 January 1903

The mathematics of the above are open to question, and perhaps stung by criticism the author came back after a few days with:

One fiftieth part of a cube foot of water
Or 'pint' as it's called, weighs a pound and a quarter.
At least this convenient relation would hold exactly if the
    pound were .997136 of its present value.
                                          20 January 1903

An ingenious advertiser cashed in on this vogue for poetry in the personal column with:

I told the rose upon her stem
'Your petals are like Kleinert's gem.'
'Oh no,' she answered, blushing red,
'The gem is odorless,' she said.
                                          22 June 1905

(Kleinert's Gem was a pad worn under the arms to absorb perspiration.)

A poet who was not 'a hireling base, who wields his pen for pay', signing himself 'W', contributed several short verses in 1906. The first, quoted here, has a certain naive power, but the rest are disappointing:

To John Bull
Oh John, you are completely scattered now,
Worse than his Lordship sprawling on the grass;
Him, anyway, a horse did overthrow,
But you are tumbled over by an ass.

Pick Yourself up again, man: quickly, too;
Or long will be the bill you'll have to pay
To those old Gaelic tyrants that anew
Expectant, rat-eyed, mark you for their prey.
                                          8 January 1906

If John Bull felt completely scattered and tumbled over, he could always spend a few days drying out on an island:

> If the drink you cannot withstand
> Come at once to Osea Island.

Osea Island for the cure of inebriety. Ladies and Gentlemen. Freedom, boating, billiards, golf, fishing etc. Resident physician. Terms 3 to 5 guineas.

Osea Island, in Essex, is accessible only at low tide by a causeway. It now belongs to Cambridge University, who use it as an experimental farm; but for many years it bore an annual crop of alcoholics – all *Times* readers, no doubt, for these advertisements are a feature of the personal column of this period which no one who glanced at the newspaper's front page could have failed to notice. The column, in 1909, is at its lowest ebb. The few advertisements which are not from solicitors or charities are commercial matter masquerading as personal: an imposture to which the column invariably becomes prey when the tide of inspiration has left it high and dry.

Among the few advertisements of the early years of the century which stand out against this depressing trend is that of an old lady thanking a gentleman for providing her with a cup of tea:

If the gentleman who travelled from Folkestone to London by the afternoon Paris train of the 20th inst., and who so very kindly procured a cup of tea for an old lady at Folkestone Station, would make his address known it would greatly please her, as she very much appreciated his unusual kindness.

29 April 1903

There is still a genteel, unspoilt England in which the values of Jane Austen are upheld:

A Lady (widow) of position, fortune and well connected, member of an old country family, much alone, desires to meet another who may have a fine house with all its appurtenances, but may be weary of loneliness, to whom she could go as it were on a visit, longer or shorter as suits, no ties on either side; she would read aloud, accompany in drives, play games etc. No salary, merely for company; in or near London.

4 August 1906

It is rather a shock, after this return to eighteenth-century tranquillity, to find that Pollaky's profession still thrives, but that its leading light is now a woman:

Antonia Moser, Detective expert, late of Arundel Street, Strand. Prompt, secret and reliable. Confidential enquiries of

every description. Agents in all cities of the world. 37 and 38
Strand, London.

8 August 1906

Some quite gruesome theories were currently in vogue about the
physical roots of criminality and the idea of criminal tendencies as
a disease, whether inherited or acquired, produced some weird
experiments:

Psychological research. – A gentleman, who for some time has
devoted his attention towards developing a process whereby
the mental activity can be controlled through the utilization of
certain waves of light upon the brain in conjunction with
psychological measures, the aim of which is towards remould-
ing the personality of the criminal and mental and moral
pervert, would be grateful for financial aid to enable him to
secure necessary laboratory apparatus. Advertiser will be
pleased to meet any prospective patron at his residence and to
explain details.

31 August 1906

The only staunchly familiar figure at this low point in the column's
history is the lunatic. It is not to the credit of the newspaper's
management that on 8 January 1904 it allowed an advertisement of
twenty lines headed 'Publicity with Authenticity' and, ten days
later, another from the same individual, 'A.C.M.', of sixty-eight
lines, headed 'Rationality, Manifestation of Divineness'; for both,
with their obsessive use of abstract nouns and general vacuous
meaninglessness, could be of interest only to students of abnormal
mental conditions.

Another message in May 1905 declares:

The seventh messenger to the Potentates, Priests and Ministers
of all nations. Away with abominations. Prepare the people for
a special manifestation of The Light. War must cease. Seven.
70.

Appeals for money are also very prevalent, and some of them
have all the appearance of emanating from blackmailers. Somebody called Ambleside, an actor possibly, regularly appeals for
support from his or her benefactor:

I scarcely dare ask you again, and believe me I would not could
I help it . . . 12 weeks' assured engagement in London has
been cut to five on account of alterations in the piece.

And a depressing sounding individual who signs himself 'Louis' regularly makes appointments, with demands for money, in 'Kelly's Library'. Can this be fitting material for the front page of 'The Thunderer'?

But even in its darkest days, the spirit of snobbery, most comic of human vices, survives:

> Riding in the Row. – Antipodean visiting England for first time is doubtful whether riding in Rotten Row is still a necessary part of the social round. Will some readers of 'The Times' inform him privately whether it is still 'de rigeur'.
>
> *29 October 1913*

Soon after this, the personal column begins to recover. The approach of war seems to be the main impetus. This shows itself in one obvious way, in that inventors have a field day advertising ingenious devices which need just a little more money to perfect them and make them into essential items of military equipment. A general awakening process seems also to occur, and messages become wittier, more romantic, odder and generally more like the personal column should be.

Perhaps some keen-eyed member of editorial staff spotted this trend, for the newspaper, with a sure instinct for priorities in a time of national crisis, ran a lengthy article on the history of the personal column a few weeks before the outbreak of the First World War. It would be tempting to suppose that this article boosted the morale of advertisers and was responsible for the generally high level of material during the war years. Certainly the author deplores recent trends towards commercialisation and begging:

> They want money. They all do nowadays. Agonists such as E. J. Wilson know of finer things. They wanted amiable females or lost children. We fear, from their continued appeals and final silence, that they got less than they wanted; while today, possibly, the numbers who 'want money' get more than they deserve.

Citing the epistolary style of Choderlos de Laclos (*Les Liaisons Dangereuses* is presumably meant), the writer suggests that someone should compose a novel entirely made up of personal column advertisements. He also suggests that there could be no better training ground for an ambitious enquiry agent than the decipherment of those 'enigmatic romances, thrilling to the curious person with detective tastes'. The Collinson cryptograms come in for some erroneous speculation and are referred to, quite groundlessly, as 'Irish looking agonies'. Evidently the memory of Collinson's own explanation of his codes, published twenty-five years previously, had already been lost.

Gallantry and courtly romance had already begun to return to the column a few months before the above appeared. Could 'Gentleman Ranker' in the following advertisement be our socially adroit Antipodean?

> If the lady who rode the dappled grey in Hyde Park on Saturday morning will do so again on Wednesday next at the same time, the gauntlet she dropped will be returned to her. – Gentleman Ranker
>
> *16 March 1914*

People started advertising for jobs, and writing lengthy essays in self-justification headed 'Fettered Abilities' or 'Grasping Life's Opportunities'. A less effective appeal from someone, who to judge from what he says is probably on the verge of some kind of breakdown, nonetheless speaks volumes for the prevailing atmosphere and *mores*:

> Appeal. (24) Victim social circumstance: no snob nor fool; every quality of gentleman (unfortunately), but willing to work (non-commissioned), and for small salary. Disgusted ignorance, vulgarity, repression, effect on health. Only asks Berth among peers or treated as should be honourable, genial, sensitive fellow. Urgent.
>
> *25 June 1914*

It is a pathetic plea. Nothing he says inspires confidence in his value as an employee and he really doesn't sound as though he qualifies for that 'berth', but I cannot help hoping he found it, all the same.

What he needed was to be a bit more self-assertive, like the inventor, first off the mark, who announces:

> Inventor of most deadly projectile extant, for use against dirigible and other airships, is desirous of selling share in world's rights. Trials are about to be carried out by Government. Fullest investigation courted. Enormous fortune awaits prompt investor. Lieut. West, Hither Green, S.E.
>
> *31 October 1913*

This advertiser has the right spirit too:

> Aviation. Cross Atlantic Waterplane Competition. – Financiers wanted for syndicate to build Naval Army bullet-proof flying boat. Guaranteed to do everything but talk. – Inventor
>
> *20 February 1914*

Less immediately useful in wartime, but no less intriguing, was the invention of a self-styled 'non-golfer' who claimed in July 1914 to be able 'by using the principle of witching waves' to turn any back garden into an eighteen hole course, through the deployment of seventeen levers, strategically placed.

Optimism was everywhere in the air:

Wanted: Person of enormous wealth to finance season at London Theatre for obscure actress.
13 February 1914

And an actress far from obscure – she was currently appearing as the star of *Mamselle Tralala* at the Lyric – advertised a few weeks later:

Miss Yvonne Arnaud, Lyric Theatre, would be obliged by the anonymous donor of the strange animal which reached her yesterday evening informing her as to the diet on which it thrives. The creature refuses to touch ordinary food.
4 May 1914

Stylishness and eccentricity are back:

Wrong. – Right. Write.
3 June 1914

Eton. – Will the lady who was wearing a small gold ear trumpet at Speeches in Upper School on June 4th help a fellow sufferer by writing and sending name and address of maker to Mrs L, care of Messrs Spottiswoode & Co, Eton?
26 June 1914

July 1st shows a terrific outburst of initiative, romance and sheer quirkiness. Here are two examples:

Won't very radical journalist who told the extraordinary story about his grandmother's bequests at Simpson's Monday night indulge enthralled listener with an interview? Nothing serious. Simply must know part of tale impossible to hear.

Having had a surfeit of motoring through police traps, yet possessing ardent love for mechanics as practised in the open air, and hankering after adventure, advertiser is planning motor-boat trip to the Faroe Isles to chase the sperm whale. Who will accept half of all the risks?

All this took place within a couple of days of the assassination of the Archduke of Austria at Sarajevo. Among the romantic messages on that fatal day was the first exchange between two lovers – 'Water Nymph' and 'The Pilot'. As is so often the way for those who resort to the personal column for their amorous communications, the course of true love did not run smooth:

The Pilot. – Do not write me direct. Post being watched and fear letters will not reach me. – Water Nymph

1 July 1914

Water Nymph. – From 10 a.m. onwards next Friday a taxi will wait opposite the P.P. where we parted. The flag will be down and the chauffeur will wear a flower you will recognize. Do not speak to him, but hand him an envelope with your initials thereon. Enter the cab and trust to me. Don't arouse suspicion by attempting to bring luggage or even your jewellery. – The Pilot.

15 July 1914

Water Nymph. – Car waited all day, why did you fail? – The Pilot.

20 July 1914

W.N. – Unsought publicity embarrasses correspondence. What am I to understand from your failure?

22 July 1914

The Pilot. – You may understand by silence that Water Nymph has had the good sense and courage and confessed everything. Your method of communicating with her is no longer available. She has had the good sense to decide upon peace and happiness under my roof rather than disaster with you. – Water Nymph's Mother.

25 July 1914

Perhaps 'The Pilot' should have taken to the air:

Young and little known, yet thoroughly experienced aviator, having found engine of extraordinary power and reliability, has undertaken to attempt a vertical flight of 1,000ft. Conditions require that he should carry a *Volunteer* Lady Passenger. Partner arranged for having failed, would like to hear from candidate who should state fully age, weight, say whether married, single, responsibilities, and whether parents living or under other guardianship: no fee required.

2 July 1914

Nor likely to be forthcoming? The general air of uncertainty and excitement led advertisers to make extravagant bets with each other, such as the above, organise expeditions ('retired Cavalry Officer, middle aged, anxious to start in autumn for tour round world . . .') or commit rash romantic acts. For the first time in thirty years there is a secret coded exchange between two lovers, RAYQ and YMNNSW – which readers who took the trouble to practise their alphabetic shifts in the course of digesting Chapter Six will immediately recognise as 'Jack' and 'Connie'. Exactly as happened to their grandparents in the middle of the nineteenth century, Jack and Connie's *billets doux* were deciphered and exposed – in this instance both by Connie's parents and by a friend called 'Hope'. It seems incredible that during the last week before the outbreak of the Great War people should have frantically started sending each other love messages in code and before I succeeded in fathoming the mysteries of RAYQ and YMNNSW, I assumed, as no doubt many *Times* readers must have at the time, that these were the messages of spies – which are indeed rumoured to have appeared in the *Times* personal column during the First World War. For those who may wish to follow the ciphers, and satisfy themselves that I have not missed a lurking traitor, here are two from 25 July 1914:

Qyar. – xna Wsnnmy we wfat xngmv.
Wsnnmy. – Whahi wpzgmjh htsi nogpmy emnq jwthav qnsth wunajja ijwhhao. – Wlmt.

25 July 1914

The original cipher, based on a reversed alphabet displaced by one letter, suffers the disadvantage that both 'n' and 'a' are the same in plain text and in cipher. To make things harder, Jack has started reversing the letters of each word as well. In the second message, incidentally, 'Hope' has omitted the word 'can' before 'arrange'.

On Monday there is a reply in the original cipher from Connie, who is evidently not the world's greatest cryptoanalyst, for it translates as:

Jack. – So sorry could not ring you up Mother at home must try meet you Buckingham Gate 4 Wednesday if you send another message change code. Cannot understand Saturday's messages.

She was not great at punctuation either. But she was right to say that the code was due for a change. The following 'marplot' sounds as if it must emanate from Connie's parents, who are clearly not too pleased at being judged '*de trop*':

Ymnnsw. – Allajwnhpc vahtwj anx omhtwj ajw xw hjml cwi cmg ogih ytanuw ymxw. – NMH RAYQ

30 July 1914

Another symptom of the general awakening which preceded the

arrival of Armageddon was the sudden digging out of old manuscripts which had lain for years neglected in attics:

> A gentleman who is the holder of manuscript poems and verse, written by his late grandfather, and hitherto unpublished, wishes to convince some publisher of the undoubted merits thereof.
>
> *27 June 1914*

Quixotic quests and long-forgotten dreams were dusted off and tested out:

> Advertiser desires to take proceedings to establish his claim to a well-known peerage. Will any wealthy person help him?
>
> *27 June 1914*

All this, and much else, happened in a few frenzied days. The ant-heap had been stirred, and everyone was rushing about in all sorts of directions:

> An old manuscript has come into the hands of the advertiser, in which is described a place in England where one may see a wall which is supposed at one time to have enclosed a vineyard. The wall is said to be composed of stones and human bones in almost equal parts. If any reader can identify the locality from this brief description advertiser will be greatly obliged as much depends on the identification.
>
> *18 July 1914*

This particular manuscript was, I suspect, a hoax and the start of an elaborate con-trick. The vineyard would appeal to a visionary type of personality and the search for this mystic place would absorb all the resources the con-man could extract from them; but he must have been a con-man of above average inventiveness and discernment, quite an artist at his trade. Curious finds in old walls are sometimes made: for example, an earthenware jar containing a horde of old sovereigns was found under a withy tree in the wall of a kitchen garden at Stanford-in-the-Vale, Berkshire, in 1944, though human bones are not mentioned . . .

Returning to literature with more serious credentials, it is noteworthy that members of the Diogenes Club – who were, as always, among the best informed regarding foreign affairs and the likely outbreak of hostilities – are first off in the manuscript stakes, rushing to commit important matters to print before civilisation came to an end. The Jowett in the following advertisement is perhaps some relative of the famous Master of Balliol, who had died in 1893, leaving a quantity of unpublished material:

Wanted. – Experienced writer to revise and to form for publication work of momentous interest. Scientific, philosophical and Christian. – Athenaeum. Jowett.

1 February 1914

Ordinary mortals did not realise until the Great War was nearly upon them that the last chance had come for putting all those plans into action. Had this advertiser had the prescience of a Jowett, horticulture might have been the richer:

I can grow a sky-blue rose. Will a capitalist help me to make money out of it?

15 July 1914

But it was not a good moment to embark on experiments in gardening. Capitalists had other uses for their money and there were more urgent things that needed to be done. Everyone, it seemed, was looking for some way of joining in the national effort. There is a proliferation of requests for employment. To set themselves apart from the mass, some advertisers began being self-deprecatory, and started a minor fashion for 'opposite language'. *Times* personal column advertisers have always been fond of this very English species of false modesty, and there are examples of it from the middle of the nineteenth century right up to the present day. The following, however, seem to go too far:

Idiot, age 38, fully qualified, work shy, champion idler, seeks Confidential Position. Social and intellectual qualifications really deplorable; totally uneducated; untrustworthy; horribly nervous; absolutely unreliable.

16 July 1914

Absolute rotter, dumb in six languages, served Rifle Brigade and N.I.D. Admiralty; can be trusted with money, silly ass, loves his country, perfect fool, completely brainless, but harmless with children, young as possible, has means, wants a Job.

17 July 1914

Romance continues to bloom, and lovers continue to send each other epistles as mystifying in plain English as anything in code:

White dove. – To understand message substitute 'love' for 'friend', 'at the garden gate' for 'attentive', 'nine o'clock' for 'your lemons', 'in the car' for 'in the morning', 'for a long ride' for 'to task on your progress'. – Lochinvar.

17 July 1914

Competition: devise a suitable letter from Lochinvar in which these alternative readings will fit (Jaspistos, where are you?). Next competition: what exactly was going on here – is this evidence of more 'marplotting', and from someone with rather a wicked sense of humour? The following two advertisements appear, one immediately above the other, on the same day:

A. MacT. – If your several messages, which I have only just seen, were intended for Babs, of N.B., please note that answer of July 10 was not mine. Either misunderstanding or fraud. – Still care for you. – Babs.

A. MacT. – Do not seek me. I am beyond redemption. The little needle has given me the forgetfulness I craved. – Babs.
27 July 1914

Motorists were dashing round the countryside creating an infernal nuisance:

Will the Owner of the Car passing through Stoughton to Guildford on Thursday at noon, with some children and luggage, whose chauffeur drove over and killed a young puppy belonging to my son kindly send me his address, not to make any claim, for the dog had no monetary value? It is acts of this sort which cause so many people who still care for the country and their dogs to loathe and detest motorists. – A. H. Stockley, Rydes Hill, Guildford.
27 July 1914

This is not the last hate-mail directed towards motorists nor is it the last we are to hear about dogs, which remain central preoccupations of *Times* readers throughout the war.

There are not many 'Come home' messages during these last few weeks before the outbreak of the war. Sons and husbands had every excuse for disappearing on supposedly important business too secret to be divulged. But there is one, and it deserves a special prize: it is something of a minor masterpiece. There is, as I have pointed out earlier, a marked tendency among the composers of 'Come home' advertisements to reveal in the wording of their message those very character traits which drove their 'beloved father' or 'darling son' from the all too clamorous and suffocating nest to seek peace and freedom elsewhere. The composer of 'Daddledar' gives us a prime example of this Achilles' heel of the come-homers:

Daddledar: Your room's just as you left it so long ago. Your slippers on the hearthrug where you dropped them; your

158

half-burnt cigar and your matchbox on the table; the news-paper you were reading is on the floor beside your chair. How far out of date!! The page it is open at reports the relief of Ladysmith.[1] Will you never return to those who love you so devotedly and sincerely and grieve for you so deeply?

27 June 1914

At the outbreak of war the column is splendidly in character. Portfolios are still being left in taxicabs, emerald rings and pearl necklaces have been mislaid all over Knightsbridge and Mayfair; an inventor requires capital to develop a 'fogometer, invaluable for service use'; and a schoolmaster (M.A., Oxon) is planning to take a summer holiday party to Brittany (very safe bathing). Frustrated romance and public-spirited announcements vie for pride of place: the war is to be a 'great venture', and all who are proud to call themselves British are eager to dash in:

Pauline. – Alas, it cannot be. But I will dash into the great venture with all that pride and spirit an ancient race has given me. Had I seen you before going the outlook might have been brighter. A.L'A.

1 August 1914

To all who call themselves English gentlemen. – Are you Drilled and Armed and Ready *To Defend Your Country*?

1 August 1914

---

[1] Ladysmith was relieved in February 1900.

9 *The Personal Column Goes to War*

The prevailing impression created by the personal column when Britain declared war on Germany on 4 August 1914 is one of confused and sporadic activity; muddle and patriotism going hand in hand. It was also a great time for romantic protestations, mainly from men indulging shamelessly in emotional blackmail. The position of the heroic gallant, departing for war and bidding adieu forever to his weeping consort, was, initially, one of unassailable strength in the battle of the sexes; it allowed men to get out of liaisons which bored them or to look up old flames for 'a final kiss before parting' with reckless abandon. The female sex, however, soon devised methods of counter-attack against the very citadel of masculinity, which left all kinds of psychological scars on the enemy for years to come. It was not, I believe, from the evidence of the column, the female who had been thus ill-treated who was generally roused to action, but some stronger-minded sister who had seen the whole drama played out and was looking for a legitimate way to swipe back at the male race.

Before going on to study these major aspects of the conflict, it is worth observing that the personal column was also used in a number of official, or quasi-official, ways to announce war-time measures. The German Consul, for instance, was (amazingly) allowed to insert an advertisement the day before war was declared:

German Mobilization. – Germans who have served or are liable to serve, are requested to return to Germany without delay, as best they can.

For information they can apply to the German Consulate General, 21a Bedford Place, Russell Square, London W.C. – R. L. von Ranke. Consul.

3 August 1914

Announcements in French, Russian, Italian, Spanish and German were later placed in the column by *The Times'* management to the effect that the personal column was open to citizens of all these countries for 'approved communications' with friends and relatives. There is little evidence that much use was made of this invitation, which did not apparently extend as far as free advertising. Since many of the expatriates referred to were soon interned it is hard to imagine how they could have availed themselves of the offer.

On the day war was declared the following advertisement, first of many similar, appeared:

> Professional man desires to meet others from Corps Mounted Infantry. Each provide own arms and contribute hire horse. Drill and instruction after and before working hours, August and September. Camp will be formed. Will gentlemen interested please communicate at once, mentioning age, profession and previous military experience.
>
> *4 August 1914*

All kinds of people made offers to help in various ways in the national effort. 'Mrs Cornwallis West will be glad to help in the present crisis . . .'; 'Mrs Thatcher [a happy thought, could this be Denis's mother?] will give a home to a little motherless girl (under 12 years of age) whose father (officer or civilian) has been called to the war . . . Whitstable.' And, as always, communications are less than perfect:

> Empire Ginger. Monday's message not mine. Mystery. Investigating. Hope to see you soon.
>
> *20 August 1914*

The first shot in the battle of the sexes is fired by J.G. at Agnes of Eastbourne:

> Agnes, Eastbourne. – The hope that the news of my call will melt you and prompt you to see me again – probably for the last time – has emboldened me to write to the old address. Your failure to reply will ensure my non-return. – J.G.
>
> *11 August 1914*

Agnes' defences are totally demolished:

> J.G. – All is forgiven. – Agnes, Eastbourne.
>
> *15 August 1914*

The next trigger is pulled by 'A. L'A.', whose touching farewell message is recorded at the end of the previous chapter. Pauline writes on August 18th in tones which leave her defences wide open:

> A.L'A. – I beg and implore you to allow me to expiate my
> unjustness and cruelty before you go. Will you not allow me to
> ask your forgiveness? – Pauline

The reply is instantaneous and ruthless. It purports to emanate from
'a friend':

> Pauline. – Your remorse is too late. A.L'A. has already gone.
> Your message will probably never reach him. This should be
> your well deserved punishment. – A Friend.
>
> *19 August 1914*

Someone signed 'Patriot' (or perhaps there is more than one
'Patriot'?) inserts a barrage of messages which continues
throughout the early years of the war. The first of these starts a line
of thought which eventually leads to the invention of the prime
weapon of female retaliation:

> Cricket. – Who in the name of wonder is interested in young,
> able-bodied Englishmen at this moment taking nine wickets in
> an innings and making a century not out? Why are they not,
> being so physically fit, in the fighting line with 700,000 other
> Englishmen? In the name of decency stop cricket, and above
> all stop reporting it in the newspapers. – Patriot.
>
> *22 August 1914*

This is reinforced in a matter of days by the following unsigned
missile:

> 'Flannelled fools at the wicket and muddied oafs at the goal'
> have now an opportunity of proving whether or no Mr Kipling
> was right.

Significantly, on the same day, there appears an impassioned plea
from a Brigade Surgeon's widow, for all good men and true to bestir
themselves for action. It is headed 'Attention! Men of Britain!'
There are three or four of these strongly worded declarations
inserted at considerable expense by the same advertiser, each
running to twenty or thirty lines and too long to include here,
splendid though they are in their way. She too is against cricketers,
and her strongest emotions are expended against sportsmen in
general as well as 'taxi-men, and dwellers in quiet towns'.

The first shot from the female side to score a direct hit was
published the next day:

Wanted. Petticoats for all Able Bodied Youths in this country who have not yet joined the navy or army.

27 August 1914

Thenceforth the entire male sex comes under heavy mortar fire from the regiment of women who felt it their duty to goad cowards into the lines:

Englishwoman undertakes to form and equip a regiment of women for the firing line if the lawn tennis and cricketing young men will agree to act as Red Cross nurses to such a regiment.

31 August 1914

Supporting action was provided from the organisers of Old Boys' Clubs, anxious to uphold the honour of Public School Man. The first of these to weigh in were, fittingly, the Old Wellingtonians, with a request to all Old Boys to record the date of their enlistment, a request which would have made it easy to track down shirkers and fell them with moral imperatives.

From this point on there was a rout, as anti-shirker fire was aimed with deadly accuracy at the virility of anyone who had so far failed to face the hail of lead that was raining down upon the trenches across the Channel:

Loungers at City Bars! Why not prove your manhood by assisting your country at this time of crisis? Your help is needed. Enlist at once.

7 September 1914

Suddenly an unexpected winged secret weapon, of the kind to be found only in the personal column at the height of its inventive powers, is flung back across the lines. Its opening words have a deceptively harmless air as they whizz towards their goal:

Parrot wanted to Purchase; must be good talker; good price will be paid for one that hates women. – State price and particulars to: Bachelor, care of Jones and Yarrell, 19 Ryder Street, S.W.

4 October 1914

This produced a host of replies, and the advertiser is forced to insert another advertisement stating that he will deal with them all once he has had time to go through them carefully. There was clearly a willing band of supporters on his side, awaiting marching orders.

After this there is a pause for retrenchment on the female front; then, as the football season draws on, ammunition is found for further assaults on the male sex:

Petticoats for footballers urgently required. To be found bargain basement leading drapers. Shop early. Supply limited. In this garment *Free* kick-off ensured.

28 November 1914

Why not design a 'pretty' uniform to attract the 'knuts' to the colours? Something which would harmonize with heliotrope socks, lavender gloves, spotted waistcoats and mauve handkerchiefs, would appeal irresistibly to their aesthetic sense – the only sense they possess. Khaki is so unromantic.

1 December 1914

The advertiser shows a lack of psychological insight here, for khaki was, of course, the most romantic colour in the world at this time – that was just the trouble (a 'knut', by the way, is a fop):

Khaki Clad, whose message to Brown Furs appeared here on Tuesday, much regrets that it is impossible for him to answer personally the hundreds of kind people who proffer their services in substitution for Brown Furs.

1 February 1915

After this the attacking forces make the further error of believing the enemy to be dispersed, and there is a slackness in their next sally:

Where are the Effeminate Males? 'The Nuts are being Shelled'. The abused performers of Negroid suggestive dances, male and female, are serving their country. Elderly critics please note. Bravo, gallant young Britain!

15 April 1915

With the euphoria of victory, lunacy has apparently set in. There are, however, signs that the victory is a hollow one. The enemy, far from being defeated, has undergone fundamental changes and is regrouping. A commando force, working across battle lines and employing outrageous new tactics, looks like turning the tables on the female front. They go under the innocent-seeming code name of the 'Chums'. By employing this password, they are able to form secret resistance cells, or 'Chum Pairs', which are totally unaffected by female fire-power. *The Times*, perhaps unaware of the true significance of their password, allows many such messages between the 'Chums' to get through:

Does any sportsman, really lonely, keen on country life, want a real Man Chum?

2 November 1915

164

Gentleman, aged 50, holding responsible appointment, exceptionally broad-minded, quiet disposition, desires a Chum who desires companionship, trustworthiness and steadiness. Age immaterial – strictest confidence to 'Chum'.

23 January 1916

Meanwhile, on the battlefront itself, close engagements between the opposing forces continue to be fought out. There are occasional male set-backs – most notably, a late rally at Mottisfont in Hampshire:

Mottisfont. – Invalid lady to whom wounded officer sent the book regrets that, owing to his deplorable taste, the idea of correspondence must be abandoned.

6 July 1916

But numerous invitations from the female side, such as 'Young widow will write to lonely soldiers' or 'Do you want cheering up, lonely officers?', are followed up energetically by male forces, who are now scoring sweeping victories. After the following message appeared, from an officer who had advertised a few weeks previously, the female side knew the writing was on the wall and further resistance useless:

'The most lonely officer in England' WARMLY THANKS his two hundred and fifty-two correspondents, and regrets that he cannot answer them all individually.

6 March 1916

After the Sex War among advertisers came the Dog War. As we have seen, pro-dog sentiment on the eve of hostilities was at a high point and no sacrifice was too great for our fighting men:

Lady Bower is willing to look after a Soldier's Dog while he is away; a mongrel preferred, as it is so hard to get them homes. If wanted, will be returned after the war, but must be non-fighter and used to a house, as she wishes a house-dog.

2 October 1914

The first anti-dog missile was fired anonymously some time after the significance of Lady Bower's altruistic offer had time to sink in:

Questions. – How many hundred thousand dogs round London? How much do they cost? How many famished Belgians or Frenchmen would that sum help? How many comforts for our troops would it buy?

5 November 1914

Without waiting for a reply, a salvo of unique potency is targeted at Tulse Hill:

> Tulse Hill Dog Nuisance. – If the owner of small dog (or is it a thousand small dogs?) in this neighbourhood were to have a good day's mental work he would see the desirability of sending his dumb guardian into the country, where its piercing whines, doubtless intended as a mark of displeasure at being broken into the kennel habit, would better harmonize with the many other objectionable noises for which the ordinary English village is so justly famous.
>
> *24 November 1914*

It is some time before pro-dog forces are able to retaliate:

> Dogs of War. – 'Togo', a black spaniel, appeals to all dogs who are 'sports' to help the dogs of the brave Belgian Army, who drag the machine guns and do outpost duty etc.: collapsible kennel-tents, designed by master, light in weight but securing a dog-bed, and good British hound-meal, will be promptly sent. Naturalized dachshunds and cats can lend a paw. – 'Togo', Ingham Manor, Stalham.
>
> *6 April 1915*

It should be added that 'Togo' was the name of an inventor: his collapsible kennel-tents are advertised elsewhere as indispensable to the army, and capital is sought to develop this aid to modern warfare.

Widening the field of action, there is another generous female offer with repercussions on the Sex War:

> Would any regiment like as a gift from a lady a little tame white pig for a mascot? Two months old; hand fed; very affectionate.
>
> *8 January 1916*

This was half a century before the expression 'male chauvinist pig' came into common use. Later in the war animals play a less combative role, though elephants make a useful contribution. There are numerous warnings, as the war draws to a close, of the impending shortage of dog-biscuits, and, shortly after the war ended, someone felt inspired to announce in traditional personal column 'oracular' style 'A. – Cat no use. – M.' Finally, readers may find it amusing to speculate on the significance of:

> Found, in a railway carriage near Portsmouth, a little old seal.
>
> *10 January 1916*

It is generally accepted among those who have written about the personal column of *The Times* that it was used during the First World War as a vehicle of communication for spy networks. The rumour returned to haunt the column, imposing annoying restrictions on advertisers, during the Second World War. On the face of it, the idea sounds reasonable enough. But the more the proposition is examined, the less plausible it becomes. After all, there are hundreds of methods of communication less public and less risky than advertising on the front page of a newspaper. Anyone using the classified columns regularly to transmit messages to networks of spies would be easy to identify and track down, since *The Times'* scruples concerning the protection of sources could hardly be depended upon by spies in wartime. It is not impossible that the column might have been used *in extremis* for the occasional rendezvous between agents: the agents' names could be disguised and the rendezvous would pass off as a romantic one. But even this seems unduly risky and unnecessarily elaborate, when simpler methods are available. As for the transmission of large volumes of secret matter to enemy intelligence headquarters by this route, the idea is clearly out of the question. A number of writers on intelligence and former intelligence officers I was able to contact during the course of research for this book all agreed that not only had they never heard of a single authenticated case of the personal columns of newspapers being used in this way, but it would be an odd and seemingly self-defeating exercise. However, a former MI6 officer was wise enough to add 'But don't rule it out, because the improbable is the rule in the world of espionage' – and shortly afterwards there appeared in the 'Deaths' column of *The Times* the fake 'von Hessen' notice thought by many to be just such a clandestine message.

There are also circumstantial and entertaining accounts of the activities of a German spy, Fraulein Anna Maria Lesser, who in the best spy traditions was not only extremely beautiful but a full 'Doktor' and an accomplished actress, capable of putting on a convincing Irish brogue. This paragon is supposed to have established herself in a village near Hatfield in 1916 and suborned the local scoutmaster to her evil designs, eventually disposing of him and, with the aid of some skilful make-up and a further display of histrionic talent, taking over the scout group as its leader. She then used the group as cover to spy on some tank experiments that were taking place before Lord Kitchener in 1916. The detailed results of these activities are then supposed to have been passed on to German intelligence by means of the personal column.

Apart from the intrinsic absurdity of this colourful tale, Kitchener was rather out of favour by 1916, having been stripped both of his responsibility for munitions and of his control over strategy; furthermore, a careful search of the columns of the front page of *The Times* during the war years reveals no suspect messages.

The one message that does look suspicious in this context is the following, which may on the other hand be the result of over-indulgence in the composing room:

> Do I come a nice who so not firstly sending writing him? Large all – follow issues. – L.E.
>
> *1 May 1916*

It is true that the signature contains the first two letters of Fraulein Lesser's surname; but there is probably another explanation, from the real world of espionage, for this odd message. Captain William Reginald 'Blinker' Hall,[1] Director of Naval Intelligence since November 1914, was responsible for many of the major intelligence successes scored by the British in the First World War, including marshalling the information from German coded messages which enabled the Battle of Jutland to be fought. One day a man from the City who boasted a certain skill as a cryptanalyst called on Hall with the information that he had solved the meaning of a series of secret messages in *The Times* personal column. These messages, he explained to Hall, were signals to German U-Boats betraying the planned movements of troopships in the Channel. Hall took all this in with a serious expression on his face and asked the man to return when he had further proof. The Director of Naval Intelligence then himself composed a 'cryptic' message and had it printed in the personal column. The man returned the following day in a state of excitement and explained that there had been a message indicating the departure of troopships from certain channel ports. He pointed to Hall's own message in *The Times*.

Some of the cryptic references to naval movements which so excited the amateur cryptanalyst are contained in the following exchange, which ostensibly describes the activities of somewhat lighter craft:

> Daphne. – Aren't you ever coming on the river in my punt again at Richmond? Purple, black and white. – Eric.
>
> *3 September 1914*

---

[1] Hall suffered from a nervous tic of the eyes; hence his nickname. All Halls in the Navy are now known as 'Blinker' in his honour.

Daphne, Baker Street. – Too cold for punting now, Richmond deserted. Where can I meet you? Purple, black and white. – Eric.

26 November 1914

Daphne. – Thanks awfully. Willing, but unable. Could explain satisfactorily. Like you 'I do think nature is wonderful' but very unkind sometimes. – Eric

30 November 1914

Fair Punter. – Red and white cushions, Molesey Sunday. Trust no ill effects partial submersion. Would like to hear. – Brown suit.

6 April 1915

Brown Suit. – No ill effects submersion. Would like to thank you again. Any day, same time and place. – F.P.

9 April 1915

Submarines, for the first time, were playing a vital role in this war. The railways also merited close observation by enemy agents. The 'Enigma' code machine did not come into being until the Second World War, but there is evidently some foreshadowing of its invention in the following suspicious-looking message. Or could the 'Fair Enigma' have been the lovely Fraulein Doktor herself?

Fair Enigma – who eagerly devours this column every morning on the 8.55 from Surbiton. Some humble and respectful admirers would like to see you smile.

13 October 1914

The smile is evidently granted, for things develop very rapidly between 'Fair Enigma' and fellow travellers:

Fair Enigma – the grateful thanks of the 'Seasons' and the freedom of the corner seat are hereby unanimously bestowed upon you.

14 November 1914

Eventually a working association is struck up between 'Fair Enigma' and one of the 'Seasons' on the 8.55, who signs himself 'Smiling Cavalier'. It does not take long, however, for 'Fair Enigma's' dominant personality to assert itself:

Smiling Cavalier. – Are you the culprit? If so, you may apologise personally. – Fair Enigma

20 November 1914

A second group appears anxious to make contact:

169

Fair Enigma. – the 'Seasons' of the 9.18 do hereby humbly petition that you postpone your departure by a few minutes and cast the light of your countenance upon them. By order.

28 November 1914

Whatever the true explanation for the above exchange, during those war years romance was definitely in the air. It was a time of snatched meetings and last, tragic farewells, of chance encounters and sudden passionate affairs. As the first reports of missing soldiers come in, towards the end of September 1914, the personal column acts as a clearing house for news about those believed lost in action. These stark messages, giving no more than the name and rank of the missing soldier, stand as the markers of untold tragedies, like the plain wooden crosses on a battlefield cemetery. Against this background, the attitudinising of 'A.L'A.' is shown up for the sham it is. By way of contrast there are advertisements such as the anonymous one of 25 September 1914, which simply states 'I staked my all and lost', and its answer 'You have not lost all. What of me and my unchanging love? Have faith. For the sake of past memories I entreat you communicate and do nothing rash. All made right. – V'. It is moving to come across, amidst the lists of missing men, the following unsigned announcement of joyous rebirth:

As gold is to lead, as sunshine to blizzard, as wine to water, as life itself to death, so am I to what I was.

25 June 1915

In this context those rendezvous under the clock at Charing Cross or Victoria Stations sound almost magical. Such snatched romances cannot be dwelt upon without the haunting afterthought that they were perhaps the last moment of happiness for some young soldier: that some girl was perhaps never to forget or never to love again. The poet Keats, had he been around at the time, would have found some way of freezing the following taxi race in the Mall into an enduring moment in Arcady:

Will the girl in the taxi who raced the officer in the taxi down the Mall on Tuesday morning please write to Box B. 138. – Lonely Soldier

22 July 1915

Here is another chance encounter, trapped in amber:

Haymarket 1.50 p.m. Tuesday. – You came swinging down in khaki; I, in black, turned into the stores; and, passing, you looked round: can we not meet?

31 March 1916

and a fine romance lost in the land of mists:

> Chris. – If you mislaid address given hurriedly, Tube, night of
> fog, communicate here. Would forgive and see you again. –
> 'Fog-girl'.
>
> *20 November 1916*

Lastly there appears, during the third year of the war, just as
T. E. Lawrence was stirring the Arabs into revolt and the United
States was breaking off relations with Germany and preparing to
come to the aid of the allies, a genuine St Valentine's Day message –
the only one for years. The message of 1917 – there *is* only one – is
terse compared to all the cooing nonsense one reads nowadays
every February 14th; indeed maybe it is a message from Fraulein
Doktor Lesser to headquarters telling them U.S. forces are about to
enter the war, for all it says is 'Central – May I be your Valentine'. It
is unsigned.

The First World War was also the heyday of another kind of
romantic – the inventor. Suddenly, from being a voice crying in the
wilderness, a lonely eccentric whom no one would listen to, the
inventor becomes a prophet of salvation. There had never been
such a seller's market for inventions since the height of the
industrial revolution. At first soberly worded advertisements
appear, from which it seems that the inventor is doing potential
investors a great favour by letting them in on schemes whose
financial rewards are guaranteed. Announcements beginning 'war
inventions of proved and unique utility', giving solemn lists of
backers and bankers, are typical of this period. Later entries into
the field become somewhat hectic in tone: 'Submarine devilry can
be crushed', which appeared shortly after the sinking of the
Lusitania and advertises the invention of a new form of explosive, is
a good example. This inventor found it necessary to advertise again
a few days later, in order to widen the field as far as possible, adding
that 'Zeppelin Devilry' as well as the submarine variety could be
dealt with equally effectively by means of his invention.

Signs that it was too late to join the bandwagon are apparent from
the pathetic plea of an inventor named Hawksworth Collins in
January 1916, which starts with the words 'Investigation wanted,
ridicule invited . . .' Surprisingly enough, this appeal seems not to
have attracted the requested response, for Collins is forced to
advertise again the following August: 'Investigation still wanted
(See advertisement January . . .)'. In this lengthy announcement
the inventor explains that, although in March 'a D.Sc.' had
recognised the pressing importance of his discovery, it had been
'pigeon-holed' by scientists. Furthermore, it was so simple a

discovery that it could be recognised as 'true' by three leading scientists in three hours. 'Otherwise' – and here comes the crunch – 'on August 31st it will be transferred to America. No progress in any direction can be made until a leading scientific society has endorsed the discovery, as no one will undertake elaborate and expensive experiments without previously feeling quite sure he is on the right track.' Hawksworth Collins, writing from a private address in Brighton, gives as his credentials that he is an Army tutor in mathematics, with degrees from Cambridge and London; but does not give any clue as to the nature of his discovery or invention, nor its potential value in wartime. No doubt if he had taken a leaf out of the book of this rival inventor, he would not have needed to invite ridicule:

> In the middle of costly but successful experiments of incalculable military value am forced to stop for lack of funds, although perhaps British lives are at stake. Difficult and expensive work ahead, for which financial help is needed. £1,250 already personally expended. To proceed £2,500 is needed. Write Box 100, 198 Piccadilly, London.
>
> *1 February 1916*

That is a much more hard-headed approach, even if the Piccadilly address is only an accommodation box. Poor Hawksworth Collins, perhaps, like E.J.B., he was hoping for help from a supernatural body:

> The new modern supernatural explosive now largely generating in Britain may possibly produce the greatest bombshell in present modern civilization. Will it be patented by England or America? – E.J.B.
>
> *18 October 1916*

Setting aside these isolated evidences of the divine light of genius among personal column advertisers, the tone remains during the war years both deeply English and determinedly eccentric:

> A retired Cathedral organist is willing to help any young musician wishing to take part in the defence of his country by deputising for him for a few months; London church and plain services preferred, but open to suggestions. Write to C. Lee Williams, the Knoll, Tuffley, Gloucestershire, or could arrange to interview at 40 Dover Street London W.
>
> *13 December 1915*

Betjeman would have relished that. His poem 'Exchange of Livings' is based on a personal column advertisement in the

Guardian (the 'Broad Church newspaper', as he calls it). He would also have been touched or amused by another very English attitude to religion – the idea that somehow by advertising in the personal columns of *The Times* religious doubts could be settled:

> Advertiser would like to hear from man of the world, who, having overcome religious doubts, is now firmly convinced of a future existence.
>
> *13 September 1915*

A more materialistic writer, who nevertheless seems to be hoping against hope that he may be proved wrong, tilts at the spiritualist movement, towards the end of the war:

> To Spiritualists. – The sum of 50 guineas is offered to any medium, recommended by Sir Oliver Lodge or Sir Arthur Conan Doyle, who instead of holding converse with dead men's ghosts, shall, under strict test conditions, get in touch with the spirit of the advertiser while still alive.
>
> *14 October 1918*

More Surtees than Betjeman is a character whose cheerful greetings every New Year's Day – and during the war at other significant dates – do much to liven up the page. From the sound of his messages, he must have been a crashing bore but, luckily, as readers, we don't have to listen to his views on fox-hunting or smell his porty breath. Here are his New Year's greetings:

> 1912: Fox-hunting and the Ladies, God Bless Them! – Carlton Blyth, Bude Haven.

> 1913: A Happy New Year from 'Old Coachington', Bude Haven, on the Atlantic.

> 1914: Cheeroh Friends! Carlton Blyth, Sunny Bude, North Cornwall.

> 1916: New Year's Card. – Tally Ho! Cheeroh! Good Luck! Buck up! – Carlton Blyth, (late Royal Berks), Bude, North Cornwall. Times reader 50 years.

> 1916 (October 21st): Trafalgar Day – Cheeroh! To all our soldiers and sailors from one and all in Bude. – Carlton Blyth (late Royal Berks), Sunny Bude, North Cornwall. Times reader 50 years.

> 1917: Cheeroh! Good Luck! Hats off! To Mr Lloyd George. And to all our Nurses, Soldiers, Sailors and Friends. Constanti-

nople Next! Do it now, boys. Do it now. Tally Ho! Don't Wait and See. Get there! Cheeroh! – Carlton Blyth (late Royal Berks), Bude North Cornwall. Times reader 50 years.

There is no message from 'Old Coachington' in 1918, but he reappears after the war, much the same, though sometimes hailing from more exotic scenes of jollification.

Someone of whom I am sure Carlton Blyth would have heartily approved advertises in June 1916:

Elephant wanted to purchase for heavy harness work. Hopwood, Sandygate, Sheffield.

Research reveals that in April of the same year, owing to the scarcity of carting facilities in Sheffield, Messrs T. Oxley Ltd introduced 'diluted labour' by yoking two camels and an elephant to a dray. The innovation was watched in the busy streets of Sheffield by crowds of people. The animals jogged along easily with a load of ten tons, doing the work of eight horses.

Someone Carlton Blyth would not have approved of is moved to state, on the very last day of the first year of the war:

Southport. Only fools and the dead never change their opinion. The place is really 'quite nice'.

There would, I fear, have been cold shoulders in Sunny Bude for Mr Weissberg, who changed his name in 1914 to Whitehill; likewise for Krauss, who changed to Cross, Meltzer to Milton and Weiss to Wise. On the other hand, more sympathy would have been shown to 'Modern Briton', who advertises regularly during the war with messages such as:

May God preserve the King and Christian Britain's advisers from Sentimental Racial Enemy Friends.

5 November 1915

After the sinking of the *Lusitania* by a German submarine on 7 May 1915 the personal column was full of advertisements asking about survivors. There were also those who wrote to announce their own interpretation of the event:

For how long can a crew survive on a German submarine without getting scurvy from bad air and compressed food? Study this question and look at the map! Cornwall, South Ireland, Scotland – where are the bases and the base suppliers?

22 May 1915

A scheme is also suggested, by a man of vision, for putting German prisoners of war on every ship to leave port:

What a 'Fag' for the authorities to have to put German officer prisoners on every ship leaving port. Yet it is the only safeguard. See my message to The Times April 5th last year – a month before the Lusitania was torpedoed. – J. Landfear Lucas, Spectacle Makers' Company, E.C.

27 March 1916

Rather than offering such specific advice, many advertisers were content to insert messages such as:

To the conscienceless despoilers of Reims and Louvain: 'Vengeance is Mine; I will repay, saith the Lord.' Rom. xii, 19.

22 September 1914

Others, when Woodrow Wilson seemed to be hesitating about coming into the war, inserted comments such as:

Willie – Where did you leave your hat?

30 March 1916

Willie Waits, Why?

27 January 1916

Scotia to President Wilson. Greeting. 'Nemo me impune lacessit'.

9 February 1917

Only in England could the following advertisement have appeared, in the very middle of the 'war to end all wars':

Clergyman or barrister wanted devote portion of spare time assist gentleman acquire refined accent.

22 August 1916

Civilisation appeared to be going on very much as before, despite everything, and the English were as mad as ever:

Gracious gentles grant good gay gramophone to deaden groans and grousings and gladden girl grain grower's gloamings.

25 June 1917

And perhaps it was an enraged neighbour of the girl grain-grower who advertised as harvest-time grew nearer:

Loud (second-hand) gramophone wanted for reprisals.

15 September 1917

Amid all these sturdy expressions of individualism there appears the longest 'job wanted' advertisement ever published by *The Times*. It takes up seven inches of extra fine print and, although in a short article about the advertisement *The Times* refers to 'Seven inches of qualifications', it mainly consists of the advertiser's strongly worded views on what is wrong with the war effort and what needs to be done. It gives, above all, the impression of a man driven half mad by bureaucratic muddle. Ninety lines are too many to reproduce here, but some of the comments made by the advertiser, an American by nationality, born in Britain, give a sharp impression of what the war felt like to one who, despite his very best endeavours, was prevented from contributing to the national effort:

If there is a shortage of talent surely there must be large employers or Government contractors who can use his services inside their offices or outside to travel. If no real shortage of Department Heads, then let him and similar men be told so, and they can organize themselves into regiments and march in any direction to the London Docks or to the Clyde and offer to replace all recalcitrant labour. Feels certain there are thousands of men from 39 to 55 who would be willing to do this *pro Patria*. Seems ridiculous to contemplate 300,000 old gentlemen of Home Reserve Army depicted in their shirt sleeves, according to daily illustrated Press, practising trench-digging, while goods languish at London Docks for lack of labour, or ships-in-the-building wait for men to hold red-hot rivets . . . The estimated requirements for boots for all troops fighting, if the war lasts for a twelvemonth more, are *One Hundred Million Pairs*, yet advertiser knows of one of the largest American manufacturers, after waiting five weeks in Paris, was unable to do business, and returned home in disgust . . . Advertiser offered Belgian Ambassador to organize American-Canadian Bureau for Emigration and Employment of Belgians . . . suggestion met with contumely . . . Offered services as interpreter . . . recommended by a Cabinet Minister . . . result nil . . . offered recruiting poster to the authorities . . . was informed peremptorily that they were not using such methods . . . within a week recruiting poster offices organized. If authorities would only look ahead and say what they want, men are ready to do it and take any work which will advance the cause and shorten the war . . . We must organize better to save time. Offers of employment to be sent to *Patient*.

23 March 1915

10 *Coloner Groucher, the Bul-buls and the Daring Young Men*

If there is one type of advertisement for which the personal column will always be remembered, it is that of the young man equipped with no more than an Oxford or Cambridge degree, a few modern languages and a motorcycle who is prepared to take on the world. He 'seeks adventure – anything legal', places 'self and powerful motorcycle at disposal of anybody' and is prepared to 'do anything, go anywhere'. There are also advertisements that seem specifically aimed at him: they were most frequent in the 1920s and 1930s, and they too contain the word 'adventure', often coupled with 'shooting', 'sport' and 'game'. Those were the days when there was still a British Empire for these young men to go out and explore, and beyond that empire lay parts of the world 'where the foot of no white man had ever trod'. As we have seen in Chapter 1, the most remarkable example of a 'daring young man' who found his adventure is Peter Fleming: that advertisement of April 1931 changed his life, and provided the title of this book.

There were many other advertisements Fleming might have answered. In the same month, for example, he might have joined up with this gentleman with adventure much on his mind:

> Adventure: – Much travelled ex-officer thoroughly conversant
> with film technique, seeks adventurous companions to join him
> in fitting out expedition to make adventure and travel films.
>
> *2 April 1932*

Or if he had been tempted by the lure of Spanish gold, with this group:

Adventure: – Treasure hunting, shark fishing, scientific research. Well known Topsail auxiliary schooner, expert crew, sailing for Spanish Main end of May, would take three active passengers. Total inclusive cost £350. Physical fitness imperative. Share all profits.

12 April 1932

Shackleton's last expedition in 1921, the aim of which was to explore Enderby Land, in Antarctica, advertised for a cinematographer in *The Times*. It was during this expedition that the explorer died, on South Georgia Island in the Falklands.

Wanted for 'The Quest'. – An experienced cinematographer is required for the Shackleton-Rowett Expedition to the Antarctic and the little-known islands of the Pacific. Excellent pay and all found. Selected candidate, who must be young and pass rigorous medical examination, must be prepared to leave England immediately to join the Expedition. Ex-Service man preferred.

19 November 1921

By way of complete contrast, many sportsmen contrived to enjoy a good deal of what the French refer to as '*le higlif*', and Fleming might have been tempted to join a luxury cruise, instead of going off across the wilds of the Matto Grosso with no more than a rusty rifle, half a tin of Quaker Oats and a handful of waterlogged biscuit crumbs.

Young sporting peer with luxurious, 500 ton steam yacht (eight splendid cabins with bathrooms) wishes to meet congenial sportsman or sportsmen to form a party, sharing expenses, for cruising, Cowes etc; later to Med. or Florida for big game, fishing. Open to any suggestions. – 'P', Mary's, Bury St, W.1.

10 July 1924

Alternatively Fleming might have inserted his own 'daring young man' advertisement. It would of course have been superbly worded, conveying just the right blend of romanticism and bravado in the manner of the following:

I offer my life to the most interested bidder. I can and will do anything anywhere. No risks too great. Age 22. Served Aug 7th 1914 to May 5th 1919 (Lieut. Pilot). Penchant for literature, flying and danger.

10 November 1919

That one is hard to follow – though if Fleming had written it, he would have thrown in a touch more realism and a hint of humour. It is refreshing that for once Public School or 'Varsity' are not mentioned. Alas, not all young men, even in those days, were quite so heroic; some, indeed, were a trifle limp-wristed:

> Driven by harsh family find tutorial post Christmas vacation, Undergrad, Oxford, could just bear it if work combined winter sports, Switzerland. No delicate boys, please. Been there before.
>
> *3 December 1919*

Meanwhile, roughly, in the opposite corner:

> Ex-Officer, 'a *Man*', rides, shoots, swims, drives; ex-heavyweight boxer, wants a job. – *Gentleman*.
>
> *26 May 1920*

A less ambitious applicant signs himself 'six feet of misery'; while a man in Brighton who describes himself as travelled and educated 'seeks any berth, any country; *willing to be shot to Mars*' – a safe enough offer to make in 1920. But perhaps the frankest of the 'daring young men' was this:

> Queer job abroad wanted. Ex-officer; actor, artist, singer (28).
>
> *29 September 1920*

So many of the daring young men sound as though they are really not in command of their lives at all. They offer to launch themselves into the stream 'magnificently unprepared', as Rupert Brooke put it, careless of where it might take them. Their hearts are on the sleeves of their leather flying-jackets and their heads are not screwed on very tight. It is therefore interesting to come across the occasional young man who really sounds as though he knows just where he is going, indeed has already got halfway there:

> The subject of the Evening News article 'Boy of 19 makes a fortune', thanks many correspondents for their communications which he regrets he cannot answer individually. He would point out, however, that he is not seeking investment for his capital, which is already in active use, but is desirous of obtaining one of the £2,000 a year jobs for which, it is complained, capable men are not to be found.
>
> *21 November 1921*

If that sounds a trifle brash, one could not say the same of another serious-minded advertiser who takes up three inches of column space to address 'Heads of financial houses and others with large business interests' on the subject of his qualifications, but ends, after giving his box number, with a final sentence in capital letters:

LEST YOU SHOULD FEAR SOMEONE WITH A LOUD VOICE OR AGGRESSIVE MANNER, HE APOLOGISES FOR THE TONE OF THIS ANNOUNCEMENT, A TONE HE HAS NOT ADOPTED BEFORE.

Perhaps the less said the better about the following, far from daring young man. One knows the type:

Will sporting person save graduate of famous Oxford College, who is in poor health (and has stupidly lost all his money) from having to leave the Riviera this winter? First class honours, linguist, varied competences. Any services offered. NZX, English Library, Monte Carlo.

11 October 1924

Another military man who could not be accused of aiming too high, and clearly wants to keep his head down now that hostilities have ceased, advertises:

Ex-soldier, married, seeks situation in own district as Mole-catcher; life experience; good references.

1 May 1922

The daring young men are famous, but it is less well known that the same period saw a large number of advertisements from angry, disgruntled or manic individuals, who to judge from their views were probably past middle age. They use the column to let off steam, often with highly comic effect. The tone of voice is so distinctive that the effect is that of a single advertiser, whom I picture as red-nosed, dressed in tweeds, bewhiskered, and holding a glass of port in one hand and a Purdy fowling-piece or an old bound volume of *Punch*, depending on the time of day, in the other. He makes a fleeting appearance just after the war in this advertisement:

It is hoped that the irate Colonel who, metaphorically speaking, sat on an unoffending Sub. in a West-End Tube train a day or two ago has now discovered his mistake and made peace with the third actor in the comedy.

28 January 1919

The Colonel, whom I shall refer to as 'Colonel Groucher', has parallels in fiction, most notably Nina's father, Colonel Blount, in *Vile Bodies*.

His next appearace is as a campaigner for public health:

C3 babies will arrive until production of medical health

certificate is made obligatory before marriage ceremony. A tainted-blood person who marries is worse than a Hun. And segregate infectives and by fierce penalties stop sale of foul milk. Thus and only thus (with sanitary houses) a strong nation.

18 February 1919

His political views are of the extreme right. He is of course a sportsman, and has in the main a poor opinion of fellow sportsmen:

Would the person in the green Tyrolese hat note that though it may be a custom on his own course to pocket golf balls on the fairway, it is not done elsewhere.

20 May 1919

He is, it goes without saying, an expert on what is and is not 'done':

Perhaps it would be useful to the important person in the brown Harris tweed suit to know that he will not get many games in the South London Club he contemplates joining unless he brings his own guests.

8 July 1919

The rest of the world, generally speaking, needs to be told how to go about its business. Take bus drivers, for example:

Motor omnibus drivers in London would do well to remember that they are not driving their cars over roads pitted with shell holes here; the manner in which some of them handle their vehicles is terrifying to some of the outside passengers, and the writer has observed many with the 'wind up', and frequently has it himself.

11 July 1919

People on the Underground nowadays have no manners either:

Courtesy was invented before Tubes. Fat man with offensive watch chain and manners at Charing Cross, please note.

15 July 1919

The Colonel is, one gathers, living in High Wycombe at this time. He moves about a good deal, of course, for his nature is a restless one. Apart from travelling a lot on buses and tubes, and not infrequently in his own car (he is a pioneer motorist and has a lot to say on the subject), he joins groups of commuters. He is perpetually late, and is always having to make excuses to his good lady for hours lost at wayside inns. The railways take much of the blame:

Lost – on Great Western Railway, somewhere about

Maidenhead, all sense of punctuality. Anyone – railway official included – returning same will earn gratitude of travellers on 6.50 Paddington–Wycombe train.

4 September 1914

The Colonel's lady struggles to make do on an army pension, much of which disappears during her husband's mysterious daily 'business' trips to the City. She has to do her own housework (luckily she is a practical woman), but her ideas are ahead of their time:

A slave to her own home appeals to the scientific and inventive genius of the nation to devise machinery which will perform the many distasteful, arduous and weary duties of the housewife. Such, for instance, as a boot-cleaning machine, automatic cookers, etc etc. She will further be very grateful for any information as to domestic labour saving devices at present available.

13 October 1919

However, the Colonel is blind to such banausic details, preoccupied as he is with upholding standards of behaviour:

If the individual who thought it clever to shout his remarks about a certain lady in a West End restaurant on Armistice Anniversary night has the courage to repeat them to the advertiser he may do so by making an appointment with Box Z221.

17 November 1919

People appear less and less concerned to respect even the simplest moral imperatives. The loss of his cane – a gift from old colleagues in arms – comes as a severe blow, but he puts a brave face on it:

Exchange is no robbery, but the Micawber-like gentleman at the West End Club who mistook my ebony and silver cane for his own ash mud prodder might have consulted me first.

18 November 1919

With the coming of spring, the Colonel is able once more to indulge in his favourite pastime, at the nineteenth hole of the golf club. But as he makes his way one evening, through mud and bracken, towards the welcoming lights of the clubhouse, he is appalled by the sort of people the club is letting loose on the course:

Would the individual with the handicap of eighteen and the large voice who hacks his way round a certain suburban golf course reflect that his golfing adventures do not interest other members to the extent he would think?

12 April 1920

The Colonel's lady, who has her own views about the way people go on nowadays, is also making an effort to do something about it:

Correspondence desired with serious thinking women: object cooperation women's Christian movement, working for higher moral standards.

11 May 1920

Both the Colonel and his lady are regular attendants at their local church. The Colonel also likes not to miss the major sporting events of the season – and that goes of course for the sport of kings, at which he indulges in the occasional harmless flutter, though not always with happy results:

To the smirking, top-hatted rogue who departed with my hard-earned winnings at Epsom on Friday. I have a good memory for a face, and usually get my penny back on the punching machines.

8 June 1920

During that same summer, both the Colonel and his lady are moved by the behaviour of working-class leaders to write a joint message:

The Middle Classes are at present the Corn between the Grindstones. What are they going to do if the threat of a certain section of the community is carried into effect? Will they sit down resignedly and watch the ultimate ruin of the country for which they have made, at least, their fair share of sacrifice? It is for them to show, as during a previous crisis, their determination not to be terrorised by a minority class who have been the principal beneficiaries in the vicious circle of higher wages.

24 August 1920

Later, they both join the Middle Classes Union, as some sort of defence against the outrageous demands of the miners.

It was, in fact, a near relative of the Colonel – a cousin, I believe – who inserted the following advertisement for a tutor for his two lads:

Sporty Boy Wanted, preferably Etonian or Wykehamist, age 18–23; should be resident pal to two robust boys age 7 and 6; country house, 17 miles from London; father a benevolent autocrat; mother, fat and good tempered; good wage, trough and wash. 1870 claret sometimes.

24 September 1920

The results were, as the Colonel had told him they would be, 'simply amazing'. There was an avalanche of letters. Was it the 1870 claret?

Sporty Boys. – The Benevolent Autocrat is snowed under with replies to his appeal for cub hunter. B.A. has written most likely applicants; regrets and thanks others.

30 September 1920

The advertisement was seized upon by an eccentric Vicar living in Addlestone, Surrey, who wrote an enthusiastic appraisal of it for his parish magazine. Explaining that one of his favourite hobbies was reading the personal column, he goes on to daydream in print about 'the arrival of the fortunate "Sporty" who got the job. The benevolent autocrat awaiting him in front of the fire, primed with some of his best jokes. The fat, good-tempered mother on the settee; the two robust boys, spoiled to the top of their bent. And then the trough and the 1870 claret! Attendance at church on Sundays? I *don't* think!'

Seeking to take their minds off the intransigence of the working classes on the one hand and the immorality of the Bright Young People on the other, the couple make their way up to town from High Wycombe one evening to the theatre: he going ahead in the motor, she taking the afternoon train. The play they have chosen to see is that controversial new work *The Right to Strike* by C. E. Hutchinson, about which the Women's Christian Movement had been holding discussions. Fortunately perhaps (for the Colonel is deeply shocked by the content of the play), they are hardly able to hear a thing, and the Colonel is so incensed that he insists on leaving the theatre half way through Act II:

Surely it is not expecting too much that an audience should observe common courtesy and silence while the curtain is up. The writer, at considerable expense and inconvenience, came from the provinces to witness a well-known show, and had, for his trouble, to listen to a lot of personal back-chat while the show was on. – Vox et Praeterea Nihil.

12 October 1920

The Colonel spends the following morning at his club, composing two announcements:

We are accustomed to the humours of road-makers, the inconvenience of strikes, and other minor disadvantages of living in the twentieth century, but we never shall understand officialdom which desires so much room to expand whenever it has duties to perform. Possibly it may have had some reason for entirely closing the Embankment yesterday, but whatever it was, it did not appease the exasperated businessmen – I was one of them – who were forced to waste considerable time in using alternative routes.

13 October 1920

'Pull together!' This excellent advice from our Royal Ambassador should be acted on immediately. The present conditions in the commercial and industrial world is leading the country into a state of instability which will adversely affect our prestige among those nations who have, in the past, looked to us for guidance.

13 October 1920

As the autumn wears on, the bad weather and the inconvenience of strikes evoke many more heartfelt cries from the Colonel:

It was said 'We will make this a land fit for heroes.' True! The speaker will probably turn out to be a greater prophet than he thought. If the present ruinous course of action be continued by those who would gain all and give us nothing it will only be heroes who will stay the course.

16 October 1920

The only thing to do was to organise and unite. In a moment of inspiration the Colonel remembers an old service chum who has a reputation for brains:

The Owl – Come out of retirement, old boy. There is work to do. Join me in London. We can 'dig' together. Write to Club. – Jimmy

21 October 1920

Meanwhile, the weather and the traffic get worse and worse:

One is getting quite used to obstacle dodging in Oxford Street owing to the energies of road breakers, and it seems a pity that they should ever be deprived of the amusement. An enterprising trader, however, might perhaps be able to flood the gulf between the footpaths and turn it into a 'Venetian' canal for the Christmas season. It would certainly not be more inconvenient, and ratepayers might benefit from the extra attraction to the locality.

27 October 1920

Despite the hurry and bustle of the present age, those who bark other people's shins can surely find time to utter an expression of regret. Burly man in diagonal grey, with gold chain, at Oxford Circus 1.45, please note. – Victim

12 November 1920

As the visit to *The Right to Strike* ended in such a fiasco, at the next meeting of the Women's Christian Movement the Colonel's lady decides to go up to town with another member and see the play again, just before it is due to come off. To her intense annoyance some affected woman in the row in front keeps on chattering throughout the performance:

If the lady with a lisp, who condemned a show at Hammersmith last Saturday, as being 'vulgar', would write to Box M 672 she would receive in return an exposition of the piece, showing clearly wherein she is wrong in her condemnation.

23 November 1920

Results exceeded all expectations:

That as many as six ladies with a lisp could have congregated in the same place the same day never occurred to Box M672 who however will fulfil offer made last Tuesday, if indication is given as to dress, afternoon or evening performance, and position in house.

27 November 1920

Meanwhile, the Colonel has been hearing about the new horrors which have been afflicting the sport of football, and he notices the following in his favourite column:

Missiles thrown by spectators. – Two London football grounds closed. Play the game, Englishmen. – Pure Sport.

23 November 1920

His reply, fuelled by his memory of the unfortunate incident at Epsom earlier in the year, is snappy and to the point:

Pure Sport – Abolish, as far as possible, betting on football results, and such deplorable occurrences will cease. All sport when so contaminated becomes degraded. – Old Road Rider

24 November 1920

Even as he drafts this reply, he reflects on another subject close to his heart – the infernal new taxes which are going to make it even harder to get along on his pension. To make up for the unpleasant prospect that in future his life may involve a greater proportion of 'business' and a smaller proportion of afternoon slumbers in the

Club drawing-room, he settles down to a few days of furious penmanship:

> Advertiser, realising that owing to taxes, strikes and other 'frightfulness' this is no longer a land for heroes or anyone else, would like to hear from others of a similar opinion, with a view to doing something about it.

24 November 1920

> How long is the Season Ticket farce at the Suburban Railway Stations going to last? The porter, who knows you as well as your club hall porter, is forced to make you fumble every morning to produce the wretched carton he knows so well, allowing you the honour of a ride to the City with from 15 to 18 of your long-suffering fellow citizens.

25 November 1920

> When will pedestrians be protected from the mud-splash of motor vehicles? Surely some genius can produce an effective mud-guard and Scotland Yard enforce its use. – Mud Lark

9 December 1920

The sobriquet 'Mud Lark' was chosen in a mood of irony, and causes much hilarity at the club when the Colonel reveals that he wrote this message. A fellow member of the club remarks to the Colonel that some pansy economist has been going round saying the Bosch shouldn't be made to pay for the war:[1]

> 'Pay, Pay, Pay!' – Did we win the war? If so, what about our indemnity? There used to be a custom that the loser paid, yet we are being taxed to the hilt and beyond.

16 December 1920

Owing to the grim financial outlook, Christmas and the New Year pass wearily. However, New Year's resolutions still have to be made, and one of these is in future to make more use of other facilities of the golf club than the nineteenth hole:

> Golf – Can anyone inform earnest, if lazy enquirer how he can remove rust from iron clubs without any undue expenditure of muscular energy? – Tired.

1 January 1921

Parties, such as the Bright Young People went in for, are not really the Colonel's cup of tea. He prefers to make merry with kindred spirits:

---

[1] John Maynard Keynes, *The Economic Consequences of the Peace* (1919).

'Ticklers' and such-like forms of fun are all very well, but the victims should be carefully selected. The writer had an expensive pair of eyeglasses smashed owing to the hilarity of revellers on New Year's Eve.

3 January 1921

Back in town, and now a habitual bus user, for the sake of economy, the Colonel finds time despite the increased pressure of 'business' to vent a few grievances:

Nos 6 and 6A Bus Routes – Will the two corpulent friends who habitually use these routes sit on the same seat – if they can – and give others an opportunity of sitting in comfort.

31 January 1921

Fair moustache and spats, Haymarket, 3.15p.m., 11th. – My one regret is that I did not have my riding whip with me. – Old Fogey

12 March 1921

The Colonel's lady also contributes a sensible comment:

The health of the citizen is seriously menaced by the dirt and dust that is carried by the wind from the open dust carts, especially so when they are being filled. Surely a type of cart is available that will remedy this. – Hygeia

18 March 1921

As a pioneer of motoring, the Colonel is appalled by standards of driving:

To the pseudo gentleman and party in the flamboyant cabriolet on Kingston Hill about 6.30 p.m. on Sunday. – After a few lessons in car driving I should buy a small handbook on manners. They can both be bought with *money*.

6 April 1921

A year goes by. The Colonel and his lady make a rare visit to the opera:

'During the Overture'. – Lady who was emphatic in her denunciation of 'Jim' should remember others around her are not in the least interested.

28 March 1922

The Colonel still manages the occasional trip in his motor car:

Perhaps the badly scared youth driving the new sporting two-seater near Reading will take to heart the lesson he received, and realise that a knowledge of the rules of the road, although understood by a small minority of present day motorists is helpful to those who wish to avoid the graveyard. – Pioneer

18 April 1922

During a rare train ride into town an architectural thought, born of her reflections on hygiene and the poor, strikes the Colonel's lady. Once again she is well in advance of her age and it is not until the 1950s that her vision of high-rise housing begins to be put into effect, with the disastrous results we are familiar with today:

Will anything ever be attempted to give more clear air spaces to those who live in the slums? One high building instead of 20 or 30 of the rambling hovels one passes in the train would give sunshine and happiness where it is most needed. – Visitor

20 April 1922

Meanwhile, despite the Colonel's repeated endeavours, road manners are getting steadily worse:

The time has come when motorists who are convicted of reckless driving should not have the option of being fined. Only a salutary lesson will, apparently, convince these 'road hogs' that peaceful users of the road are not out to have their nerves wrecked and their bodies maimed for their edification.

25 August 1922

That is nearly the last we hear of the Colonel and his wife. Admirers of Waugh's Colonel Blount will, however, remember his interest in the cinema – paradoxical in that the Colonel was not as a rule in favour of technical innovations – and they will recall that it led to his financial downfall. He becomes involved in making an elaborate costume drama directed by a mountebank full of high-flown talk about the cinema as art (a concept Waugh himself was always highly sceptical about). Here, surely is that mountebank, advertising in the personal column, and in view of the fact that the Colonel only makes one more brief appearance on the front page, a good deal to the west of his usual haunts, it may be that he too got involved in making a film, lost what savings he still had and was unable to make further announcements in the column:[1]

All interested in the elevation of the picture theatre by the introduction of a higher grade of film – Historical, Geographical, Classical – and willing to facilitate by the loan of armour or

---

[1] The cost of advertising went up in January 1923 to 10 shillings for two lines.

189

costumes or old houses (for photographic purposes) in the campaign of a well known film producing company with ideals and experience in this direction are invited to communicate with Box K 171.

31 August 1922

His last, brief, advertisement reads:

To the unmitigated bounder disguised as a gentleman motoring through Ledbury early Monday. – May you really get lost one day.

6 December 1922

There is, however, a footnote – an announcement inserted the following year by a wealthy bachelor, perhaps a cousin of his, which has some of the same robust assertiveness:

Advertiser is a hardworked bachelor who has to earn his living. Recently he was changing houses and had occasion to get rid of 20 trusses of hay for which he had no use. He had the temerity to suggest to his housekeeper that she, or one of an adequate staff of servants might walk 15 yards to the local dairyman or 50 yards to the local butcher and do the deal. He is informed haughtily that it is not part of the duty of a housekeeper to sell hay. Advertiser is intrigued and has purchased 20 five-shilling postal orders, which will be sent to the first 20 housekeepers who have ever been similarly insulted, and, having born with the insult, have sold the hay. – Write 'Bachelor', Box Z 148

28 March 1923

What exactly was it that made Colonel Groucher and his like so angry? Naturally, it was those Bright Young People, whose flippant and immoral goings-on were conducted in the most public way possible. They did not ignore the use of the personal column in their efforts at self-publicisation. Their goings-on included the use of stimulants of all kinds, including alcohol, and cocaine, which had become fashionable during the war. *The Times* published a strongly worded article on the subject on 14 December 1918, in the aftermath of the scandalous death of the twenty-two-year-old actress Miss Billie Carleton. The following advertisement appeared in response to the article:

The cocaine habit. – Will those interested in forming a strong anti-drug movement please write 'North', c/o Pool's, 180 Fleet St E.C.4.

18 December 1918

The abuse of alcohol was made fashionable by the cocktail craze, which made gin respectable for the first time, instead of being something drunk by Mrs Gamp. Colonel Groucher, who was shocked by cocktails and detested gin, was nonetheless hardly the man to join the anti-drink campaigners, who were soon to appear in Britain, headed by the notorious American, 'Mr Pussyfoot' Johnson:

Tanks. – Beware, Pussyfoot has arrived.

12 July 1919

'Mr Pussyfoot' was eventually routed by the united medical student population of London, who seized him during a public debate that November, and submitted him to various indignities, including sousing him with a large bottle of Bass. Colonel Groucher, who was no doubt somewhere at the back of the hall during these proceedings, must have been gratified by the students' constant refrain of 'Old soldiers never die'.

The first signs of 'The Game', which was all the rage for the next four years, appear in January 1919, with an announcement which reads: 'Shiver my timbers, I like it not', signed 'Spindles'. Such pseudo-piratical slang appears in many later advertisements, and is part of 'The Game'. Next, there is a joke, which is referred to several times during the four years of 'The Game': a joke which anyone who was a schoolboy over twenty years ago may remember. It seemed very daring and grown-up when one first heard it. The advertisement which first appears may conceivably refer to the original incident, handed down from one generation of schoolboys to the next; if so it gives some clue to locations as well as dates, a pleasing touch of authenticity. The joke itself revolves around the notorious difficulty of distinguishing between one bedroom and another in a large country house, and the similarity between one brother and another when dressing for dinner, at the point when the dress-shirt is over the head. It is a young bride who utters the words, in bell-like tones, of course, suiting her action to the words; though this announcement would appear to have been inserted by a mischievous teenage nephew:

To Father and Uncle: – 'Tingaling – aling – darling, dinner's ready.' (Peebles and Manchester papers copy.)

22 February 1919

Signs that spring is in the air are evident from the next, though the tone is still very much of the war years:

If the enthusiastic young lady, Bakerloo, Thursday afternoon, who made such charming remarks concerning a certain G.G.

191

will travel same route, same time Saturday, she may confirm
her opinions.

7 March 1919

The Bakerloo line must have been fairly humming that Saturday if
the following may be taken to be the outcome:

Failia. – And then you awoke. What a night! A great 'hold up'
certainly. Do you think the intellectual one could stay the
course? Anyway the fun is worth the money. – The Boys.

10 March 1919

'The Game' was a means of keeping in touch, challenging the wits
of fellow players, and getting as many *risqué* jokes and *double
entendres* printed as possible. It was in part a game of word
association; it had anagrammatic elements, and it even contains
occasional references to some of the personal column advertisements of the past reproduced in Alice Clay's book *The Agony
Column*.

It should be remembered that crossword puzzles had not yet been
introduced; when they were in February 1930 they absorbed some
of the functions of 'The Game'. The difference is that 'The Game'
was an active sport – you had to devise your own puzzles as well as
solve those of others – whereas crosswords were, indeed still are, a
one-way process: they set them and you work them out. The spirit in
which these coded messages and cryptic announcements were
inserted was entirely different from that which had hitherto
prevailed. Until 1919 codes had been used in all seriousness –
however ineffectually – by lovers trying to escape detection, or at a
still earlier date by men with clandestine business to conduct; now
that the telephone had been introduced, and the moral climate had
changed, the serious use of codes became obsolete. It became
instead an entertaining pastime to write coded *billets doux* and
cryptic challenges to one's friends. 'The Amalgamated Agony
Column Association' was a privately formed club, which behind a
mask of solemn mystification, concealed a group of players of 'The
Game' who specialised in anagrams, classical references and simple
codes. The content of messages was mostly very trivial: it was about
flirtations, parties, and so forth. Many of the participants were
'Pansies' or 'So's' as they were then called. The messages were
always short:

The Greater. – You may consider yourself top dog, but wait. –
The Lesser

5 April 1919

Humpty – Don't fail me this time. Two pink one white. – Printemps

10 April 1919

Fluffy – What did you do with the other two rings? – Fifi

16 April 1919

Brown Dog – Those that live in glass houses etc. This is applicable to you. – Grey Cat

21 April 1919

Robin. – It is most unkind of you, and if you insist you, not I must bear the consequences. – Lark

22 April 1919

Lucky – Don't expect me again. Company too mixed. – Sixpence

1 May 1919

Dehra – Not another rupee. Blame yourself. – Sing

2 May 1919

Punch – Nothing. Is it loss of affection or loss of memory? – Judy

2 May 1919

The 'pair' signatures are characteristic of this phase of 'The Game'. There are endless examples: Queen to White Knight; High Road to Low Road; Light to House; Match to Cigarette; Dandy to Dick Swiveller; Nina to Nautch Girl; Fly to Dragon; Kestrel to Hawk; Saucer to Cup; Pilot to Skipper; Quaver to Minim, and so on. The messages sound cryptic but are written in plain English – the style aimed at seems to be that of the famous Sibylline or oracular *Times* announcements of the genre of STOP THAT PIANO or DOORMAT AND BEANS TONIGHT. Later, codes begin to appear and the management of the column at this period seems to have been quite content to allow 'outlandish' typesetting, including Morse code, Chinese characters, astrological signs, Rosicrucian code (an example is given in Chapter 6) and even bars of music.

The criminal fringes of the Bright Young People's set, including dope pushers, betting touts and, once or twice, burglars – no doubt of the Raffles variety – can be traced in these messages. Mostly, however, it was all innocent fun. Jokes abound. Flirtations are rife. The 'So's' scintillate and tease. Some at least of the following are their work:

Match and cigarette. – Jermyn Street. Same place, same time and day this week, or write Box R.

2 June 1919

Clytie – Won't you communicate with Tongue?

25 July 1919

Argus – Retiring disposition and Victorian prudery forbade fulfilment of suggested directions. Future still masked. – Cough-drop.

29 September 1919

Jack – Rouse yourself up and be a man, and remember there are others that have more than a sneaking regard for your 'dainty little daisy in the dingle' – Pedlar Tom.

13 November 1919

Bowlie Hatt. Have you got a cough, old boy? CBDB Bot.

3 January 1920

(This may be a reference to Brian Howard, doyen of the 'So's', who is portrayed as Sebastian Flyte in Evelyn Waugh's *Brideshead Revisited*. Brian Howard while at Oxford managed to deceive the art world by mounting an exhibition of ludicrous 'modernist' paintings signed 'Bruno Hatt', which is both a reference to his name and to the slang expression 'Brown Hatter', meaning a homosexual. There is an advertisement of 4 January 1917 which appears relevant: 'Will Brown Hat communicate at once with the painter of "The Spot".')

Memphis – You will have to be fitted up with a pair of gyves, if you continue at your present rate. – Louis

8 January 1920

Bowlie Hatt – See you soon; imitaçion not verra goot. – Cocky

10 January 1920

Richard – The older the fiddle the sweeter the tune, my gay young buck – Uncle Syd

26 January 1920

Martello – Go, take wing, you shameless one, you boldfaced thing – W.J.

3 March 1920

Henrique – Don't ye hear mas'r a-callin'? – The Whip

17 March 1920

Basil – You will be meeting slap-up-to-date sporty boye-e-e-es, so don't swing the lead – Lew

7 June 1920

Nero – I will accompany you on my one-string fiddle. – The Major

12 June 1920

The following sounds like a communication between the police and an informer:

G.W. – Rumour has it that you are going to render a sweet little song on the 31st; be sure and don't fail the expectant multitude. – Old Bill

8 July 1920

However, subsequent messages every day until the end of July – 'Only four more days', 'Only three more days', and so on, ending with 'The curtain's up, the stage is set; they're waiting' and finally 'G.W. Your understudy top-hole – B.' (2 August 1920) – tend to disprove this theory. Also involved in this 'performance', whatever it was, is 'Pimpernel', who is admonished by 'Laurustinus' – 'You naughty, wicked man – don't go!'; later, 'Parsnip' appears. These two names were used by Evelyn Waugh as pseudonyms for the writers Auden and Isherwood (still in their teens at this date, so there is no suggestion that the famous pair are actually involved).

The prize for this period goes to the following dedicated follower of fashion:

My spring suit just loud enough asphyxiate snakes who dare hiss 'unfashionable'.

23 March 1922

Other popular forms of slang are the 'pseudo-piratical' (seemingly inspired by *The Pirates of Penzance*), the Latin or Hispanic, the pseudo-medieval and 'Brer Rabbit'.

The 'pirates' send each other messages such as 'Land crabs leave no trace' and 'the reef will tell no tales', and there is talk of poops and fo'c'sles, and the skull and cross-bones. 'Smuggler Bill' advises 'Starkey': 'Wait till the rocks are nearly covered . . .' and a fine roar emanates from a 'pirate' to his 'bul-buls' (nightingales), indicating that he expects to be back in action before long:

Bul-buls – 'Vast there, ye lubbers; wait till I'm out of dry dock, and ye'll want every stitch of canvas ye can clap on. – Ole Ben Dick

5 January 1923

'Brer Rabbit' slang includes:

Bob & Al. – You fellahs sut'nly take dat biskit. – Rastus
24 June 1920

Rastus – Wait till de kettle am a-singin' on de 'ob. – Loo
17 July 1920

Octoroon – Dere aint nuff to go round. What yo' gwine ter do den, fo' dis chile am nearly snuffed? – Ebe
17 December 1920

The Latin or Hispanic genre is dominated by a preposterous figure signing himself 'The Muleteer', who keeps up a regular correspondence throughout the five years 1919–24, with a series of cronies named 'The Don', 'The Matador' and, with a bit of a geographical leap, 'The Gondolier'. Various other peripheral figures – 'The Grandee of Aragon' and 'The Matelot', for instance – also join in. They are always issuing 'solemn warnings' that their patience is exhausted, or uttering threats such as:

Arouse the tiger of Hyrcanian deserts, strive with the half-starved lion for his prey: lesser the risk than rouse the wrath of – The Muleteer.
17 February 1920

Nothing, so far as one can tell, ever comes of these threats. There is a rather nightmarish illogicality about the messages, with their endless posturing and windy exclamations in Spanish or Italian. The impression they ultimately convey is of an amateur theatrical group disrupted by a sado-masochistic intruder. They irritate rather than entertain. When, after an interval of some months, the Muleteer and the Gondolier return to the scene, the Matador, no doubt echoing the feelings of other readers of the personal column, declares:

Caramba! Mios bravos, Senor Muleteer and Signor Gondolier, carry on with your siesta once again; your awakening has upset my digestion. – Matador
12 April 1922

Later in the year the exchanges seem to reach some sort of *dénouement* in a treasure hunt. Such a development at any other point in the history of the personal column might have offered a most interesting field of investigation, but after all those empty 'Olé's' and 'Ho! Ho!'s' it is hard to take it seriously. We are at too many removes from reality:

The Don, if he has a lanthorn face and black earrings, is my man, and I claim him – The Muleteer.

18 July 1922

To the Don – Stay your hand until you learn the ritual. – The Muleteer

20 July 1922

To the Don – Be at Oxford Circus 3 p.m. today. Long-arm will be there to hand you the plan and instructions. Take up usual position and drive straight off. – The Muleteer

22 July 1922

To the Don – Herewith the ritual: 'When gilded vane and turret gray are in line with ash, steps 3 × 3 and 8 × 6 shall bring you to the stones. Dig beneath the one thou seest first, for that reveals the tomb.' – The Muleteer

25 July 1922

Per Bacco! Nothing but rust and dust. – The Don

29 July 1922

The Muleteer – Zounds, Sir, you suggest I am a ninny and cannot read? Retract or you will regret ever having met – The Don

4 August 1922

There are a few examples of Irish brogue and even of Australian, but these are not memorable. There is also a large pseudo-Tudor, Olde England contingent. At a time when 'stockbroker Tudor' was becoming fashionable, it is interesting to see a corresponding trend in the Bright Young People's slang.

Perkin – How sayest thou, a goodly draught from the old leather bottle – Pistol

6 July 1922

Pistol – By the marry maskins, trow the bonny brown bowl to me. – Perkin

7 July 1922

A favourite resort of the 'Olde England' group seems to have been the public house Jack Straw's Castle, on Hampstead Heath. One is even addressed as 'Jack Straw':

Jack Straw – What ho! Thou scullion, I trow thou hast been having thy fill in mine absence. – Rufus

12 September 1922

Were some of these inserted by clever publicans, hoping to drum

up trade? Possibly, but 'Brother Merry Meads' and his 'revellers' do
not appear to be connected with any particular establishment.
Another club – probably theatrical rather than homosexual, or at
least more the former than the latter – was 'The Pixies', whose
'Master of the Revels' was always issuing exhortations such as 'All
report at H.Q. immediately' or 'What fools these mortals be!'
'Fairy' language represents the soppier side of 'straight' romance;
and when a reader signs himself 'Peter Pan', no *double entendre* is
necessarily intended:[1]

> To those responsible. – Please give us back our Kensington
> Gardens before the Spring has quite gone. – Peter Pan, on
> behalf of his friends, the children, old people and dogs.
> *7 June 1921*

'Will o' the Wisp' and 'the little elf' remind one of that bane of
Bertie Wooster's existence – Madeleine Bassett, who used to tell
him that every time a wee fairy shed a tear, a new star was born.

> Will o' the Wisp – A little elf thanks you very, very dearly.
> There were lots of horrid giants around. You saved her from
> them. The fairies bless you.
> *2 February 1921*

> Accushla – The little people whisper in your ear – Lucky Little
> People! – Dennis
> *18 July 1924*

In the midst of all this jolly light banter one or two faintly sinister
messages appear, such as 'Erb – You can roll a hedgehog, but you
can't bite it, my lad – Alf'; and these, surely, are burglars?

> Screw – First floor; frosted panes; barrel key; easy approach. –
> Tom Thumb
> *1 September 1920*

> Le Loup – Third floor, frosted. – Pierre
> *9 November 1920*

'Nutmeg' and 'Grate' sound as though they might be handling
cocaine and 'Needle' some other drug, while the following may of
course refer to an offer of winter fuel, but I doubt it:

> Celia – Kind of you, I'm sure, but I don't require any coke,
> thank you. – Quaver
> *26 November 1920*

---

[1] Any more than when, during the Second World War, a *Times* article noted after
an air-raid: 'The Peter Pan statue in Kensington Gardens has been damaged. Peter's
pipe has been wrenched downwards, though it is still held firmly in the hand'.

The conviction that *The Times* was read by burglars and other members of the criminal fraternity was firmly held by advertisers such as the following:

If the accomplished gentleman who inadvertently took Mr Harold Terry's suitcase from the Brighton–London train Tuesday last is not contemplating a histrionic career, will he return to Mr Terry at the Garrick Theatre the box of pre-war grease-paint, now unobtainable, and the manuscript of the play?

29 March 1921

Warning! Avis! Guardase! Whoever appropriated near Barnes, gold hunter (engraved RB) and chain with lion's tooth charm attached, take care! For the charm, endowed by the Keeper of the Shining Light with the power of good over evil, may cause its present owner to become acquainted with Mr Coroner, unless Box R420, The Times, is speedily notified.

31 March 1921

When players of 'The Game' were being cryptic or mysterious the rule seems to be 'the greater the code, the lesser the content'. By this time, the idea of passing serious messages by advertising in *The Times* seems to have died out altogether. 'Unnecessary anonymity and anagrammatic ambiguity spell F-O-G. – Irresolute', complains one unhappy advertiser in March 1920. It is surprising that at a time when advertisements still cost only 7s 6d for two lines, it was considered worth the expense of setting material such as:

PAMELA.   *6 May 1922*

The reply was 'M.Y.O.B. I know my notes, I count each bar' – Pamela.

And when Morse code was used, as it was on several occasions:

Dot· ·--- --·-·· ·------ ·-- - ·-- --- - - ·---- ·· ·· ·· – Dash

30 April 1920

it translates to nothing more mysterious than 'You're dotty i i i'.

The number of personal column advertisements did, however, grow considerably during the period, increasing from a column or less at the end of the war to three or four, the last of which went over onto page two, in 1919. These remarkable proportions were sustained until the mid-twenties, when 'The Game' lost its impetus. The cryptic messages helped to focus interest on the column and increased trade; and it is not impossible that when there was a dearth of real material, *Times* staff may have made some of it up themselves. When the column stretched onto page two, they took good care to see that a number of 'romantic' or 'cryptic' advertisements appeared at the foot of the column, to draw the eye down, so the rest of the column would not be ignored. Some of these were virtual repeats of material in Alice Clay's book. A trio of characters forever sending each other teasing messages, with no apparent conclusion, are 'Clarry', 'The Count' and 'Poppa'. In a direct reference to an advertisement from 1854 by E. J. Wilson, 'The Count' inserts 'Pyramus – He has sneezed' on 14 June 1922, which is followed by 'Poppa – Pockey hanky hi. Would you not like to see him? – Clarry', an obvious echo of a similarly worded advertisement from 1866. When one comes across advertisements like 'X – I can see through you. – Ray', the suspicion mounts that this is a staff insertion; and the advertiser of 'Triumph C.B. combination 4 h.p. countershaft 1917 – as brand new (£95)' must have been less than pleased to see, immediately above his offer, the line 'Rowley – She'll have to get out and push it – Dido' (16 September 1920).

That there was enormous curiosity about the column at the time is clear from an advertisement of 31 March 1922:

> I have closely studied this amazing column for 28 years and would be glad to receive any interesting views about it from others who have done likewise.

There were so many replies that the advertiser had to apologise a week later for being unable to answer more than a fraction of them. A similar advertisement appeared in January 1965. This time no apologetic follow-up was needed.

There are few truly oracular advertisements at this period. A series starting 'One, two, buckle my shoe' in May 1922 and going through the nursery rhyme at weekly intervals does not convince. However, 'Eighth step – The Lantern – Grey Goose' sounds exciting in a Buchanian sort of way, and 'A Timberwolf Bites Deep' is every bit as good as 'A Newfoundland Dog Has Teeth' from 1843. The prize for the most fatuous 'oracular' advertisement of the period goes to:

> Terra Incognita. – If you want to kindle a fire – use wood.
> *28 April 1920*

Very twenties: ligneous in every sense, embellished with a Latin tag, and including contemporary references to exploration and the unknown.

Sir Arthur Conan Doyle must have been gratified to see a number of examples of his work taking on the flesh of reality in his favourite column during the nineteen-twenties. But Sherlock Holmes's hackles would have risen when he read:

> Required. – Healthy person able to sleep during the day. No work, but good healthy sleeper essential; good wages; references. – Apply Abel-Harry, Shetland United Knitters.
>
> *16 June 1920*

For Holmes it was axiomatic that such advertisements betokened no good at all, and he would have regarded with the gravest misgivings the action of those who responded to A. C. Inman's famous advertisements in the Boston newspapers:

> Persons Wanted – who have had interesting experiences and can tell them interestingly, to talk to an invalid. One dollar an evening. Telephone Back Bay 5358 from 9.0 to 10.30 a.m. or call at Garrison Hall, 8 Garrison Street, Boston, from 7 to 8 p.m. Mr and Mrs A. C. Inman.

The results of these talks were the famous Inman Diaries (published in 1985 by Harvard University Press and edited by Daniel Aaron) of which, in view of the extensive insight they give into the sex lives of the people who came to talk to the invalid, Holmes would most certainly not have approved.

The great detective must have been keenly afflicted by nostalgia when, reading his *Times* (front page first, of course) in the cottage on the South Downs to which he had by this time retired, he came across:

> The Red-Headed League. On account of circumstances not unconnected with the bequest of the late Hezekiah Hopkins of Lebanon, Penn., U.S.A., lucrative employment for One Day Only is now available for twenty CURLY, RED-HEADED MEN who are sound in mind and body. Those who have served in H.M. Forces and have some knowledge of acting preferred.
>
> *20 January 1920*

The advertisement was, unfortunately, not evidence of anything so ingenious as Conan Doyle's story, but merely of the making of a film. There were many advertisements at this time for film actors: 'Parts guaranteed to complete novices' reads one in May 1920, 'looking for youth, beauty, personality (riding and driving essential)' reads another.

Several readers, including no doubt the retired bee-keeper of the Eastbourne chalklands, would have been highly intrigued by:

Holmes – Lxxhl – 26 xlcx 521ppk – Watson

> *23 February 1923*

Times readers of the 1920s liked to think of themselves as a fairly high-brow bunch. Occasionally they produce advertisements which might have come straight out of the Members' Queries Book of the Athenaeum:

Will any reader kindly demonstrate to Advertiser the possibility of there being any truth in Goethe's words, namely: 'To live in the idea means treating the impossible as though it were possible.'

21 July 1919

Some of those who played 'The Game' congratulated each other on their braininess:

Terry – The brilliancy of your notions leads me to think you are of a xylophagous species. – Vi

10 May 1920

Terry was a woodworm – perhaps a bookworm is meant, or was he merely boring?

'To her with the prettiest name in the world' declares an advertiser in June 1920, and then goes on with seven groups of code: NLMZN – JQGSU – SDPZT – KRLNZ – MCFOU – SQCAO – UBKCA. What she could have made of that, unless she had the relevant code book to hand, is anybody's guess.

In 1921 readers became preoccupied with Egyptology. Howard Carter's excavations in the Valley of the Kings, which led the following year to the discovery of the tomb of Tutankhamun, aroused the curiosity of the public and started a new pseudo-scientific cult based on the measurements of the pyramids and the mystical properties of the number '17'. The 'Pyramid Inch', a measurement applied to the sepulchral chambers, was supposed to reveal the dates of major historical events and to predict the future. Those interested in such dark corners of the human psyche may like to consult the personal column of 28 October 1921, 3 February 1922, 14 March 1922 *et seq*. It is not recommended to the faint-hearted.

Two code puzzles from this period are given in the Appendix. They certainly defeated me. Nor can I offer an explanation for 'Francis – Heggs is heggs – B', to which the reply is 'B – And your tortoise [*sic*] is a "ninsec" – Francis'. An advertiser asks, in January 1923, for 'a code, simple but precise, for transmitting private affairs, not business'. Three weeks later the following appears: '4 – 51 – H.e.: vy: 328. bd: 3abl: hr: 8mr: D 82: Contry – 2'. That the management was beginning to find the burden of cryptic advertising excessive is indicated by notices such as 'Will the sender of the cryptic advertisement for this column – "Goodfaith, Carbon" etc. please communicate name and address to the Chief Clerk, *The Times*, as these announcements cannot be inserted without this information, which of course is confidential.'

In the midst of 'The Game', a lone voice, clearly scandalised by the signs of decadence on every hand, appeals to a higher power:

> The clouds which have arisen from the marshes of our sins need new bursts of the Sun of Righteousness to melt them away. Shine Forth! Shine Forth!

4 September 1920

Another four years were to pass, however, before the last traces of 'The Game' with its hectic slang and racy undertones were to disappear from the front page of *The Times*. Meanwhile, in addition to the 'lone voice' just mentioned, another mystic message, first encountered nearly a century before, is repeated on seven isolated occasions. That message consists of a single word. As always, it bears no signature. The word is EXCALIBUR.

11 *Homage to Copernicus, Darwin and Freud*

The romantic side of the 1920s has dated less than its crazy, slang side. It is not hard to imagine today's equivalent of the love affair which took place in 1919 between a 'fawn costumed lady' and a man sporting a 'red and gold hat-band' who met at a library in Hove, Sussex. One can guess from his garish taste in headgear and his choice of the timid, demurely dressed lady in the library, whom he is not forthright enough to approach openly, that the man is probably a 'thumping crook' and she is 'a very ordinary little woman' (Betjeman). For the personal column daydreamer, a whole September seaside romance is evoked by this one glimpse:

> To the red and gold hat-band, Hove. – The 'fawn costumed lady' is recalled to the country, but hopes to return to the library soon. She is short-sighted, and dreadfully afraid of making a mistake. Would you really like to speak? She would be very happy.
>
> *2 September 1919*

A more sophisticated but equally romantic vision is offered by this:

> Ritz – Will the lovely lady with the slight foreign accent write to the gentleman who was fortunate enough to render her a slight service outside the Ritz last Wednesday after lunch?
>
> *4 October 1919*

Gallantry and *politesse* were still the rule rather than the exception:

> If the little lady in green velvet who dropped her lace handkerchief outside the Burlington Arcade on Saturday at

noon cares to be on the same spot, same time on Wednesday next the finder would deem it a great privilege to return it to her.

13 October 1919

Towards the end of the war, an advertiser states that he wishes to see a girl who resembles a painting illustrated in the Christmas number of the *Strand Magazine*, entitled 'Wood Nymph'. His ambitions evidently go no higher than actually wishing to view the object of his passion. His wish seems to have been granted, for he advertises again a number of times, and eventually seems most pleased with the outcome:

Wood Nymph. – Wonderful, splendid; I was spellbound. – The Watcher

15 June 1920

'Shy Lady' and 'Silent Worshipper' also correspond through the column for several weeks. Eventually, after a chance, unspoken encounter in the Members' Friends' Pavilion at Lord's Cricket Ground, of all places, the following engagingly taciturn exchange of messages seems to promise the hope of some form of consummation:

Shy Lady – Silent Worshipper in train Southampton August 31, much wishes appointment.

22 September 1920

Silent Worshipper – Shy Lady equally anxious. Write R., c/o Newsagent, 11 Henry Street, St John's Wood.

27 September 1920

The more glamorous version of 'fawn costumed lady' is her London cousin, who causes a sensation in the vestibule of the Trocadero. But 'Kindly Act', although he is to all appearances a finer and a better man than 'red and gold hat-band', does not look as though he stands much of a chance:

Lady in Tête de Nègre, Troc., Vestibule, February 3, 1.15. Will you communicate with performer of 'kindly act'?

5 February 1920

'Kindly Act'. – I cannot think why. – Brown Lady

8 February 1920

Brown Lady. – Disappointed. Thought might arrange meeting or note at least. Surely must have mutual friends if opportunity to discuss. – 'K.A.'

11 February 1920

205

That is the last we hear of the unlucky K.A. and his romantic aspirations. A romantic no doubt, in his way. Some of the 'romantics' were poets too:

> Fallen on sorrowful days. Love let me thank you for this: you were so happy with me wrapped in youth's roseate haze, wanting no more than my kiss by the blue edge of the sea.
> *31 October 1919*

> Miss Blue Mist – I, in my garret, all forlorn, think of my ladye fayre, and wonder if she thinks of me, and wonder if she cares.
> – The Wight in Grey   *3 March 1921*

But poetry has a notorious tendency to be counter-productive in affairs of the heart. A certain detachment, a sense of humour and the 'giftie' to see oneself as others see us brought success to this advertiser, as the answer shows:

> Most Beautiful Bobbiedazzler. – May you one day learn to think of him, who ever thinks of you, as other than – The Bore
> *12 February 1921*

> The Bore – Do write; so interested to hear after last Monday. – B
> *24 February 1921*

Wit, when employed by the fair sex, seems often to take the form of a put-down:

> Monty – A man, however well behaved, at best is only a monkey shaved. – Clara
> *3 March 1920*

> Toby – Manners makyth the man, not a fat cheque book. – Hilda
> *10 March 1920*

> You dear old thing – your name's Jasper: you only need a cigarette, riding breeches, hunting crop, hair the colour of a raven, and to utter innumerable 'Ha! Ha!s' and you'd make a most delightful villain for melodrama. – Joyce
> *12 July 1922*

Among the most persistent, but least successful romantic pairs of this period are two people, both of whom use the signature 'Telepathy'. They clearly believe in and to some extent rely upon this extra-sensory method of communication – and only resort to *The Times* when it lets them down, which it not infrequently does:

To my unknown friend. – Implore you to write as power of telepathy has ceased.

16 February 1920

Telepathy – Nothing would induce me to return. It is a washout.

21 February 1920

Telepathy – Not my advert, dear. All misunderstanding. Please write 'Faith', Box N.391

27 February 1920

Telepathy – Why did you not read the personal column of The Times last Friday?

13 September 1921

If 'Telepathy' had done so, he or she would have seen a note requesting a letter. The process of telepathy was evidently even more open to confusion and interference from the 'marplot' than the codes used by mid nineteenth-century lovers.

Other forms of romantic mishap are also recorded. The Grand Hotel, Eastbourne, a magnificent pile then in its heyday as a venue for the Bright Young People, saw more than one such incident:

Peace Night, Eastbourne. – If the flapper whose arithmetic or eyesight was so defective that she was unable to distinguish between room 169 and 196 will communicate with box H888 The Times, she will have the opportunity of apologising to the astonished officer in the blue pyjamas.

23 July 1919

If ---, Beachy Head, whose comments on Flapper, G.H., appeared in this column, would cultivate a little charity and less hump it would distress greeneyed monster and improve general appearance.

29 July 1919

Another seaside accident, which sounds as though it might have had thorny consequences, is tactfully laughed off:

Fair Ladies – The gentleman who collided with a rosebush at North Foreland, and his friend, thank you sincerely for the charming smiles which relieved their embarrassment.

28 September 1921

This leaves room for interesting speculation as to how the two fellows came to be entangled in the rose bush.

Even Love sometimes deferred to Class:

Eileen – It is nothing more than a question of caste; whatever others may say, I am a sahib. – Lance

6 November 1919

And if the sahib erred, there were rules laid down to correct matters, under the social code of the day:

B – The 'Amende honorable' is that your brother give me a jolly good hiding for my intentions towards you, and then, will you forgive me? – R

13 January 1920

Rupert – I suppose you will now order coffee and pistols for two, what? – Bunty

5 February 1920

The personal column does give the most revealing insights into the *mores* of the age. Changes in attitude and new crazes are instantly detectable, particularly from the messages of those who most deplore them:

Roman d'un Jeune Homme Pauvre. – Cadet, old military family almost extinct, having grappled with post-bellum conditions and achieved modicum artistic and commercial success, desires resume social intercourse with such of the breed as do not consider trade ignoble. Requisites, brains and birth. Plutocrats taboo. Dancing anathema.

18 February 1920

The 'jeune homme pauvre' was making a mistake in excluding dancing from his social life. Dancing was of paramount importance:

Will the lady in the crinoline and red velvet hair-band who danced so beautifully at the Savoy, Monday night, kindly disclose the address of her dancing teacher to Lady V., this column?

10 October 1919

No matter which sector of society one belonged to, dancing was essential if one were to get along and make new friends. People have a rather affecting way at this date of forming parties via advertisements in the personal column, a practice which says much for the degree of trust which prevailed in post-war society. Members of a particular 'set' were able to recognise each other with complete confidence, even if they had never met before, and could then establish links through mutual friends (as 'Kindly Act' hoped to do after his meeting with the lady in Tête de Nègre in the foyer of the Trocadero). Society today is too fluid for such advertisements to be a practical proposition; and the naive acceptance of class distinctions which enabled people to respond to invitations such as 'Jolly Winter Sports Party – only Sahibs need apply' is now virtually extinct. There is a special absurdity in the application of these standards to 'Bohemians' – surely 'not our type' and the least likely people to take *The Times*?

> Dancing – Few jolly Bohemian people required to complete party Victory Ball Albert Hall, and other dances and rags. Write fully Box GS92
>
> *8 October 1920*

And clearly Trev was not quite Phyllis' type:

> Trev – The ripple of the brook was very entrancing, but I prefer a good jazz band. – Phyllis
>
> *21 September 1922*

Throughout the twenties there are advertisements for teachers of the tango and the Charleston; among them, frequently, 'Varsity man, gold medallist, gives private lessons' and 'Syncopated music taught by professional expert'.

Another indication of the way things were going appeared in 1924, when the wilder flights of 'The Game' had ceased and the column was returning to a more sober state. This was an advertisement by the British Fascists, a movement which had recently been formed in the wake of Mussolini's seizure of power in 1922. Their future leader, Sir Oswald Mosley, was at this time a newly elected Labour M.P. and did not embrace the cause until after his visit to Mussolini in 1932. The Fascists' lack of any ideological base is clearly shown in these early advertisements, which offer nothing more than the hope of combating Communism:

> British Fascists. – Those interested in fight against Communism, and who wish to join and help, apply Hon Sec, 71 Elm Park Gardens, S.W.10.
>
> *4 June 1924*

A most romantic-sounding series of advertisements appeared in 1930, but in fairness to the reader I should point out that their meaning is not quite what it might at first seem:

> Oswald – Merci pour les fleurs. Oui j'ai trouvé le petit mot dedans. Trop de monde au Palais de la Mediteranée, trop de monde au Majestic. Cherchez autre combinaison. – Diana
>
> *3 January 1930*

Diana – Can't you get D. to arrange skiing party to Beuil? – Oswald

5 January 1930

Oswald – Truly, pleasure never dies. 'Twas immense sweetness to be with you at D's skiing party in the great white ocean of snows at Beuil. Mother is talking of going for a weekend of skating at Piera Cava. How vivid the Mediterranean looks from the mountains! – Diana

7 January 1930

Diana – At last we'll have a grand opportunity to meet, I hope. You know the 'All Spain' masked ball at the Palais de la Mediteranée, February 15? Well I hear the mystery room under the grand stairs will be open that night. When you design your costume, let me have its description. – Oswald

9 January 1930

Oswald – How do you get that way? as my American friend says. Mother and D. waiting for me at the opening of the Casino at Juan-les-Pins. I don't propose to see you again. – Diana

11 January 1930

Diana – So, after all, he and your mother have won. I don't believe you ever cared for me. I saw you at the Majestic, as you were strolling in its gardens. – Oswald

14 January 1930

Diana – Your silence confirms my belief. If you had ever really loved me you wouldn't have minded. I talked it over with J and B. I went over to the Provençal to see them. – Farewell. – Oswald.

16 January 1930

Oswald – I may forgive you. Meet me at the Palais de la Mediteranée. Perhaps I'll tell you my costume for the 'All Spain' Ball. – Diana

19 January 1930

Oswald – Please see me. Peter has cleared the way. Really, he was Peter's friend, not mine. Why won't you answer? I saw Jane at Le Provençal and she has promised to talk to Mother. – Your Diana

21 January 1930

Oswald – Please be nice. I'll meet you anywhere. Mother is so worried. I can't tell her. I didn't know it was possible to suffer

so, and in such a lovely place. O! why did I ever listen to you? –
Forever your Diana

22 January 1930

Diana – I will give you one more chance. Everybody on the
Riviera is preparing for the wonderful costume ball, 'All
Spain', at Palais de la Mediteranée February 13. That 13 may
be your lucky number. How recognise you? Will you wear the
shawl your grandmother gave you? – Oswald

5 February 1930

Oswald – Wonderful! Mother has consented to let me go to
Palais de la Mediteranée 'All Spain Gala'. She hopes I'll win
prize for most beautiful shawl. Meet me Majestic garden –
night – you know – Diana

8 February 1930

Diana – I have telephoned England send out my Toreador
costume for Palais de la Mediteranée 'All Spain' Gala. Great
enthusiasm Riviera about it. Dancing, I'm told, allowed till 8
morning. Peter is looking for a partner. Whom do you suggest?
The one from Le Provençal with the motion-picture eyes? –
Oswald

11 February 1930

Although no more than a clever piece of advertising copy, the piece
has considerable period charm and the choice of those two names –
Oswald and Diana (a clear reference to Lady Diana Cooper, whose
'motion-picture eyes' were the most famous of the age) – was sure to
catch the attention of the socially conscious.

The number and quality of romantic messages fall off markedly
after this date. (Perhaps lovers did not want to risk sounding
like advertisements for hotels.) The column's quota of oddities
and idiosyncratic announcements of all kinds does not diminish,
however.

Just after the war a Mr Clarkson prints an apology, very much
regretting that in decorating Mr & Mrs Claude Watney's house, at
No 20 Charles Street, Mayfair, in honour of the state visit of
Marshal Foch to London, a German flag was by mistake exhibited.
(Foch, it should be remembered, was commander in chief of Allied
forces at the end of the war, so this was an error of rather
magnificent proportions.) The eccentric Colonel 'Black Sheep'
Meinertzhagen writes from the Hotel Majestic, Paris, appealing for
details of observations of migratory birds; a Mr Gulliver seeks to
hire a dirigible from which to drop bags of sweets by parachute on
Peace Day; and someone with a rare sense of priorities regards the

theft of his sportscar as less important than the loss of a borrowed book:

> Will the kind friend who removed a yellow Perry Coupé from the Winter Gardens, Bournemouth on Wednesday evening last, kindly return the copy of 'Rough Road' found in the pocket, to the address on the flyleaf, Chelmsford, as it was borrowed?
>
> *18 September 1919*

Unusual medical advice is offered by an elderly lady:

> Yellow belting – To achieve desired results absolutely essential violently shake patient before applying treatment, which should then be quite satisfactory. Otherwise patient derives scant benefit and has little chance of responding to treatment. – Grandmother
>
> *26 September 1919*

'Maskelyne's Magic Theatre' requires the services of the ugliest woman in the world to appear in an illusionist's act ('no stage experience necessary') and Carlton Blyth, 'Old Coachington' to his many friends, who did so much to boost morale during the war years, continues to send messages of good cheer:

> Cheerio To All Dear Old Friends. – Carlton Blyth, Cap d'Ail, 'A.M.', France
>
> *2 January 1922*

> Tally Ho! Good Luck! Cheerioh! 'The Captain', 'Old Times', London and Brighton Coach. Peas Pottage New Years Card. Captain and Mrs Carlton V. Blyth wish their very many friends and relations a Bright and Happy New Year. – Tilgate Forest, Crawley and Bude, Cornwall.
>
> *1 January 1923*

Carlton Blyth's move to Peas Pottage betokens the start of a campaign of agitation to improve the London–Brighton road, and messages in 1925 and 1926 add rhymed slogans such as 'Council awake and cease to snore: A Path provide and sleep no more!'

Someone offers advice on feeding newts; a Mr Seiveking has a full-grown skeleton (male) for sale in a crate, for £10; Box K has for sale a genuine Russian icon presented to the present owner and signed on the back by the notorious Rasputin; and a Mr Reid Moir advertises for information as to the whereabouts of the Foxhall Jawbone:

> Jaw Bone – Information wanted regarding whereabouts of

human jaw-bone found in 1855 in coprolite pit at Foxhall, near Ipswich, Suffolk and described by R. H. Collyer M.D. in Anthropological Review 1867. Supposed to have been taken to America. – Reid Moir, Ipswich

11 March 1919

The interesting feature of this jawbone is that, if genuine, it proved the presence of man on this planet during the Pliocene age, which lasted from roughly twelve million to two million years ago. Discoveries at Piltdown in Sussex a few years earlier had proved to the satisfaction of some the existence of a 'missing link' going back to the beginning of the Pleistocene (roughly two million years ago). The Foxhall bone was distinguished by a curious metallic lustre, deriving from the fact that it was completely impregnated with salts of iron, which abound in the Foxhall coprolite beds. Nothing more has been heard of the bone, but in this context it is interesting to recall the case of the dinosaur's rib-cage, also showing ferrous stains, found in Morocco in 1930, which proved, on the discovery of the manufacturer's name-plate, to be the remains of an American hay-making machine.

Something of the luxury of life in those early years between the wars can be seen from some of the more mundane advertisements. A 36 h.p. Delaunay-Belville is offered for sale in 1919 for £850 ('seats five, finished in Spanish mahogany with separate armchairs and silver toilet set; crystal accessories'); a young married couple are offering a lift to Monte Carlo by Rolls-Royce ('extra smart chauffeur, sporting body'); a lady 'having lost all her money in Russia' wishes to sell her priceless Russian sable cape; a Villa at Èze-les-Pins is offered to let furnished for the season ('eight best bedrooms, eleven servants' rooms, hard and soft tennis courts'); and Joan of Arc's breastplate and sword are for sale ('Best offers, inspection invited'). Oh yes, and there's a lighthouse for sale in perfect order ('immediate possession, magnificent position').

There is a fondly-worded dog obituary – something of a rarity:

Beelzebub, a brindled bulldog, with a large circle of acquaint-ances, died suddenly, 3rd February 1921. Inquiries or ex-pressions of sympathy will cause additional pain to his Host and Hostess.

More than one legless female advertiser – or perhaps it is the same one – asks for advice as well as help of a more tangible kind: 'Would sympathiser provide impoverished lady with artificial leg?'. Silks from Napoleon's dining room, as well as hair from Nelson's head ('given to Peninsular officer, with authenticating papers'), are on offer, as is Captain Cook's telescope; and a 'genuine Rubens painting', *The Head of Circe*, is offered for sale by a Mr Churchill in Fulham.

The comedian Stanley Lupino wants a parrot ('only African Greys, Amazons or Macaws considered. Must not swear. Good fee paid for one taught to say "Good morning, Stanley Lupino" ') and an odd but invaluable piece of advice is offered to visiting tourists:

> Visitors to London are perhaps unaware that it is not customary to offer gratuities of sweetmeats to policemen for services rendered. – Bow Bells

8 July 1921

There is an announcement from a Professor Soddy to the effect that someone is fraudulently using a letter written by him, referring to tests made of a process alleged to make gold. Schemes for making gold by alchemy were enjoying a vogue at the time, particularly in Germany, owing to the effect on the economy of reparations. The efforts of alchemists reached a peak in 1931, when a charlatan named Tausend caused a lump of gold to appear from nowhere in the presence of leading German bankers, including Herr von Lentze, Director of the Administrative Council of the Deutsche Bank, who pointed out that, after all, Frederick the Great had supported the work of alchemists, so why shouldn't the tradition continue?

More easily bankable assets awaited an Oxford man who in December 1921 is the subject of one of those advertisements all personal column readers dream about:

> To Charles Lionel Howard Hannay Esq (formerly of Oxford and who resided in Cape Town about two years ago). There is a substantial sum of money awaiting you in respect of a portion of your interest under the will of your late uncle . . .

In reality, these advertisements are exceedingly rare and the chances of finding that one is to benefit from a bequest by reading of it in the personal columns are even smaller than the chances of winning the football pools.

One of those unsung pioneers of industry, who can have derived few bankable assets from his far-sightedness, advertises:

> Atomic Power. – Will all persons interested in this important scientific subject write at once to Major Huntley, 1/4 Copthill Chambers, E.C.2.

25 January 1922

The interest aroused by the above advertisement was very much less than that produced by an advertisement inserted by the manager of the Savoy Laundry, in June 1922, for a girl with a university degree, to answer the telephone. Even greater amazement was caused when the same gentleman, after a few days, was forced to announce:

> The Manager of the Savoy Hotel Laundry thanks the many hundred ladies who replied to his advertisement in The Times on Friday last and regrets that he is unable personally to answer all the letters. The position will be filled by one of the thirty applicants holding a university degree.

'I wanted a trained brain', explained Mr Neame to a *Times* reporter. 'This is not telephone operating in the ordinary sense . . . it is a job that requires judgement and tact of a higher order.' The candidates were made to pass a series of tests designed to test their tact, resource, pertinacity and speed of judgement. They were invited first to get into telephonic communication with someone not on the telephone; then told to deal with a customer who rang up asking for the van to call half an hour after it had left the laundry – the problem being to ascertain where the van was likely to be at that moment and then decide which of the next few customers would least mind being asked if they could speak to the van driver on their telephone. The newspaper featured the story on the centre page between 'Sunshine and breezes – Need to Conserve Water Supply' and 'The Prince's Return – Royal Welcome Plan'. It must have been a slow day for news.

Among other bizarre advertisements which appear at this time are 'Wanted for chemical research: mistletoe grown on oak. Please write without sending plant'; 'inspiration in rotation – poet journalist supplies rhymes for the new advertising'; 'the hand in relation to evolution. Appointments. Hotel Vandyke'; and an early advertisement for yoghurt:

> Bulgarian Lactic Acid Bacillus. Metchnikoff; proved to eliminate self-poisoning, gastritis, dyspepsia and all stomach complaints. Write for leaflet, New Research Co, Blandford Road, Teddington.

> *7 January 1926*

A good try at an out-of-the-rut campaign, but lacking in mass appeal. As with the gas industry in 1806 and atomic power in 1922, so with the milk products industry in 1926; readers of *The Times* personal column were given the chance to get in on the ground floor of major technical innovations – but how many of them took that chance? The gap between the innovator and his market has never yawned so wide; not even the rotational inspiration of the poet-journalist was adequate to bridge it. (The mistletoe research chemist, we may one day learn, invented super-glue, but lacked the marketing ability to make it stick.)

'Homage to Copernicus, to Charles Darwin, to Sigmund Freud, and to Truth', someone announces on 13 January 1926. 'Homage to Frederick Winsor, to Major Hartley and to the New Research Co. of Blandford Road, Teddington' would seem a fitting response.

A small advertisement appeared on 11 December 1926 which failed to attract any attention:

Friends and relatives of Teresa Neele, late of South Africa, please communicate. Write Box R.702

It later transpired that 'Teresa Neele' was the name under which Agatha Christie had registered when she arrived at the Hydro Hotel in Harrogate at a time when she was under great mental stress. The reasons for Agatha Christie's mysterious disappearance from her house 'Styles' at Sunningdale and her flight to Harrogate under an assumed name lay in the two great emotional blows she had recently received, from the death of her father and the break-up of her marriage with Colonel Christie. Her car was found halfway down a slope at Newlands Corner near Guildford. Various mysterious clues were found by reporters, who swarmed everywhere, having the time of their lives and, despite heavy mists, several hundred people combed the area, assisted by a lady with three pedigree blood-hounds. But no further clues were found.

Exactly what happened during the 'lost fortnight' is not known, except that the writer seems to have lost her memory and wandered off to Yorkshire in a state of confusion. It was not until December 14th that the real identity of the occupant of the hotel room in Harrogate was discovered. Colonel Christie escorted her back by train, taking elaborate precautions to ward off journalists. The couple were granted a divorce two years later, and in 1930 Agatha Christie married the archaeologist Sir Max Mallowan.

Agatha Christie herself made use of agony column advertisements in a number of her books – most notably in *A Murder is Announced*, which was written over twenty years after the events just recounted. Clearly a personal column enthusiast, she describes how nine out of ten readers of that lesser organ the *North Benham News & Chipping Clegham Gazette*, after a cursory glance at 'Correspondence', turn straight to the personal column, where a host of fascinating messages are grouped together higgledy-piggledy. However, enthusiastic as Agatha Christie might have been for the idea of the personal column *per se*, she was no friend of *The Times*:

> Mrs Swettenham, pushing back the little grey curls from her forehead, opened *The Times*, looked with lack lustre eye at the left hand centre page, decided that, as usual, if there was any exciting news *The Times* had succeeded in camouflaging it in a respectable manner; took a look at Births, Marriages and Deaths, particularly the latter; then, her duty done, she put aside *The Times* and eagerly seized the *Chipping Clegham Gazette*.

It is in the *Gazette* that the sinister announcement is inserted of the murder which is to take place at Little Paddocks. Of course nobody takes it seriously – but that is ever the way with agony column announcements.

An advertiser who appears to be positively asking to be written into an Agatha Christie novel makes a curious request on 2 May 1929:

> A solitary old gentleman, who must not read much, seeks advice on how to employ two long weary hours per day.

It is to be hoped that the old gentleman did not take up the offer made a fortnight later by someone signing himself 'Joe, 41 Half Moon Street' advertising cases of '1830 Brandy, genuine' at 30s a bottle ('few cases for disposal at this incredible figure'). His neighbours would not have had to call in Miss Marple to discover the cause of death.

Many people's memories of the year 1929 are far from happy ones, so it is pleasant to know that there were those around who made a sincere effort to cheer up their fellow men:

> A few jokes on accountancy, banking, insurance, law and shipping required. Can anyone oblige?
>
> *31 October 1929*

Probably not. This was a time 'when jokes were few'. The Wall Street Crash had occurred the day before.

It is with a feeling of relief that one turns from this to the usual pot-pourri of oddities. Mr Nigel Playfair (grandson of the inventor of the Playfair Cipher) has lent a pair of valuable black velvet curtains to someone for a play and cannot remember who. Would they please communicate with him at the Lyric, Hammersmith? A small party is to be taken to hear the nightingale next week (apply to the Homeland Association, Covent Garden); an historical Royal

bath of white marble which cost Sir Robert Peel £550 is being sold
for 200 guineas; a lady with a two-seater seeks engagements at 6d
a mile; and, on St Valentine's Day 1931, 'Do any Anglo-Indians
remember the Curse of Delhi?'

There is a rather special car for sale in November of the same
year:

> 1929 45 h.p. Special Hispano Suiza 'Barker' Sedanca de Ville –
> battleship grey with polished aluminium specially lengthened
> bonnet, silver-plated fittings, etc . . .

The car belonged to Lady Louis Mountbatten, who was going away
to Malta with her husband for two years.

Returning to the theme of inventors and marketing, a remarkable
labour-saving device, not yet in widespread use, was advertised as
follows:

> Domestic invention of the age needs marketing. Cheap,
> simple, labour-saving bed-making device; irresistible appeal to
> millions. – G. A. Shakespear, 20 North Common Road,
> Ealing.

18 August 1933

The idea caught the imagination of *The Times* and is given top
billing in Home News the following day, where details are provided
of how the bed-making machine worked. The device apparently
consisted of three specially prepared rods. Bedmaking proceeded
by placing the sheets and blankets in alignment at the foot of the
bed. The loose rod was then placed across the bedclothes, which
were wrapped round it once, and on top of them was placed a clip
consisting of the two other rods, held together by springs which
were passed over the 'loose' rod so that it was firmly held. The
bedclothes were then hung over the mattress at the end of the bed,
so that they retained their orderly position. The unitary effect
produced in this way saved at least five minutes per bed per
housewife per day – an enormous boon to mankind. Had the device
caught on, we might have been spared the horrors of the duvet.

During the Spanish Civil War the personal column served as a
means of contact among those who formed voluntary groups to fight
for the Republican cause. Advertisements such as 'Jack – Situation
clearer; get in touch or report to D.E.N.I.N.O.', which appeared
in July 1936, testify to this activity. Another side of the war can be
seen in:

> The passengers of M.V. Palacio desire to express by this means
> their appreciation and thanks to the commander (Capt. V. St.

J. Phillips) and crew of the vessel for their devotion to duty, whereby all on board were brought safely out from Seville during the Spanish Revolution.

28 July 1936

The following Christmas a lady living in Eaton Square caused a great stir by advertising, very simply, 'Wanted – A brown donkey'. In a number of articles celebrating these four words Robert Louis Stevenson's *Travels With a Donkey* are cited, suggestions are offered as to which big London stores should stock donkeys as seasonal pets and editorial eyes grow dewy with nostalgia and Christmas spirit. It seems unfair that a similar degree of publicity was not accorded to the much more unusual advertisement placed by a Scottish Colonel a few years earlier:

To scientists, zoologists etc. – A freak of nature for sale. A Clydesdale horse hermaphrodite, aged, very quiet, good worker. – Offers to Col. Forbes, Rothiemay Castle, Banffshire

11 August 1919

A worrying note for lovers of the personal column is struck by reactions to a small announcement made in February 1938 by the Torquay Jig-Saw Puzzle Club. All the Club's advertisement offers are a few vacancies for new members, but the moral drawn from this is that, while of course jig-saw puzzles were all very well in the good old days, now that most homes had a wireless set and crossword puzzles had become so popular, the days of the jigsaw puzzle were numbered. The advent of the crossword puzzle in February 1930 was indeed a severe blow to devotees of the personal column; somehow, its fate and that of the jig-saw puzzle seemed linked. One could scarcely imagine all those scientific brains who devoted so much of their time to solving and devising coded messages for the column having enough spare time left over to continue doing so after solving a *Times* crossword every morning. The evidence is there in the column, for codes virtually disappear after 1928. The personal column, as a haven for cryptic brain-teasers, was on the way out.

The other functions of the column, as a place to buy and sell unlikely objects, air one's grouches, warn the populace of the loss of one's animals, and make clandestine appointments under the clocks of railway stations all continue to flourish. There are subtle changes as the years go by, from which the social historian may be able to derive food for thought. A 'Come home' message of the late 1930s shows a new and altogether more enlightened attitude to erring offspring:

Jack – Admire pluck: come home when you like; anxious to know how you are. Telephone home on transfer charge, no cost to you.

29 June 1937

Only seventeen years previously another parent had advertised:

Boy – It isn't for you to make conditions, but for us. – Father.

And in 1920 another anxious autocrat asked: 'Will any parent having similar anxiety give an Englishman advice as to successful treatment of son 16½, of gentle birth, lacking all sense responsibility and truth?' and went on to state that the boy, although of excellent physique, charming manners and 'no vice', was unbalanced and unreliable. 'Medical hypnotic treatment' had proved unavailing.

A different kind of problem was posed by a headmaster's dog advertised in the column in January 1938. The headmaster had just retired, but the dog, Pan, a four-year-old Newfoundland, refused to retire with him. Whenever Pan saw a group of boys, he would rush up to them wagging his tail and refuse to be parted from them. The headmaster therefore announces that he is prepared to make a free gift of Pan to any other headmaster prepared to offer the animal scope for the continuation of his scholastic calling.

Animal lovers were alarmed to see, in March of the same year, the announcement: 'Wanted – 10,000 budgerigars'. Suspecting that (as a *Times* leading article put it) 'behind such a demand lay designs for Apician ecstasies of the palate' and speculating grimly on the relative mass of the tongue of the budgerigar as compared to that of the flamingo, a well-known delicacy in ancient Rome, wise men of the newspaper decided that this unusual advertisement needed investigating and deputed a humbler member of staff to look into it. However, the humbler member of staff discovered that the BBC had a programme called 'In Town Tonight' which was broadcast every Saturday evening, and that a few weeks previously a budgerigars to recite nursery rhymes, and the Camden Town pet-rhymes on the programme. The popularity of the bird had soared since this performance. Everyone, it seemed, wished to train budgerigars to recite nursery rhymes, and the Camden Town pet shop which inserted the advertisement – it was in fact the same pet-shop in Parkway from which the five children in E. Nesbitt's books rescued their magic 'Psammead' – was desperate for supplies. Dr Johnson, *The Times* leading article concluded, would not have approved. 'Not for any clever artifice would it be worth while to risk the enchanting ways of the untutored bird.'

In the months leading up to the Second World War there are indications of various makeshift attempts by advertisers at 'digging in for the duration' in situations as safe and comfortable as could be devised. The contrast between these months and the period immediately preceding the First World War could hardly be more marked. No more 'To all that call themselves English Gentlemen – are you ready to defend your country?' No more 'dashing into the great venture'. As early as February a hotel is advertising bomb-proof shelters alongside their other luxurious facilities, specifying that these were 'deep underground concrete Air Raid Shelters with filtration plant, telephone and every convenience'.

Two months before the beginning of the war a visionary, oracular voice declares, with uncanny accuracy:

Savannah – Six lean kine – Pete.

30 June 1939

The war indeed lasted just six years.

In order to prevent the exploitation of the personal column by German spies, whether female and glamorous or otherwise, no codes of the more obvious sort are henceforth allowed to appear. The suspicious might nevertheless view the following as an odd request, possibly concealing some more sinister intent:

Uncle! – How can I keep two fishes for nine weeks?

12 July 1939

Eight weeks will do, nephew.

No inventors come forward with 'fogometers' or other indispensable aids to battle, but the marketplace is full of curiosities: a fragment of the Holy Thorn, 'with authentication document', and Napoleon's couch are for sale in August; meanwhile the letters ARP (Air Raid Precautions) creep into more and more advertisements, and appear as an essential stimulus to all sales – houses, dogs, yachts, even the services of 'Universal Aunts' – all could be seen to offer new advantages under the alluring light of ARP.

A sardine's eye-view of rural cosiness is conjured up by the following advertiser, who had perhaps not experienced at close hand the corrosive effects of the artistic temperament on the bourgeois conventions of manners and personal hygiene:

ARP Evacuation – Offer to share with professional woman quiet pretty cottage in heart of Cornwall; preferably writers or painters; sleep eight in emergency.

25 August 1939

How long that cottage remained quiet and pretty one dreads to

221

think, for the creative life, as the advertiser was no doubt soon to discover, is one continual emergency.

A more worldly wise advertiser, with an intuitive grasp of the priorities in a survival situation, announces:

> In the event of war. – To let furnished. Sussex cottage, large well-stocked garden, 2 reception 4 bedrooms; electric light, telephone, excellent ex-naval manservant, total exemption, remaining.
>
> *25 August 1939*

The word 'exemption' is the key, soon to acquire in the eyes of the market-place a value far exceeding those peacetime epithets 'qualification', 'experience' or 'training'.

'ARP Movable Home Luxurious Steel Barge Yacht'; 'ARP Strong Cellars'; 'ARP – a happy retired life awaits you in Sunny South Africa'; 'ARP solid stone warehouses, Dorset'; 'ARP chose your own safety zone: full-size buses (seats make excellent beds)'; and, last but not least, 'ARP Dogs':

> ARP Dogs. – Happy temporary home for your pet dog. In the heart of the country. Personal care and attention. Mrs Bell, Colmouth, Beds
>
> *29 August 1939*

Phrases such as 'If storm bursts' occur in personal messages, and there is a rare public announcement concerning Tower Bridge:

> ARP Tower Bridge: Notice is hereby given that on receipt of an Air Raid Warning the Bascules will be raised and Tower Bridge closed to road and pedestrian traffic. – Alfred T. Roach, Town Clerk
>
> *31 August 1939*

The storm burst on September 4th. Readers of the personal column were not allowed to remain in ignorance of events. The top right hand corner of the front page of *The Times* for that day carries, above the usual advertisements, in letters nearly half an inch high, the announcement BRITAIN AT WAR: LATEST NEWS.

12 *Battling with Sea Monsters*

To the great credit of *The Times* and of those who advertised in the
personal column there is not the slightest indication that it was ever
used during the Second World War either for espionage or by black
marketeers. Of course there were rumours – that the names of
battleships were contained in crossword puzzle clues, for instance,
but these were all without foundation. Critics may cavil at
the newspaper's staunch advocacy of appeasement in the years before the war, but the front page, at least, remained blameless.
Furthermore, although owing to restrictions on newsprint the
newspaper itself was cut down to a fraction of its former size, the
whole of the front page continued to be devoted to classified
advertising. Aware of its importance as a means of communication
in wartime, the management, while keeping a watchful eye open for
suspicious-looking messages, continued to promote the column in
pamphlets headed 'Front Page News'. They point out that not only
did *The Times* carry a greater volume of classified advertising than
any other daily paper, but its 'small' advertisements could be
described as a 'national institution' and as a part of 'the great social
register of the nation'. Despite wartime shortages, space would
continue to be found for the personal column.

No fault could be found with any of these sentiments or
provisions; the same spirit, however, did not prevail at the offices of
The Daily Telegraph. Far from purging the columns of their
classified section of all cryptic material, the editorial staff (I have
this on the authority of the widow of an Assistant Editor) made up
some coded messages to make the column more interesting. Soon
afterwards they received a visit from 'Intelligence'. Experts, it was
explained, had been unable to decode certain suspect messages in
their columns . . .

No doubt *Times* staff were fully aware of the provenance and true meaning of every message that appeared in the column during the war years, but at this interval of time it is interesting to speculate whether, for instance, it was Evelyn Waugh who inserted 'Elaine – Hope your strange adventure ended happily – E.W.' or Humphrey Bogart who was being addressed in 'Bogey, I'm coming along, with me shillelagh under me arm – P.A.' There are few traces of the illustrious in the columns during the years of the six lean kine.

The day after the outbreak of war a far-sighted advertiser, with an eye to ensuring the safety of Whitehall administrative staff, announces:

> Bomb-proof – Westminster. – For those who must stay in London, small house near St James's Park: concrete roof, staircase, 4 very thick concrete floors, basement sitting room, safe. No agents.

Careful precautions were taken by a Member of Parliament who inserted one of those notices declaring that he would not be responsible for his wife's debts – or his daughter's, he adds, to make doubly sure. For once, to the credit of the female sex, wife and daughter answered back, stating that they had read the notice inserted by the Honourable Member and for the protection of their reputation desired it to be known that neither of them had incurred or had any intention of incurring liabilities justifying the insertion of such a notice.

Shortly after this, a sea captain called for Service offers for sale his African Grey parrot ('exceptional talker, mimic, sings, dances, entertains'); shoppers are enjoined, on the advice of Professor Hilton, to save paper by using string bags ('your purchase will help toward the maintenance of the war blinded'); an antique church bell is for sale (engraved '1680 James Bartlet made me weight 1c 3q 16');[1] a lady giving a telephone number offers a hand-vibrator for sale ('price available on application'); and there are many other indications of the survival of the entrepreneurial spirit. Barry Neame, of the Hind's Head Hotel, who offers his seasonal greetings to readers throughout the war years and bids fair to outdo 'Old Coachington' in popularity, announces:

> Eton College. At the request of several parents a motor coach will run on Sundays at 1 p.m. from 'The Burning Bush' to the Hind's Head Hotel, Bray, returning about 3.15 p.m. When

---

[1] The bell would not have been of much practical use, as there was a ban on bell-ringing during the war.

possible, seats should be booked in advance. – 'Mine Host'
Barry Neame.

11 October 1939

Mrs Horace Farquharson, who in the years immediately before
the outbreak of hostilities, had offered her advice on the conduct of
debutantes, weddings and social affairs generally, now, sensing the
emergence of other priorities, announces 'War brings family
problems. Mrs Horace Farquharson advises'; various basement
restaurants in Soho point out the advantages of the fact that they are
'completely underground'; and a writer with an optimistic attitude
advertises:

Author of 'War, wine and women', expert French scholar,
would represent any newspaper on French front.

Someone else, with the right spirit, announces:

Win the war. – All willing to help rouse national will to victory
write Box E.

22 December 1939

As during the previous war, however, advertisers' main priorities
are bound up with 'Man's best friend'. In the first week of the war
'Louie May's Dog Shop' in Elizabeth Street is quick off the mark
with 'All plans complete for the immediate evacuation of your dog
and cat to a safe country place'; and an appeal from Mr and Mrs
Ionides for wartime homes for their pet poodles meets with an
overwhelming response:

Mr and Mrs Ionides desire to thank the several hundred
sympathisers (known and unknown) who have written, telephoned and telegraphed them at Buxted Park offering help and
accommodation for their poodles. Owing to this kindness none
of the dogs need be destroyed.

3 January 1940

Someone signing herself 'Mae' declares 'Do not destroy old
fashioned English fox terriers. They are far better than cats for
killing rats, mice, black beetles and wild rabbits.' Later in the war
there are advertisements from bodies such as the Canine Defence
League, some of them quite strongly worded:

Dog owners. – Please do not pay more than controlled prices
(6d and 8d a pound raw and 7½d and 10d a pound cooked) for
meat for dogs. Also protect your dog's health by refusing to
buy mixtures unless you know their contents and that your dog
will not suffer from them.

In 1941 great alarm was caused by an advertisement asking for 'One thousand male kittens' and a *Times* leader raises the horrid notion that 'that ingenious pieman, Mr Brooks, is reincarnate':

'They're all made o' them noble animals' says he a pointin' to a wery nice little tabby kitten, 'and I seasons 'em for beefsteak, weal or kidney, 'cordin to the demand.' Dismissing this hideous thought . . . a more pedestrian surmise: the kittens may be wanted for training in the Home Guard against invading mice.

Evidence of the survival of the proper spirit of gallantry at a time when nerves were frayed by the stress of war is contained in the following public-spirited apology:

Taxi-cab dispute, Liverpool Street, evening of the 2nd September – The advertiser wishes to express his regret at his lack of good temper and good manners and to offer his sincere and humble apologies.

4 September 1940

and evidence of the survival of the spirit, *tout court*, was to be obtained from:

Survival – London Spiritualist Alliance Ltd, 16 Queensberry Place S.W.7. Bereaved invited. Public meetings Tuesdays 6.30. Read 'Light' 3d per week. Marianne Bayley Worthington. Trust helps the Poor.

27 May 1941

The rich too were not beyond the help of such bodies, and at this tragic time there was inevitably a heightened demand for such consolation as the Alliance was able to offer. 'Minim', who a day or two later addresses 'Crochet' with the message 'Being charitable, I will only say that you are being misguided', puts the point nicely, for guidance was much needed by all concerned.

In November 1941 an elderly couple of 'French *Haute Noblesse*', stranded in England since May 1940, appeal for hospitality through Colonel Ponsonby, M.P., who describes them as 'exceptionally charming companions', adding that 'Monsieur is a very good bridge player'. The appeal illustrates a point which came up later in the war when a lady announced in the personal column her desire for 'two charming paying guests'. As a *Times* writer pointed out 'even those who in their secret hearts feel themselves gifted with that indefinable quality called charm generally leave it to other people to proclaim.' This elderly French couple did exactly that and one can only hope, for their sake, that they were not obliged to fall back on

226

the doubtful charms of another institution of the personal column (the horrors of which are briefly alluded to in the previous chapter), the 'Jolly House Party'. One such is advertised the very next day – 'Jolly House Party, Surrey. – Officers on leave welcomed. £5 5s per week.'

The wants of wartime were as varied as those of peace, or more so. A serving officer with an oddly medieval attitude to twentieth century warfare wants a crossbow; hockey sticks, musical instruments and billiard tables are all in demand by 'isolated companies'; ladies with invalid husbands require one or two new-laid eggs 'for a short while'; four narwhal horns – 'state height and girth' – are wanted (could they have been for some latter-day Boadicea's chariot?); a 'blind nature lover' wants 'a reliable clock with strike such as bugler or trumpeter'; and towards the end of the war someone appeals urgently for an ice-axe. But perhaps the most intriguing want of all, which one can only assume was inserted by a passionate lover of Hardy who had just read *Two in a Tower*, is this:

Wanted. Apparatus for erecting Camera Obscura at the top of a high tower.

18 February 1942

Far exceeding all other wants, however, through the war years is the clamour for new golf balls: 'New golf balls – price no object for well known make' appears more frequently than any other single 'want' advertisement.

Ship halfpennies (the older type, last made in 1932) are wanted by the Royal Naval war libraries. An ingenious idea, which caught the imagination. The essence of wartime charity schemes was to make an appeal of this slightly illogical, haphazard kind, which none-theless conveyed some idea of the sort of purpose to which the money was to be put. Early in the war a woman canteen-worker named Margaret appealed for all other Margarets to make donations toward military canteen funds. It was good psychology and the idea was soon taken up by Marguerites, Marjories, Margots, as well as Peggies, Pearls and so on through the alphabet.

There are, as I have indicated, many mysteries still to be cleared up about the personal column during the war, despite the fact that codes and cryptic utterances were banned. Why, one wonders, did Box F wish to form a study group with 'practical interest in Heard's Pain, Sex and Time Theory'? And why did Radclyffe Hall, author of *The Well of Loneliness*, together with her friend Una V. Troubridge, announce her thanks 'to Guy de Fontgalland for a great favour'?

A further mystery was created when the Home Secretary,

Herbert Morrison, borrowed all personal column papers on 13 January 1943. Did he suspect that *The Times* was being used, once again, for nefarious purposes by an enemy? Later that year two slightly odd messages appear, which may have nothing to do with the war:

> Robinson Crusoe – I see smoke on the horizon – Man Friday
> *17 November 1943*

> Man Friday – Alas it has drifted away – Robinson Crusoe
> *26 November 1943*

Soon afterwards an over-optimistic advertiser announces: 'Reconstruction – Landowners' postwar problems examined and recommendations made.'

But the real issue, as the Reverend Parsons explained, lay elsewhere:

> Hatless women in church – The Real Issue, as expounded by the late Rev G. M. Parsons. Booklet 10d post free from publisher, Loughborough.
> *19 March 1943*

Not everyone perhaps would have shared the Rev. Parsons' view of the priorities at this dark hour of the war. But the truth is that this was not a war to which the personal column was able to make a very notable contribution (mercifully, Government propaganda and public notices were kept out of it). Prevented from being cryptic, too weary to indulge in much display of gratuitous wit, the advertiser was content to sell his model railways (Hornby 'O' gauge was as common as cornflakes), or his boots (£3); apologise for missing appointments; and advertise his charitable causes. It was not a romantic war so far as the personal column was concerned – not by comparison with the previous one. No one sent any Valentines, though there are many 'keep in touch' messages and Universal Aunts arranged a special 'keep in touch' service. Apart from that, the main impression is of endless perfunctory apologies – for being late, for missing you ('alas impossible communicate'), for lost tempers, lack of trust, despair and irritability ('sorry I was a cross-patch'). A war not of love, but of charity:

> 'My hat! I've forgotten to send it to Guy's!' Felt Hats in large quantities are still one of our needs. – Appeal Secretary, Guy's Hospital

And there are some remarkable bargains on offer:

> Nazi flag, captured on retaking of Tobruk, intended for display

in Alexandria. 6ft × 3ft. 2ft black swastika in white circle. £25. Also Luger Automatic, captured Alamein, best offer.

5 April 1944

Bugatti Grand Prix 1½ h.p. Full road equipment. 100 percent condition, 103 m.p.h. £350. No offers.

1 May 1944

Tails by Drew. Chest 40, leg 14, one sleeve frayed, £4. Handmade Jodhpur boots, little worn, 8½ £4.

2 June 1944

A buyers' market, if ever there was one. Emotions too were frayed and spent. Hatless, irritable, exhausted, with virtually no money and nothing to spend it on, the young serviceman emerging from the war can scarcely have been in a flirtatious mood. Yet the signs of a re-burgeoning of romantic sentiment begin to appear in the spring of 1945:

Urgently required for Wren bride, black silk stockings, size 9 or 9½, also new Maison Pearson hairbrush.

4 April 1945

Mosquito pilot very much wishes to purchase Adonis 'Blue Grass' perfume for honeymoon present for bride, mid-April. Please can someone help? Even very small quantity much appreciated.

5 April 1945

A lonely colonel's wife asks 'some kind person' to forward fortnight-old copies of the *Tatler* and *Sphere*; the barrel is being scraped by impoverished gentlefolk who offer gold pencils, dinner jackets and Mah Jong sets at bargain prices; and someone wants a standard lamp, a *Who's Who*, black coffee cups and a cookery book – modest essentials with which to begin the reconstruction of war-torn England. However, after the war, for many months, even at only 7s 6d per line, the column barely manages to get over halfway down the front page. February passes without a single Valentine, but there is the occasional lyrical outburst during the following months:

'Lord W' – 'The lark is singing on high', now and forever.

30 May 1946

Someone called 'Weakley' changes their name to 'Fletcher', and increasingly the column is filled with the names of Germans and East Europeans taking on British nationality. Old Etonians continue to offer a variety of services; and silver fox furs, belonging

229

in the main to ladies about to depart for warmer climates, are for sale, as are cameras, pianos and more model railways.

An Anglophile 'from the great heartland of America' sends New Year greetings in 1947 to 'the sterling English people – courteous and gallant beyond words'. His message goes on to advocate that 'Missouri's great motto "Salus Populi Suprema Lex Est" be a guiding star to you all'. Immediately below his message is a less than 'sterling' New Year's greeting:

C.A. – Happy Christmas! What a farce. Send your address. You are very cruel and heartless. Distracted Mom.

'B.S.' is also concerned with matters of address, though his logic is open to question:

A. – Please write old address Brighton. Do you remember it? – B.S.

27 January 1947

Committees of Old Boys for erecting war memorials to the fallen from the Public Schools, which fill the columns the following year, have not yet been formed, but Winchester College remembers an old and faithful servant:

Old Wykehamists – A fund has been started to provide a testimonial for Wilkins, who is retiring having completed 50 years as boatman down river. – Cheques should be made payable to Hon. Treasurer, Old Wykehamist Rowing Club, Huntercombe Manor, near Taplow, Bucks, and crossed 'Wilkins Fund'.

20 February 1947

Tiers of slim hulls, stretched canvas and varnish pots in the gloom of the boathouse, and outside the sparkling river Itchen full of trout and weed – over these you presided, Wilkins, let them be your memorial.

The Guards Club announces on January 13th that its Ladies' Annexe is open at 48 Charles Street, W1. On St Valentine's Day the Convent of the Sacred Heart in Hove is moved to express its thanksgiving to, appropriately enough, the Sacred Heart.

With print and paper restrictions still in force, advertisements for second-hand copies of popular books are frequent. Someone writing from 'Treetops', in an inaccessible corner of the Kentish North Downs, appeals for any book by Georgette Heyer and plenty of twelve-inch gramophone albums (the advertiser does not specify what kind of music, but presumably any sort of tuneful noise would have been welcome in those dark days). Such is the enthusiasm for one book, *Forever Amber* by Kathleen Winsor (published back in 1944), that hardly an issue appears for months at a time without at least one appeal for the work. The popularity of this book was so remarkable – two million copies sold 'first time round' – that one is tempted to wonder whether these advertisements should be taken at face value. Did the publishers deliberately 'seed the ground' by inserting them? Or was this a coded invitation to erotic advances? The book has recently been republished[1] and seems innocent enough by modern standards.

A notable success for the column was scored in May, by the following request:

> Drake's Bowls. – Are the woods used by Drake on Plymouth Ho! in 1588 still in existence? The Weston-super-Mare Bowls Committee are seeking them to enable the Mayor to start their Silver Anniversary Open Tournament with them on June 23rd.
> – Any information regarding the woods or their present location will be appreciated by the Tournament Committee, Town Hall, Weston-super-Mare.
>
> *5 May 1947*

The principal difficulty about this request was that scholarly opinion tends to doubt whether the game ever took place. Despite this initial problem, an enormous response resulted and the Bowls Committee received letters mentioning locations from Magdalen College Oxford to Elstree Studios. The owner of Drake's Drum, at Chard, turned out not to have them and a Committee member quotes 'the historian E. F. Benson' (whose name came up earlier in this book in connection with a sporting challenge in *The Times* which was definitely fictitious) as being certain the story of the game of bowls was an invention. A Mr O. R. Bagot of Levens Hall, near Kendal, came to the rescue with the 'authentic wood', as well as the Admiral's snuff box. The 'wood', it turned out, had been bought by Mr Bagot's uncle from an old Cornishman; even if that is not sufficient proof of provenance for the E. F. Bensons among us, the 'wood' was at any rate an object of great age, and was carried by special messenger and insured for a considerable sum for its journey to Weston-super-Mare. On arrival it was displayed in splendour, but, owing to its great antiquity, was not actually used by the Mayor for the opening ceremony.

Towards the end of the year the cost of advertisements went up by a swingeing 2s 6d a line to 10s. However, the quality and variety of material, from a reader's point of view, declined. 'Porky wants

[1] Macdonald & Jane's, London, 1984.

work. Offers or suggestions' reads one ultra-brief advertisement, giving a rural address and no doubt eliciting more of the latter than the former. New Year's greetings in 1948 came from the Swiss-German proprietor of a *pensione* in Locarno; and on January 17th a gentleman with a Turkish-Greek surname sends birthday greetings to 'the great Philhellene, Compton Mackenzie'. The novels of Georgette Heyer remain in demand; and there is one plea for 'anything by Angela Thirkell'. The previous December, says another announcement, an Australian boy boarded a No. 15 bus by mistake: 'Will the lady to whom he spoke communicate with Box 3014?'

There follows a St Valentine's Day message notable if only because it perpetuates the belief that burglars read *The Times*:

The Burglar who burgled the bungalow is begged to return to Dr Josie Oldfield, Ash, Sevenoaks, Kent, the miniature of her father which he took; to him valueless, to her precious.

Amid all the pleas for books there is one which particularly stands out. Colonel Baker's request, which indicates a pressing need, evokes images both desperate and bizarre:

Mitchell Hedges Book BATTLING WITH SEA MONSTERS urgently wanted – £3 per copy will be paid. – Reply Colonel Martin Baker, Earldoms, Landford, Wilts.

12 March 1948

Towards the end of this year there appear a number of advertisements in rhyme. Their author, 'A.E.L.', has a bee in his bonnet about a building that is being misused – the Pump Room at Harrogate:

The Plight of Harrogate's Pump Room
I was proud; far have I fallen from my first estate;
Comely was I but an annexe mars my grace.
Restore me to my dignity and pride of place
And I'll remain the living loving heart of Harrogate.

7 December 1948

The waters of Harrogate, which rose to prominence as a spa town, attracted visitors from all over the country from the seventeenth century onwards. By the mid eighteenth century the sulphur baths and spa waters were becoming so popular that an Act of Parliament had to be passed to enclose two hundred acres of land near the main wells as a 'stray with free public access' for those taking the waters; a stone monopteron supported by slender pillars was erected in 1804 to cover the well head, and finally in 1842 the present 'Royal Pump Room' was built. Some illustrious figures were to be seen taking the waters there during the following hundred years. Byron, Tennyson and Dickens all tried the cure, with what degree of success I do not know, and at one time, in August 1911, three queens were present simultaneously – Queen Alexandra, her sister, the Empress Marie Fedorovna of Russia, and Queen Amelie of Portugal. So the Pump Room earned its epithet 'Royal' many times over:

> *The Plight of Harrogate's Pump Room*
> Where health-giving waters were served with propriety –
> Stories and quips once exchanged by Society,
> Converse is now quite reduced to a mockery
> By hissing of steam and the crashing of crockery.
>
> *6 January 1948*

And after this the verses flow forth, month after month – not quite Tennysonian perhaps, nor quite Byronic (he wrote better stuff for Mrs Warren), but good workmanlike messages pointing the finger of shame at the municipal authorities who had permitted this vandalism: 'O'er the gushing fountain's lips rose the far-famed stone-girt hall: "Waitress, bring me fish and chips, tea and crumpets, cakes and all!" '

It turns out that the Pump Room has been made into a cafeteria: 'See my interior, called "Cafeteria"! Could aught be drearier? But I'm up to date!' Isaac Shutt's domed neo-classical octagon a cafeteria! The *fons et origo* of Harrogate's fame and prosperity, where three queens stooped to drink, demoted to the rank of canteen! A.E.L. is back the following month, driving the message home to his growing band of sympathisers:

> *Harrogate's Pump Room and a Parish Church*
> St Wilfrid and I are like brothers,
> Though he's very young and I'm old;
> He renders High Service to others:
> In me it's High Teas that are sold.
>
> *2 June 1949*

After that, A.E.L. presumably thought the point had been made. There are no further messages in 1950, but in 1951, the year of the Festival of Britain, a last vigorous dig at the authorities seemed judicious, for evidently the matter had aroused some controversy and alternative uses for the octagon were now being mooted:

Harrogate's Royal Pump Room
Ding, dong, Bell! Gone to earth's my well!
Who'll put it back? Quack! Quack! Quack!
In this Festival Year of one nine and five one,
Who'll champion my cause to see justice is done?
Museum, Cafe, Cloakroom – who's having the fun?
Alack! Alack! Alack!

15 February 1951

The story has a happy ending, for in 1953 the cafeteria was driven out, and the Pump Room became a museum. At the time of writing the museum is planning to reopen the wells, and visitors will be able once again to take the waters.

During this period there was little enough else to entertain readers of the front page. Indigent vicars, with large parishes in poor districts, appeal for the loan or gift of a small car. (A surprisingly large number of indigent vicars were able to afford these advertisements; and several indigent authors, seeking type-writers, also caught onto the idea.) One vicar, admittedly an exceptional case, in St Leonard's, Bucks, complains of the loss of fourteen goats which had brought him in an income of £400 a year. Deprived of the use of these animals – he had one left, but it was a billy and more of a liability than an asset – he could but cast himself upon the mercy of readers of *The Times*.

Early in 1949 a valet asks for work – 'Real country not considered'. This caught the eye of a leader writer, who remarks that, after all, 'in town, even the most incorrigible debauchee does not bring home great clots of burrs on his nether garments; his shoes are not caked with clay nor filled with fronds of dead bracken, in the lining of his pockets no rabbit's blood congeals and his clothes do not steam as they hang amorphously before the fire.' The moral is never to be what Stevie Smith called 'too far out'.

Another advertisement at this time reminds one that although they could now pick and choose their employers, servants had not yet become an endangered species:

Wanted: A scullerymaid who will not break all the commandments and then say they were cracked already.

A few days later, the Welfare Officer of the fifth R.T.R., B.O.A.R., appeals: 'Belsen. – Troops in this lonely spot would be grateful for second-hand books of all types'. And on St Valentine's Day: 'For Sale: Early editions of Henry Miller's *Tropics*, *Black Spring* etc'.

234

A proper humility and respect for intellectual attainment is shown by several advertisements of the following kind:

Bridegroom, anxious, unintelligent, lost for wedding speech. Any humorous suggestions welcome.

This was swiftly followed by someone appealing urgently for the 'Macmillan edition, selections from Catullus', giving a phone number.

January 1950 starts with a reminder to readers to send their donations to the Simon Memorial Fund. The Fund is remarkable among the many memorial funds recently opened on behalf of the war dead in that the hero 'Simon', the eponymous hero, was not a human but a cat. In July of the previous year a British frigate, the *Amethyst*, was involved in a daring escape from Communist-held territory on the Yangtze river. Slipping her moorings silently at night and navigating in the dark without a pilot, she reached the open sea despite heavy firing from a Communist shore battery. During this action Simon, the ship's cat, was fatally injured. However, until the last, he continued his vital work of keeping down rats on board, thus preserving the ship's dwindling food supplies. He was awarded, posthumously, the Dickin Medal for valour – the first cat to receive this award. (Admirers of feline bravery may, by the way, remember the Russian cat, Mourka, who played a crucial role in the defence of Stalingrad, carrying messages under fire from a beleaguered scout observation point to the company kitchen.)

The People's Dispensary for Sick Animals, who inserted the announcement of the Simon Memorial Fund, specified that it was to help man and beast alike; and aid was disbursed both to the Yangtze disabled and sick animals in seaport towns.

As always, the 'daring young men' advertise from time to time, though few are as terse as this:

Single gentleman (27) seeks dangerous or diplomatic work (legitimate) abroad; recommendations.

9 January 1950

No plea for 'adventure' here, no boasting about effete linguistic accomplishments, expensive schooling or powerful motorcycles. One can imagine 'M', at the start of a busy day, drawing a circle around just such an advertisement and giving it to Miss Moneypenny to pass on to Personnel.

'Buy the truth and sell it not', reads the suitably austere text for St Valentine's Day 1950. It was a bitter February. In the midst of all this bleakness it is hard not to feel a pang of sympathy for the advertiser who wants to hear of a 'really *warm* hotel, sunny and heated throughout'; on the other hand, 'Author, famous but broke, at the top of his literary form, needs patron urgently' has a somewhat self-contradictory ring about it. I am more inclined to believe in:

> Bad luck will dog the footsteps of the person who took the sacred bulls from the Japanese Garden at The Node, Codicote, Herts – Seki
> *2 February 1951*

And Sherrinford Pollaky would no doubt have been able to make some sense of:

> St Vincent set a rip back and become ----- tonight. Filling the blank saves walking the plank. – G.G.
> *13 July 1951*

This was the day on which the Sherlock Holmes Society was formed. Needless to say, it was Friday the thirteenth; the name of the Chairman of the society is given as 'Ivar Gunn'.

Several times during the next two decades a terse and forbidding advertisement appears: 'Hands wanted for long voyage in small boat; no pay, no prospects, not much pleasure.' This was inserted by the sailor and mountaineer Major Harold William ('Bill') Tilman. Setting forth from the Royal Lymington Yacht Club, which heralded his departures by firing a gun in salute, Tilman accomplished many daring sea voyages in small boats without radio, liferaft or insurance until in 1977, when Tilman was seventy-nine, his boat *Mischief* was lost with all hands somewhere south of Rio.

The 'Three Peaks Race', a round Britain race which gruellingly combines sailing and mountaineering, taking competitors from Ben Nevis to Snowdon and back again, was started in his honour and more than one lonely Antarctic peak bears the name of his yacht *Mischief*, though he never allowed his geographical discoveries to be named after himself. Tilman, though a hard man, was also a witty one. He once received an answer to his usual *Times* advertisement from a sailor who claimed to have crossed the Atlantic thirty-four times; however, when he met the man, it transpired that he was the bass-drum player in the orchestra of the *Queen Mary*. Tilman was delighted by this joke, and took the man on right away.

It is not often that personal column advertisements have repercussions on international relations. Of all the innocuously zany requests, the following seemed the least likely to cause a stir:

> Tutor with Scottish accent urgently required for intelligent parrot.
> *18 August 1952*

The story was seized upon by the official Czech Communist Party newspaper, *Rude Pravo*, which explained to its readers: 'British capitalists are at present earning so much money on armaments that any one of them can afford to engage a tutor for his parrot provided that the tutor speaks with a Scottish accent'. It contrasted this example of revolting opulence with the plight of State education in the British Isles, and said there would soon be a million children without schools or teachers. These statistics were based on a recent speech by the Secretary-General of the National Union of Teachers, deploring the fact that 628 school buildings declared unfit for their purpose in 1925 were still in use. *Rude Pravo* ended its attack with a glittering account of progress in Czech state education. The British press was not slow to return the charge, for there was, as the Vienna correspondent of *The Times* put it, some distortion of the statistics. It was true that expenditure on State kindergartens in Czechoslovakia had increased, but Church and private schools had been abolished since the Communist *coup d'état* in 1948.

The native inventiveness and talent for original thinking of the British continues to be much in evidence during the middle 1950s. In November 1953 an ingenious idea is launched for dealing with smog by sucking it into town drains. The advertiser explains that the idea could only be made to work if various civic authorities and industries, which he lists, would cooperate by carrying out some experiments 'to ascertain practicability', and suggests setting up a meeting – 'confidential as advertiser does not wish create raree show'.

More work in a pioneering spirit is undertaken by a journalist touring the British Isles, looking for hotels 'where if you check in at opening time and ask for an omelette and a bottle of wine they serve it with delight'. He must have come out of this assignment a disappointed man; nor would he be much luckier thirty years later. A writer who could not be called a journalist, but whose name appears increasingly in the column during the succeeding few years issues a useful reminder on Christmas Eve:

> Sir John Anderson, Bt., reminds humanity that if everyone today would adopt Right Thinking this earth would become a paradise overnight.
>
> *24 December 1953*

Meanwhile 'J.17', addressing 'J.16', declares:

> Here only may I speak my love; my worship silenced. Yet the leaves and every place cry my love always.
>
> *2 November 1953*

Powerful emotion, though very differently motivated, is also expressed by 'S.B.', who announces:

> This, Johnny, is a sliding scale for Officers' Pensions. Guaranteed to slide down but not up.
>
> *13 February 1954*

Lighthouses are regularly offered for sale in the personal column (on average about once every five or ten years), but only on one occasion has someone actually advertised *for* a lighthouse:

> Disused lighthouse required immediately. Write Box T133
>
> *2 January 1958*

This advertisement excited great interest even before its appearance, for on New Year's Day the newspaper printed a short article at the foot of the centre page, underneath the main news, revealing that the advertiser was a lady and that she visualised a lighthouse out at sea 'but not too far out'. Her intention was simply 'to get away from it all' to a very wild place. 'I like the sea, I like waves', she resentfully told reporters. 'What's so odd about that?'

During the 1920s a number of 'gallant' advertisements are addressed to a certain 'Cherry Ripe'. If this is indeed, as I believe, the model for Millais' famous painting, she establishes a record among advertisees, by appearing in the column four times in forty years. In 1958 the painting was put on display by the Royal Academy and apparently the sitter, now an old lady, came to see it in the company of a young man. Hearing of this, the Academy inserted the following advertisement in *The Times*:

> Millais' 'Cherry Ripe' – The Royal Academy of Arts, Piccadilly, wish to contact the lady who sat for this famous portrait, now on view there in the exhibition of Sir J. B. Robinson's collection. She was born Edie Ramage and married Signor Francisco de Paula Ossorio. She was the niece of Mr Thomas, editor of *The Graphic*, which commissioned the painting and published the familiar colour reproduction. It is believed that she may have recently visited the Exhibition.
>
> *8 August 1958*

On January 1st we find:

> The Wooden Horse Club wishes a Happy New Year to all its members.

The club had been formed shortly after the war for survivors of a German prison of war camp who adopted a gymnasts' 'horse' as a means of camouflaging the digging of an escape tunnel (the story is told in Eric Williams' book *The Wooden Horse*, of which a film was also made). Several other clubs of lesser fame also advertise reunions, including the Adelaide Club, which meets every October 1st under the statue of Eros at Piccadilly Circus, the Club of the Three Wise Monkeys, which advertises balls at the Hyde Park Hotel, the Plato Society, the Pro Dicktri Society, which celebrates the birth of King Richard III every October 2nd, the Escapers' Club and the British Jigsaw Puzzle Club. There are many minor clubs and associations which advertise in the column – some of them, not surprisingly, short-lived. Despite extensive enquiries I have been unable to track down the Immorality Abatement Society, which was advertising as recently as twenty years ago. Has immorality now abated, or were members forced to give up the unequal task?

Peter Fleming, ever a friend of the personal column, had the happy idea in 1958 of suggesting to the assistant editor of *The Times*, A. P. Ryan, that the newspaper could attract extra classified advertising by circularising subscribers with a leaflet suggesting they insert notices saying 'Mr and Mrs X will be making a donation to ------- charity this year in lieu of sending their friends Christmas cards.' This, he pointed out, would have the advantage of exploiting to the maximum the *Times* monopoly of snob appeal, for the advertiser would be publicly identified not merely as a 'Top Person', but as a 'Top Person' whose friends were all 'Top People' too.

The suggestion fell on fertile ground, for it was very much in tune with the mood of the 1960s, a time when old established practices were abandoned with a will, even by older people and the Establishment itself. There is a distinct parallel between the witty, flamboyant mood of the column during the next few years and the similarly ebullient mood which prevailed in the period immediately after the First World War. In this mood, the personal column seemed to grasp at Peter Fleming's idea, which soon became a cliché. However, as deserves to happen to all clichés, it was eventually shot down by a shaft of wit:

> Mr and Mrs Frank Muir will not be making an announcement in The Times this year. Instead they will be sending their friends Christmas cards.
>
> *14 December 1964*

Advertisers were delighted by this joke, and variations of it were extended to Valentine cards and Easter eggs:

> Julia Murless, Alex Scrope, Henry and David Cecil regret that owing to the rising cost of confectionery and a surfeit of friends they will not be sending Easter eggs this year.
>
> *17 April 1965*

It is one of those messages which could not have existed outside the *Times* personal column . Nor could this, which appeared on the day of Prince Andrew's birth:

> The New Royal Baby will receive many gifts, but every baby in the land born within five minutes of the Royal birth will be given a soft cuddly toy to mark this joyful coincidence, if Matrons of Maternity Hospitals or Certified Midwives will telephone Abergavenny 473 to claim the present on the child's behalf.
>
> *19 February 1960*

Similarly, there are certain offbeat requests that seem almost deliberately created for the column:

> Bombing strongly stimulated the adrenal glands: genuine enquirer urgently seeks a substitute.
>
> *5 February 1960*

> Cephalosporins. – Original investigator and name giver seeks collaboration author. Remarkable story.
>
> *17 May 1960*

It is a remarkable story which has only been told in learned magazines such as *Mycologia*, the international journal of mycological research. First discovered in 1952 by J. M. Roberts while working for the Michigan Department of Health in the United States, Cephalosporins are a series of antibiotics derived from a substance synthesised by the mould *Emericellopsis minimum*. The three drugs derived from this source – Cephalothin, Cephaloridine, and Cephaloglycine – work by inhibiting cell-wall production in bacteria and their principal use is in treating patients allergic to penicillin. The plot and characterisation of the Cephalosporin story may not rival 'Dallas' – but you can't compress a ten-reel series into a hundred words, as those who are allergic to penicillin would be the first to agree.

Where else, apart from the personal column, could one advertise with any hope of sympathy:

> Can't dance. – Unmusical professional man has tried hard to learn without success, would be grateful to hear from past sufferers of dedicated teacher, or whether best to regard situation as hopeless, declaring oneself a non-dancer, and concentrate on the food.
>
> *6 July 1961*

Or where else appeal, with any hope of success:

Sonorous bell wanted for fine church worthy of more than its tinkler. The Rev. John Bickersteth, Hurst Green Parsonage, Oxted, Surrey.

28 September 1960

The church did not have to wait long for its bell, for one was purchased when an extension was built in 1963. The present incumbent, the Rev. G. Russell, writes 'It is certainly more sonorous! The old bell still reposes in a store room', and John Bickersteth is now Bishop of Bath and Wells – all of which has a resounding ring of success.

Self-confessed old buffers and mildly archaeological widowers too would naturally be avid readers of the personal column, and advertisements such as the following make good grist for a daydream:

Old buffer not yet gaga seeks another for serious work of catching sea trout and occasional salmon, Eire, 24 August to 9 October.

16 January 1963

Grass widower seeks another, 50–70 share lazy holiday, February 1st two weeks, Gozo, Tarifa or Algarve. Mild archaeological, literary interests (The Times crossword level) and backgammon favoured. Estimated cost £90 including tips, drinks, fritterings and losses.

21 January 1965

A verger with whom I discussed the following advertisement, which is for a verger's job, started talking to me in a rather confused manner, verging on the cabbalistic, about his working conditions, explaining that 'When you come right down to it, it is all a question of bread 'n stone, O.K.?' Not for him the spiritual calm of a rural rectory:

Stoke D'Abernon verger is retiring after nearly 10 years. The small ancient church is well known and beautifully set in the grounds of the old Manor House. The Verger's excellent modern house overlooks fields in the green belt and is 30 minutes by train from London. The position is not full time. £7 per week plus free house. Write Stoke D'Abernon Rectory, near Cobham, Surrey.

6 October 1964

The latest news of this perfect opportunity for an old buffer to go to grass is that the post was vacant again in April 1986 and was to be advertised this time round in the *Church Times*. There is to be a modest increase in salary, but there will still be plenty of time left over for solving crossword puzzles and backgammon. The job of verger might not be everybody's cup of tea, of course; nonetheless, for a committed Christian with an adequate retirement pension, Stoke D'Abernon sounds the ideal spot.

Possibly the least encouraging advertisement for a job ever printed in *The Times* (again ecclesiastical) appeared a few years earlier. Indeed, it is not clear that there is a job on offer at all, unless you read it through slowly several times over:

> To advertise for an assistant curate in ecclesiastical journals is the last desperate hope: to mention here a future vacancy can but serve to bring before the reader the possibility of his being called to a second curacy in Stonehouse, Gloucester, and may bring to the mind of some other young men that they may be called to serve in this ministry.
>
> *9 November 1960*

A very much more successful piece of advertising was:

> Narrator required for the London Planetarium to present Astronomy in entertaining and challenging terms; sound cultural background and considerable experience in public speaking, broadcasting, repertory essential.
>
> *25 April 1960*

which secured the services of the writer and broadcaster John Ebdon, and a few years previously the following request signalled the start of a famous television series:

> Practical joker with wide experience of British public's sad gullibility organizes, leads, and guarantees success of large scale hoaxes. – Routh, 26 Chepstow Villas, W.11.
>
> *15 February 1957*

As a result, Jonathan Routh became the creative force behind the BBC's 'Candid Camera', one of the most popular television programmes of all time.

A television producer looking for talent might also have made something of the following:

> Have gun will travel. Versatile veterinarian, 29, no ties, frantically seeking greater outlet for intelligence and sensitivity, requires challenging adventurous or creative position. Literary and artistic interests, sporting tendencies, rakish appearance. Anything legitimate anywhere.
>
> *1 November 1961*

The phrase 'have gun will travel' was highly fashionable at this time. It took over from 'angry young man', which enjoyed a brief vogue as a result of John Osborne's play *Look Back in Anger*, and scarcely a 'daring young man' fails to use the phrase for the next five years. Later, it became fashionable for such advertisers to describe themselves as 'bored'.

As in the market for young men, whether daring, angry, gun-toting or bored, so the spirit of the sixties can be strongly felt in the world of nannies. Dr Spock is all the rage, and his advice is taken very much to heart. One mother declares 'Not wanted: nanny only interested in manners'. There is also the fear that nannies might turn their charges into 'stunted adults', so advertisers seek nannies capable of 'developing latent talent' in children. The search is on for the swinging nanny of the sixties, who must be a paragon of enterprise and adaptability.

It is this spirit of adaptability, as much as the fashion detail and the *argot*, which makes the following so typical of the period:

> Actress, tired of trekking round agents and finding the upkeep of stiletto heels ruinous, will take doggies for walkies London; pedigrees exchanged.
>
> *2 May 1960*

The advertisements of an association calling itself 'Offbeat' are particularly redolent of the flower power years. 'Offbeat', which refers to itself as 'the organisation which pops the rainbow of kindness through your door', also offers to 'sprinkle the world with chuckles, charm and chunks of kindness'. It invites readers, 'if it is jaded you are', to write to them at an address in Ladbroke Grove. Conventions are being broken down everywhere – 'why use an agent when you can sell your house directly to tall stooping man and young spreading wife?' Employers can still afford to offer jobs which 'might suit public school educated captain of games with a few "A" levels who feels he should now start work'. The Establishment has been identified as an 'Aunt Sally', and it is now smart to drop references to it in advertisements:

> Fine, upright young man, 1936 model, hardly used, imaginative, brash, oodles of background; suffering from Establishment blues; elegant dead-end job; self-respect easily restorable by exacting career; French, German, many extras; unrepeatable value.
>
> *10 January 1962*

Since the publication by Nancy Mitford and Professor Alan Ross of *Noblesse Oblige* in 1956 the term 'U' had come into the language, and is sometimes to be seen in job offers, such as the following:

> Penelope D'Artington Cooper de Stuart or any other young lady or ex-debutante 5ft 9 or taller (and proud of it) with the requisite poise, personality and 'U'ality. A cocktail bar, at the Horn and Trumpet, Worcester, requires your presence – to grace and manage same. Basic weekly salary, 3/6 per inch of height plus incentive bonus, and the aurora of a charming job with nice people.
>
> *18 May 1961*

It is often not appreciated how important a deciding factor height can be in certain occupations:

> Happy Dwarf wants to meet fellow dwarfs to offer lucrative job and plenty of fun. Write Box X 1528 and we'll have a get-together and tell you all about it.
>
> *31 August 1960*

Another advertiser, really carrying things to extremes, appears to be looking for a diminutive equivalent of Gilbert's Modern Major General ('Modern Model Admiral Wanted: not exceeding four inches high . . .'), but the remainder of the advertisement makes it clear that he is looking for a china figurine. It must be said, however, that there are some fairly bizarre job offers at this time:

> Duelling expert (pistols only) needed urgently. No theorists; must have practical experience. Age no bar.
>
> *19 May 1960*

> Rickshaw driver wanted urgently for a few hours in London.
>
> *20 August 1964*

And there is a distinctly discriminating offer of employment:

> An exceptional cat required for something in the City. Oysters etc, to suit special diets. Only reliable, intelligent and clean cats need apply. Phone for details and appointment.
>
> *14 July 1964*

The job was evidently soon filled, but the occupant seems to have got bored rather soon, as cats do:

> Cat, sated oysters, weary curiosity, seeks replacement next week. Application in person to Hodge, Royal Exchange, E.C.3.
>
> *25 July 1964*

Not surprisingly the advertisement says little about what the animal is supposed to do – not that cats *ever* do much unless there are mice around. There is room for speculation: few cats, after all, are adept at telephoning and not many bother much about reading *The Times*, though Hodge would obviously be a 'Fourth Leader' fan because of all those quotations from Dr Johnson. But the danger of being too mysterious in advertisements of this kind is that people are liable to get the wrong idea:

Miss Teal (Common) with nesting feeling seeks husband with similar interests.

4 May 1960

Miss Teal, regretting misunderstanding with human admirers, still seeks genuine Teal drake.

13 May 1960

There was, I recall, a young lady who used regularly to bring her pet teal, in its wickerwork travelling hutch, to the Round Pond in Kensington Gardens for exercise. Her coiffure was upswept at the back in duck-like fashion and streaked with a white band. Such devotion to ducks is rare. Could this have been the same young lady?

A much more unmistakable signal was emitted the day after St Valentine's Day 1963:

Male skunk (mephitis) wanted immediately for breeding purposes; sale or loan.

Animals are indeed remarkably well represented in the personal columns of the 1960s. All the best jobs and social openings seem to come their way:

All monkeys smaller than chimp welcomed to country house in lovely garden; any length of stay; ample open air exercise; heated quarters.

24 May 1960

I 'Bodger', an aristocratic bull terrier accustomed to moving in 'county' circles require a furnished flat near a tree in London, as clot of a master has been transferred to town. Two bedrooms required. Please make rent reasonable as meat ration may be in jeopardy. Any offers to Gawdy Hall Cottage, Harleston, Norfolk.

4 January 1963

Before she herself became a star, a well-known figure advertises a star pet:

Ripe for Development. – Would anyone sick of viewing so

much degrading material from abroad care to back, or make, series of films, or feature film starring 'Junia', Great Dane successor to Juno, who at 7 months old, has already acted in delightful feature film and is impeccably trained. – Barbara Woodhouse, Campions, Croxley Green, Rickmansworth.
18 May 1962

There is a curious request from two famous comedians:

A Chung ling soo (unstained) required – Morecambe and Wise, Birmingham
20 July 1962

The unstained ones are so much harder to find . . .

Hard work would also have been needed to come up with:

Conkers – Up to two million (no strings attached) required; will pay 2s per 100 for good specimens.
21 August 1962

The list of things for sale is even more mouth-watering. Rudyard Kipling's Rolls-Royce, for example:

On 18th July 1925, this majestic Phantom I landaulette was delivered to the Poet of the Empire. Recently overhauled this historic car is now offered to Kipling lovers, literary societies, motor museums or Empire Loyalists, for only £800. Please write to Corfe Castle, Dorset.
7 April 1960

It is true that Kipling was somewhat out of favour at that time; also, perhaps the value of antique cars was not so high then. Nevertheless, as a devoted Kipling fan, I was dismayed to discover that the car was on offer again three weeks later at the astonishingly low price of £540. More extraordinary still, it was offered a third time in November, for only £500. In the faint hope that it might still be available, I wrote to Corfe Castle, but received no reply. Another interesting vehicle is the old Brighton bus offered for an undisclosed price in October 1961 and described as having 'air of middle aged gallantry, greying at the sides elegance, distinguished English bus pedigree in omnibus society archives'. But final proof that in those days no one knew a good thing when they saw it appears earlier the same year:

1938 Daimler, FREE. – Good condition though aged. Good and worthy home wanted.
4 January 1961

It was also the right time to pick up Spitfires, or helicopters: 'Four Spitfires (Mk 9), flyaway condition, £2,200 each', reads an advertisement in December 1961. They don't give the price of the 'Eight Dragonfly Helicopters Mark 5 for sale (ex Royal Navy, seen Blackbushe airport)' in May 1965, but you can bet that a generation that was giving away Daimlers and selling Mark 9 Spitfires for the price of a second-hand family saloon car would not have wanted much more than a case of whisky for a Dragonfly.

Among other items for sale were rhinoceros horns; Stanley Baldwin's pipe; four full-length portraits of Hitler; and a 'Treacle' Bible for only £200. The 'Treacle' Bible, published in 1539, is so-called because the translator, Miles Coverdale, rendered the phrase 'There is no more balm in Gilead' (Jer. 8:22) as 'There is no more treacle in Gilead' – a minor quirk in an otherwise magnificent translation, parts of which (the Psalms, principally) are preserved in the Authorized Version. All because of that one slightly inappropriate word, the Coverdale translation has been relegated to the museum of oddities, like the 'Breeches Bible', in which the phrase 'they sewed fig leaves together and made themselves aprons' is 'improved' by the substitution of 'breeches' for 'aprons'. Then of course there was the Bible in which the word 'not' was omitted before the seventh commandment. You only have to get one detail like that wrong, and years of scholarship are demolished at a blow . . .

Perhaps the most bizarre item on offer, though, is this:

Warbleton Priory Skull. – This gruesome and well-documented relic for sale. 10 guineas.

8 May 1963

The Warbleton Priory Skull is said to have been uncovered by workmen from the walls of the Warbleton Priory Farm, near Hailsham, Sussex. According to *Sussex Archaeological Collections*, 1861, 'the tradition of the neighbourhood is that the skull belonged to a man who murdered an owner of the house and marks of blood are pointed out on the floor of the adjoining room where the murder is supposed to have been committed and which no washing will remove'.

R. T. Hopkins, in *Ghosts over England*, illustrates the skull and tells the story of the farmer who tried to bury it, but was forced to give up after being struck by 'a tremendous blast, like a whirlwind'. It was afterwards supposed always to utter 'fearful sounds and unearthly screams' when anyone tried to move it. The antique dealer who was offering it for sale had already been troubled by complaints from an elderly woman neighbour of bumps and bangings in the night and was somewhat anxious to get it off the premises. Taking no chances, he wrapped it tightly and secured it in a biscuit tin before bringing it to London.

Several notable objects are advertised as lost. Saddest perhaps was Lady Diana Cooper's photograph of her deceased husband, Duff, in a silver frame, and a small silver box with an inscription to Duff inside the lid. A blue enamel Fabergé cigarette case with a moonstone clasp, with words of thanks engraved on it in the writing of the late Grand Duke Michael of Russia is sought in April 1963; the society hostess Viva King advertises the loss from her house in Thurloe Square of a gold Byzantine coin of the Empress Theodora set in a hand-made glass locket; and a painting by Marc Chagall depicting houses with a cockerel in the foreground is advertised as lost between Queen's Gate and Piccadilly the following year. The oddest and most inexplicable loss, though, is:

Duke requests return of coronet loaned by father for coronation 1937.

10 August 1962

That sounds suspiciously like a case of what Lady Bracknell would call 'carelessness'.

Those specialities of the personal column, the unfathomable pronouncements, are all but absent during these last few years; people with unfortunate names are careful to keep quiet about them, and in these boom times of the 1960s inventions are so scarce that once again, as in 1845, someone actually advertises for them. Interestingly enough, the sum of money offered in 1960 is pretty well the same as it was in 1845:

Essential ideas or inventions. – £1,000 and small old factory available for partnership.

10 April 1963

The following are the nearest the column gets to being 'oracular', and – a sign of the times – both examples also admit of a 'conservationist' interpretation:

Hedgehog convention soonest – Eilis.

23 February 1960

L – There's something wrong with Noah's Ark – W.

12 August 1964

Some hangover from wartime restrictions prevents anything in the nature of code from appearing, but MI5 should perhaps have looked over the garden fence at:

26262 – Geraniums (red), Delphiniums (blue) seem to be well planted – D.

26 February 1964

A fashion begins for announcing that one's name is what it is and not something else. Leading this new trend is:

Caroline and Anthony Wedgwood Benn are continuing to use these names and would like to be known as such.

28 December 1961

Questions of identity also arise in the strange and tragic case of Anastasia. In a lengthy declaration, the supposed Grand Duchess of Russia appeals directly to *Times* readers. This is hardly the place to retell the story of Anastasia, nonetheless this advertisement, appearing some months before the Appeal Court hearing in Hamburg, is another example of the personal column serving as a home for lost causes:

Anastasia Nikolaievna (63) or Franziska Schanzkowska (69)? Grand Duchess of Russia or Polish factory worker? Even recently, useful evidence has been brought to light by people who had assumed that their personal knowledge was unimportant. There may yet be someone who can help to establish the truth in this tragedy, where it is so hard to resolve the differences of those who should know her best . . . The controversy has continued since 1922, two years after the patient's emergence from the shadows . . . Many witnesses whose testimony was heard in the previous Courts of enquiry had since died, and their statements (particularly, by the callous rule of fate, many of the favourable statements) had disappeared inexplicably from the files. It is still possible that timely intelligence or incidental disclosure could end the litigation, but time is short. *17 March 1965*

The following year the terrible predicament of the parents of a seven-year-old boy who is dying of cancer, despite everything medical science can do, is laid before readers. The latest drugs, the most powerful X-rays and, finally, the most drastic surgical methods have all proved of no avail. A malignant tumour is once again growing rapidly. The word 'hopeless' is used by the medical profession with greater reluctance than any other, but, the advertisers tell us, that word has been used of this child, and they ask, very simply, for the advice of readers: can anyone tell them of a single case in which anything other than classical medicine has succeeded?

Real emotion of any kind is a rarity in the personal column of the 1960s. There are very few advertisements such as that just cited; also missing are the pleas of the passionate and the appeals of the deserted. There is no more agony in the column.[1] Love, in the 'swinging sixties' can express itself more easily through other channels. There are signs of wit, of exasperation, of ebullience and liveliness, but true love, if it still exists, does not need to bare its heart on a newspaper's front page. One lone exception is 'Miranda'. A sort of time-warp seems to surround her. Her two advertisements, one thanking 'G' for the lovely flowers and the other declaring 'Miranda disagrees silly – romantic? surely. Mysterious? – certainly. Has G. decided?' could have been inserted in 1862 just as well as in 1962.

There is also a touch of romance in the agony of a small boy, expressed through his mother, in June 1963:

Small boy, seven, has always wanted to be a page at a wedding. – Please ring his harassed mother who hates to see him disappointed.

21 June 1963

A *Times* reporter, in an interview with the boy's father, elicits the information that the boy possesses a page's suit and a pair of Cromwellian shoes. The boy, it seems, is much in demand socially and regularly wears this suit at parties; but it is a page's suit and he feels, understandably, that it should be worn at an appropriate occasion. The film of Princess Alexandra's wedding the previous April had been the final straw. The cameras had panned in on the page's Cromwellian shoes, with wildly exciting effects, and after that the boy had given his parents no peace.

This strange story and the lone voice of Miranda combine to prepare us for the only proposal of marriage the column has ever carried in the one hundred and eighty-one years of its existence on the newspaper's front page:

Elfreide, let us get married. Propose end of February. – Harry

6 December 1963

---

[1] More recently a fifteen-year-old boy from Bruton, in Somerset, advertised, in May 1986: 'The great Greg Perkins has decided to have major heart surgery but would first like to do something exciting.' He was inundated with offers to help him realise his dream of 'living a bit more adventurously' before undergoing the dangerous eight-hour operation.

IN MEMORIAM

The End of a Proper Facelessness

On 3 May 1966 *The Times*, for almost the first time in its history, carried a front page devoted entirely to news. On only one other occasion had this happened: 25 January 1965, the day following the death of Sir Winston Churchill.

A few words are in order to serve as a memorial notice in honour of the passing of a personal column from the front page. Most of those words can be supplied by the advertisers themselves:

> The Times – Suggest that all readers protest vigorously at proposal to alter layout of this paper which will completely ruin its well known and beloved character. – A.J.B.R.
>
> *1 April 1966*

On the eve of the event, the last day of the old style front page, the column is bursting with interesting advertisements, from *Son et Lumière* in Salisbury Cathedral to trout-fishing on the Itchen, and a long advertisement by Jonathan Miller, who is looking for 'an enormous corridor at least 100ft long in an 18th or 19th century house' and a 'very sinister, cranky indoor swimming pool, very old and very peculiar' for the BBC television version of *Alice in Wonderland*. Other advertisers, however, simply lament the impending change:

> Thou'lt come no more, never, never, never, never, never! H.P.S.

> Last front page to wish personal the best to all sad people. Stud 153401 Leiden.

The following day the messages are mainly congratulatory:

> 'Paging The Times' – Best wishes and congratulations to the newspaper and members of The Times Publishing Company on being front page news. – A.J.H.

But there are still dissentient voices:

> On this sad occasion, love to all people like Jane. In fact, love to everyone – Paul.

And 'Simon Treen', to whom birthday greetings are sent by 'Susan', is reminded that yesterday he would have been front page news.

There is no message of thanks to St Jude on either day – but before closing this account of the history of the personal column, St Jude must be mentioned. His is one of those names that always crops up in any discussion of the subject. What, you may ask, is all that business about St Jude? Who is it who keeps thanking St Jude? The answer is that it is you, it is I, it is all of us. St Jude – and St Rita – are the patron saints of lost causes.

And, in addition to St Jude and St Rita, there is a whole calendar of other saints who are addressed from time to time, such as:

> Saint Martin de Porres, half caste and illegitimate, cure us of intolerance – J.P.
> *12 May 1962*

St Martin de Porres is the saint of inter-racial relationships. Born in Lima, Peru, of a Spanish hidalgo father and a Panamanian Indian mother, he lived from 1579 to 1639. His life combined aspects of animal liberation (he had a special affection for rats and mice) with work as a marriage guidance counsellor, as a retriever of lost diaries and as a pioneer in the field of precognition.

To make up for all these saints from the Roman calendar, in 1963 there is a spate of 'Thanks be to God' announcements, from what sound like Evangelical hands:

> Thanks be to God for the Reformation's blessings, which we still enjoy. J.B.P.
> *10 July 1963*

> Praise be to Almighty God for our Protestant heritage. – A.L.K.
> *11 December 1963*

Similar in spirit, although the object of devotion could hardly be referred to as a saint, are the annual messages recorded from an admirer in Worksop, Notts., in honour of Marilyn Monroe. Memorial notices are also inserted on behalf of the passing of such intangibles as:

Press Freedom – In memory of the Death on March 6 in the House of Lords, aged 191 years. – C.P.

8 March 1963

(The above referred to the Vassall spy tribunal. Two journalists who had refused to reveal their sources were imprisoned, namely B. J. Mulholland of the *Daily Mail* and R. Foster of the *Daily Sketch*. The Lords Appeal Committee refused an appeal against sentence.)

On the subject of death, 'In Memoriam' clauses are sometimes written into wills, stipulating that a certain person should be remembered every year on the day of his birth, and some of these notices have become institutionalised. The Byron Trust found in 1922 that the sum of £90 in Consols set aside for inserting memorials to the poet was now producing too small an income to meet the expense, every April 19th, of both a notice in *The Times* and a wreath on Byron's grave, which cost 'at least one pound'. The newspaper's management kindly agreed to allow the trust to continue paying at the old rate. Several such notices are now inserted free by the management – that of Hardy, for example, as well as those in memory of the great Delane (editor 1841–77) and manager Moberly Bell, who died at his desk in 1911.

An 'In Memoriam' notice published on 20 Sept 1932 read:

Pattisson – To the memory of William Ebenezer Pattisson, barrister at law, and his wife, Sarah Frances, who were both drowned in the Lac de Gaube, Cauterets, Hautes Pyrénées, while on their honeymoon Sept 20 1832. 'One autumn moon they scarce had wedded been.' (J.H.P.)

The story of this touching and tragic death is reported in *The Times* in November 1833. It seems that the boatman who had been in the habit of rowing strangers across the lake had died four days before the arrival of the honeymoon couple and in their eagerness to view the scenery they took the boat out alone. From the shore they were observed to rise suddenly, both at once, from their seats 'as if struck by the splendour of the scene'. The little boat upset immediately, and both were drowned.

It is to be hoped that another memorial to the couple will be inserted in 2032.

On hearing the news that the personal column was to be removed from the front page of *The Times*, Mr James Macintosh, a history student at Christ Church, tabled a motion for debate by the Oxford Union that 'This house deplores the announced alteration to *The Times*, which it regards as the wanton destruction, from ill-conceived commercial motives, of its proper British facelessness.'

In opting to remove classified advertising from the front page *The Times* was, clearly, bowing to commercial pressure. The step had been advocated in a number of reports, notably that of a firm of chartered accountants in 1958. The immediate result of the change was a dramatic improvement in circulation, which rose twenty per cent in six months. It would therefore seem that Mr Macintosh was wrong: the commercial judgement was anything but ill-founded. Unfortunately, the increase in circulation was not accompanied by a corresponding increase in advertising revenue. Far from welcoming the opportunity of the increased market for their wares, the advertising industry deplored the change. *The Times*, they decided, was no longer the exclusive province of 'Top People'; it had become a newspaper like any other. The consequent withdrawal of advertising support outweighed the benefits of increased circulation. The financial burden became too great for the Astor family, and *The Times* was sold to Lord Thomson.

A curious postscript to the perennial rumours that the personal column of *The Times* is used by spies for clandestine messages was provided on 24 August 1985, when the following announcement appeared in the 'Deaths' column:

> Von Hessen – On August 21st at Penzance, Cornwall. Timothy, Mark and James. Dearly beloved sons of Margarita von Hessen and the late Count Richardt. Funeral service to be held in Germany. Donation to the NSPCC.

No such deaths had been reported in Cornwall, and a Coroner's Court requested a police investigation. The Special Branch was called in, but no further light could be shed on this apparently fictional announcement. It so happened that at this time the Princess Margaret von Hessen bei Rhine, of Wolfsgarten Castle, Hesse, was staying as a guest of Her Majesty at Balmoral. The 72-year-old Princess, known by British royals as 'Princess Louis' after her late husband Louis Ludwig, has no children of her own. There is no other 'von Hessen' to whom the notice could apply.

Earlier the same week the leading West German counter-intelligence agent Herr Hans Joachim Tiedge had defected to East Germany, blowing an enormous hole in NATO security. A wholesale flight of East German agents from West Germany was reported in the following days, and an East German couple named Schulze were charged with offences under the Official Secrets Act at Horseferry Road Magistrates Court a few days later. Did the fake 'Death' announcement have something to do with all this activity?

In MI6 the notion that the personal column could be used in such a way is something of an office joke. Nonetheless, as a former member of intelligence put it, 'in the looking-glass world of espionage the more bizarre the story the more likely it is to be true.'

And much the same is true of the personal column. No one could ever have invented the material which the column has sieved out, like a fishnet of human experience, over the years. As a register of the preoccupations of society, at every level from the most trivial to the most momentous, it has few rivals. Beyond that, it has a fascination as literature of a vernacular kind. Though often cranky, eccentric and snobbish, it is also capable of poignancy and passionate intensity, wit, irreverence and, sometimes, poetic flights of the imagination. Although by its very nature it is a record of the ephemeral, Edward Bulwer-Lytton, novelist, parliamentarian and author of *The Last Days of Pompeii*, was in no doubt about its appeal to future generations: 'If I desired to leave to remote posterity some memorial of existing British civilization, I would prefer, not our docks, not our railways, not our public buildings, not even the Palace in which we hold our sittings – I would prefer a file of *The Times* . . . No such file would be complete without the first page.'

APPENDIX

Undeciphered Codes

E.A. *** A.F. —— E.H. *** F.C. —— B.V. *** A.B. ——
B.A. —— E.I. —— A.R. —— C.K. *** F.E. —— B.L. ——
C.O. *** A.6 —— E.J. —— b —— E.G. —— lu —— C.X.

2 August 1821

E.A. * * * F.A. * * * F.G. * * * B.L. * * * A.R. * A.U. *
A.W. * B.G.

1 April 1823

A.J. * E.E. * E.F. * * * A.B. * E.J. * B.A. * c.a. * * * F.A.
* * * F.C. * C.F. * * *

3 May 1823

F.B. * C.K. * * * A.L. * C.Q. * E.H. * * * F.B. * A.J. * * *
A.J. * E.D. * * * F.E. * C.Q. * * * A.S. * A.T. * E.I. * B.T. *
C.P. * * * A.J. * E.E. * * *

3 September 1823

A.B. * E.I. * B.U. * E.J. * B.T. * C.S. * E.J. * B.A. * C.T.
* * * A.J. * K.C. * * * A.I. * E.E. * * * F.B. * C.G. * * * F.F.
* C.R. * * * F.G. * B.V. * C.T. * * * K.B. * A.J. * * *

3 October 1823

E.A. * * * E.B. * A.J. * E.E. * * * A.Z. * E.H. * C.R. * * *
F.C. * B.F. * C.M. * * * F.E. * C.Q. * C.Q. * C.T. * K.U.
* * * F.G. * R.V. * C.R. * * *

1 January 1824

E.A. * * * A.J. * E.C. * * * A.Q. * A.R. * A.U. * A.W. *
B.U. * * * A.B. * B.A. * * * F.E. * C.B. * * * F.C. * B.F. *
C.M. * * * F.F. * C.A. * * * A.L. * E.H. * C.P. * * *

31 January 1824

The following series looks like a simple substitution cipher, but the odd placing of apostrophes is puzzling:

Qbe'bl. – zauoyhgk – zahgdy – iel'ybgny – Khxebgn – dbgk – Mh'gs – suox – elzlx – fs – yuel – jugyuehzbug – Koxbgn – pushnl – ql – hxl – um – glplx – knoiz – fs – eupl – mux suo – nuk – iely – suo – Khxebgn.

9 July 1853

Qbe'bl – Suox el'zlx by hnhbg nol'ylk! Zxs ugjl fuxh!! Mh'gs.

13 July 1853

Mhg's. – Khxebgn. – b'eupl sno ilz'lx zahg lplx zabgel iely' sno mux fhxdv vhvlxy nuk iely sno fs nqg yqlz Mhg's sno abpl gu z mux nuz'lg – Qbe'bl.

20 May 1854

Thirteen – ylvz – alheza – ahv bgly' – zusuo – klhxlyz – mhg's – bhf – yzbe' – yhfi gu – fhxdy – eugn – zbfi – xlfefilx – flyufizbfiy nuk – Jeysuo.

21 September 1854

Thirteenth – Mhggs – Nuk – iclyy – suo suox – Gu – fhxd – guq – zbfl – jhguz – otyug – hmljzbug – qbeu.

13 September 1856

Several coded messages inserted by Pollaky's Private Inquiry Office in the 1860s have all the appearance of being communications to or from E. J. Wilson. Those addressed to 'Passe Partout', 'Paean', 'Diplomat' and 'NAB en voyage' have an especially Wilsonian flavour:

PAEAN . . . 3d CIPHER. – 0'5714. . 031'371 'Rote' . . . 064'3790. . – . .005(0) contex 57ii Codicil Nov 17th 1857 – Pollaky's Private Inquiry Office, 13 Paddington Green.

19 January 1865

PAEAN . . . Sixth Cipher advance double – 078154 . . . – 34'1152 – . – 00'567809 – ?33 – Letter dimissory – 323'560,7 – – "Euku"667 Rote 36 12'24'48. 16 – 579,24'8 – – ? virago, femme covert . . . 5736 12'101.4 – due 510.207 33. G. 15.C. 9 Part 4 J.C.S. 3.2.5.9. ii. 7J. quinto exactus – Pollaky's Private Inquiry Office, 13 Paddington Green, London.

25 January 1865

I:- Your telegram was duly forwarded, and fortunately in time to

$$\ddot{\cdot} \; \vdots\!\mid\!\!\cdot \; \equiv : - \; \dot{\cdot}.\mid \cdot \; \cdots \; (\cdot) \; \cdots \; \doteq \; \vdots\!\mid\!\mid .$$

I shall return to England about the middle of June. – Pollaky

16 May 1865

DIPLOMAT – 7'59362,0' – 5, 16" 71,402 – 562 = '207,, ? 43563 – '25,76.410 – 2'63592'0'34'5,922" – aut quas sibi fabula finxit. – Pollaky's Private Inquiry Office, 13 Paddington Green.

23 November 1865

The above merely indicate the style of code involved and may be of interest to those possessing some knowledge of mid-nineteenth century code systems, since they clearly cannot be cracked without the relevant code-book. That of 16 May 1865 is inserted as a curiosity; it is presumably a cipher based on similar principles to the Rosicrucian or pig-pen ciphers, with affinities to Morse code. There are many different ways in which the arrangement of dots and lines could be used to build up an alphabet. This sample, isolated as it is, may not contain enough material for decipherment to be possible.

In the years following the First World War several coded messages appear, some of them fairly simple 'brain teasers', others more intricate, while still having the look of a puzzle which the amateur cryptanalyst can solve. 'The problem of the White Muffler can be solved on request to Box Y212, *The Times*, giving some evidence of bona fides', says an advertisement of 5 April 1922. No 'white muffler' is mentioned in the period immediately preceding this announcement, but perhaps the following is somehow related:

Sailors don't care? Deadly 51 bee 25; 1805; sailor 74, don't get in between: sac 81 54 sack the lot? m.hinterlands, suggested basis for settlement, harmony 94 Euclid 47 smallest squares clear; caution.

4 April 1922

In the following, the positioning of the letters and numbers appears to be significant:

```
    C       2 F J Y P 4 D E E P X J  –
            S L 4 C C – + x + 3     3
            I Q R R W 2 H M S S X
    Y       3 4 M 3 x 3 – 3 W 3 –
                G – J – x 3 W x
  P E Z F –
```

13 June 1922

Cannot Comply. 5080X

15 June 1922

```
    C       8 2 0 – – 4 G M R x x S S
            9 2 Q – Z   5 0 6 1   T R
          2 0 8 Z   x       Y         0
                        U V
          5 3
```

16 June 1922

S 2 0 3 B – July 13 or 14

19 June 1922

Index

advertising industry: personal column as early progenitor of 6; reaction to *Times* layout changes 254
alcohol abuse 190–1
Amalgamated Agony Column Association 192
amateurism, and appeal of personal column 6, 37
Anastasia 249
Angel, J. 11
animal magnetism 49, 56
animals 166, 174, 225, 245–6; flying models 43–4, 47–8; imagery 93, 94–5; lost and found 21–2, 219, 234; St Martin de Porres 252; *see also* birds, cats, dogs, horses, pigs
antibiotics 240
apology messages 211
appeals 28–9, 43, 144, 156, 179–80; emotional 249–50
appreciation messages 16–17
April Fool's Day 95
archetypes 2
Athenaeum, The 141, 157, 202
automata 43–7, 48–9
aviation, *see* flying

Babbage, C. 102, 105–6, 109–10, 111, 122
balloonists and ballooning 44–8, 50–4, 143, 211
beer advertising 31
bequests 214
Betjeman, J. 172–3
bets 2–3, 8, 154
birds 39, 86, 211, 220; ducks 245; lost and found 95; mechanical 45–6; messages 80–1; use of carrier pigeons 143; *see also* parrots
births, marriages and deaths 61, 240, 253; *see also* matrimonial, memorials
blackmail 83, 150; emotional 87–8, 160, 161–2
bones 212–13, 247–8
books: 'book-plugging' 9, 80; theft 212; 'Treacle' bible 247; wanted 229, 230–1, 232, 234

Brazilian expeditions 9–13
'Bright Young People' 190, 207; codes as parlour games 124; slang use 197
Bulldog Drummond 9
Bulwer-Lytton, E. 255
Byron, Lord 35; memorials 253

Carbonari (I) 105, 124–5, 127
cars: for sale 200, 213, 218, 229, 246; theft 212
cats 226, 235, 244–5
caution messages 17, 30
charities: appeals 144; Christmas card messages 239; wartime schemes 227
'Christmas card' messages 239
Christie, A. 216; inspiration of personal column for fiction 216–17
Church, F. E. 121
church: bells 241; leaders enthusiasm for personal column 7; sale of 'advowsons' 144; verger's job 241–2; *see also* vicars
Churchill, W. 3, 251
cinema, *see* films and film-making
classified advertising 1; ambiguity and misinterpretation 44, 236–7; increase in 61, 144; origins of 2–3; *see also* personal column advertisements, trade advertising
Clay, A. 96; *The Agony Column* 1, 143, 192
clubs 95–6, 141, 198, 230, 239; Diogenes Club 156; expulsion from 145–6; Old Boys' 163; Wooden Horse Club 238; *see also* Athenaeum
code-breaking 103–5, 109–11, 117–18
coded messages 74, 78–82, 84–5, 96–7, 112–17, 122–5, 202, 256–8; earliest 29, 102; interference with 112–14; problems of 202–3; wartime ban on 221, 227; *see also* cryptograms, 'marplots'
codes and ciphers 99, 102, 106–9, 112–13, 117; backwards alphabet 106, 112, 155; backwards language 104; diagrammatic 124–5; 'jargon' 122–3, 135, 137–8; 'Keyword' 121–2;